D1601265

Over the last several decades, functional theory in the social sciences has fallen into disfavor. Alleged to be a static form of theory incapable of explaining social change, methodologically impotent and ideologically tainted, functionalism stands accused of being socially and politically reactionary. In this book, Michael Faia challenges the view that functionalism should be rejected. He shows, on the contrary, that the more developed theories in the social sciences tend (or should tend) to move toward a "functionalist culmination." He claims that because functional theories are causal, multivariate, time-ordered, and characterized by reciprocal causation, they are in fact *inherently dynamic*, demand the highest methodological rigor, and also force sociology to transcend its infamous "paradigm disputes" by recognizing that the social sciences have already achieved an "integrated methodological paradigm."

Drawing a sharp distinction between functionality for *interests* and functionality for *organizational survival*, Faia suggests that, in terms of the latter, stable population theory and life-table analysis provide ways in which an evolutionary view of society may be restored to a central place in the discipline. He also argues that "requisite analysis" as a major undertaking of functionalism should be replaced by "neo-evolutionary" inquiries, emphasizing a social-selection perspective.

The central arguments of the book are illustrated by a wide variety of examples drawn from several academic disciplines. These range from the incest taboo to witchcraft, from tenure in the U.S. Congress to duration of marriage, from Malthusian population theory to the Club of Rome world model, from Malinowski on magic to Zerubavel on social definitions of time, from Blau's "macrosocial theories" to Szymanski's Marxist formulations, and from the alleged deterrent effect of capital punishment to the impending "sex pre-selection" of children. The reader thus gains a strong appreciation of the wide applicability of the functionalist mode of explanation.

The Arnold and Caroline Rose Monograph Series
of the American Sociological Association

Dynamic functionalism: strategy and tactics

For other titles in this series, turn to p. 187.

Dynamic functionalism: strategy and tactics

Michael A. Faia

College of William and Mary

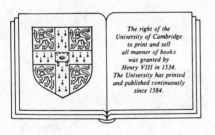

The right of the
University of Cambridge
to print and sell
all manner of books
was granted by
Henry VIII in 1534.
The University has printed
and published continuously
since 1584.

Cambridge University Press

Cambridge
London   New York   New Rochelle
Melbourne   Sydney

Published by the Press Syndicate of the University of Cambridge
The Pitt Building, Trumpington Street, Cambridge CB2 1RP
32 East 57th Street, New York, NY 10022, USA
10 Stamford Road, Oakleigh, Melbourne 3166, Australia

First published 1986

Printed in the United States of America

Library of Congress Cataloging-in-Publication Data
Faia, Michael A.
Dynamic functionalism.
(American Sociological Association Rose monograph
series)
Bibliography: p.
. 1. Functionalism (Social sciences)   2. Social
structure.   I. Title.   II. Series.
HM24.F28   1986   305   85-30855

British Library Cataloguing in Publication Data
Faia, Michael A.
Dynamic functionalism : strategy and tactics. –
(American Sociological Association Rose monograph
series)
1. Functionalism (Social sciences)
I. Title   II. Series
301'.01   GN363

ISBN 0 521 32657 5

For Nina, Gus, Lucille, and Wanell

¿Solo así he de irme?
¿Como las flores que perecieron?
¿Nada quedará en mi nombre?
¿Nada de mi fama aquí en la tierra?
¡Al menos flores, al menos cantos!

— Cantos de Huexotzingo

Contents

Figures and tables

Preface

The thesis of this book is that Kingsley Davis, in his famous presidential address before the American Sociological Association (1959), was mistaken in the claim that all sociologists are functionalists and that the functionalist paradigm is basically unsound. Using explanations of the incest taboo as an example, I argue in the first two chapters that functionalism has unique elements that are not fully exploited by most social scientists, and that this uniqueness has to do largely with the way the functionalist model focuses on the survivability of social organizations as they age.

Chapter 3 contends that the stable population model, specifically the life table, provides a way of analyzing one of the major dependent variables of functionalism – the survivorship of social organizations – and that, because the stable population model is a means of understanding population dynamics, functional analysis based on the model is inherently dynamic, that is, oriented to the study of social change.

Chapter 4 shows that the major prolegomenon of any functional analysis is to trace the behavior of relevant variables through time: If there is insufficient variability ("noise"), there is an insufficient basis for functional analysis. Using the Club of Rome world model as an example, I show that the functionalist paradigm readily comprehends the vast amount of change implied by the model, that the Club of Rome thesis is a clear instance of Marxian catastrophism, and that there is therefore no strong incompatibility between functional analysis and Marxist analysis.

Chapters 5 and 6, which make up Part II, provide copious illustrations of dynamic functionalism, followed by a brief introduction to time-series analysis. It becomes clear in these chapters that, for the present, dynamic functionalism is more readily illustrated by contrived data than by real data: The latter, in general, are far too static, that is, far too likely to be essentially cross sectional.

Part III concludes that functionalist propositions ought to be considered the summum bonum of the social scientific endeavor and arrives at the ironical conclusion that insofar as Kingsley Davis argued that functionalism is indeed the summum bonum of the sociological enterprise he was entirely correct. The problem is that the lofty spheres of functional sociology are rarely attained, due in part to our tendency to waste energy on paradigm disputes. The Appendix, essentially a supplement to Chapter 1, argues that the celebrated shortcomings of earlier functionalists, from Malthus to Parsons, do not inhere in the functionalist paradigm itself but derive rather from the idiosyncrasies of its practitioners.

John Gottman (1981:44–45) begins his excellent treatise on time-series analysis with an overview in which he lists a series of questions that he promises to answer. I have a similar list, although I make no claim of having fulfilled my promises as thoroughly and convincingly as Gottman:

1. To what extent can structural features of social organizations be explained with reference to actors' intentions, and, on the contrary, what are the circumstances under which intentions have little impact on social structures?
2. What is the probability that a given type of social organization will survive over a given period of time, and what are the structural and environmental factors that influence survival prospects?
3. What are the survival prospects of individuals as possessors of given status roles (e.g., the role of student or the role of congressman), and what are the structural features of organizations and environments that influence these prospects?
4. What are the survival prospects of small social entities such as marital units, and how are these prospects influenced by "internal" and "external" structural features – for instance, the presence of children from earlier marriages?
5. What are the fundamental social variables that provide significant time-series variation, and is it possible to classify these variables as exemplifying stationarity or as departing from stationarity due to trend, due to changes in degree of variability, or due to changes in "momentum" (i.e., autocorrelation)? Can we then explain the presence or absence of stationarity in a given instance?
6. What are the social consequences of particular forms of time-series variation? When a time series has a high frequency of change with high amplitude – for example, consumption of electricity in the United States – does such oscillation tend to create a "social problem?" Are structures such as regional power grids a way of adapting to these problems?

7. What are the factors that determine whether a variable oscillates as in Malthus's original formulation of his theory of population or follows an explosive trend as in the case of the Club of Rome world model or the Marxian theory of a rising surplus?

8. Does it make sense to look upon "evaluation research" as a form of research that tests "adaptation" hypotheses, where adaptations either preserve optimal values of particular variables or contribute to the survival prospects of organizations?

9. When there are complex interactions between adaptive processes and the variables they regulate, do time-series data enable us to sort out the causal dynamics of these interactions? Can we ascertain "lead and lag" relationships between such variables as "magic" and "anxiety" or supply and demand? Can we identify instances in which a "disturbance" stimulates an adaptive effort that, in turn, reduces the disturbance?

10. Is it possible to transform "idiographic" hypotheses about social origins (e.g., Zerubavel's hypotheses about the origins of the standard-time system) into "nomothetic" hypotheses about social dynamics (e.g., the ways in which the standard-time system is maintained [or breaks down] through time and space)?

11. How do technology and human volition combine to interrupt a nearly stationary time series such as the sex ratio at birth, and how (or when) do the social consequences of such interruptions develop over time to restore an optimal value of the interrupted series?

12. How would we explain positive feedback processes such as the self-fulfilling prophecy from a functionalist standpoint, and does functional analysis show how positive feedback processes may transform themselves into negative feedback processes, or vice versa?

13. Is it possible to simulate time-series causal processes in a way that has heuristic or didactic value?

14. Can functional analysis show that various studies of social change – among them studies employing Marxian perspectives – have not been sufficiently dynamic and have therefore failed to identify important patterns of social change?

15. Is it possible to show, through a "value-added" process involving the logic of Guttman scaling, that functionalist propositions are (or should be) the most highly developed form of social science theory and that dynamic functionalism provides clues as to how sociology might achieve paradigm integration?

Although I do not claim to be "the soul which hath the longest ladder and can go deepest down," I have certainly done my utmost to answer these questions adequately. The broken rungs, of course, are part of my own ladder.

Another major purpose of this inquiry is to begin taking more seriously, in my own work, Robert Merton's injunction that we integrate theory and research methods. We have not yet done so. One of my student assistants (Gary Dodson) recently completed an investigation in which, first, he listed all the "sophisticated," empirically grounded studies of recent years that have used the General Social Survey (GSS) and have appeared in the *American Sociological Review*, the *American Journal of Sociology*, or *Social Forces* (T. Smith, 1982): There were 57 such studies by October 1982. He then ascertained the frequency with which authors of these studies made reference to any of the traditional theorists discussed in detail by both Barnes (1948) and Martindale (1960), including prominent names such as Comte, Spencer, Durkheim, Toynbee, Sorokin, Simmel, Ross, Cooley, Tarde, Giddings, Weber, Thomas, Tönnies, and Marx, along with several others.

Among the many hundreds of citations provided by the 57 articles, there was a grand total of eight references to traditional theorists: several to Marx and Weber, and one to W. I. Thomas. All other traditional theorists were either ignored or (at best) relegated to the level of the subliminal. Perhaps this lamentable state of affairs would be tolerable if the authors of contemporary theory books were willing to act as go-betweens, integrating traditional theory with studies such as those using the GSS. However, a perusal of Abrahamson (1981), Alexander (1982), Ritzer (1983), and Turner and Maryanski (1979) reveals that these authors devote little attention to the strictly empirical studies listed in the Smith (1982) bibliography.

In the preparation of this volume, I have had help from many sources. In particular, I thank the College of William and Mary for two semester grants and a summer grant, I thank my colleagues David Aday and Gary Kreps for their encouragement and their careful reading of countless drafts, and I thank my wife, Susan, for her incredible tolerance and her occasional willingness to escape with me to Mexico.

Xalapa, Veracruz
May, 1984

Part I. Allegations, definitions, and illustrations

Though Functionalism in the United States is involved in a crisis, its world career is far from at an end. Indeed, the career of Functionalism, and of Academic Sociology more broadly, is now just beginning in Eastern Europe and in the Soviet Union. Both are becoming increasingly attractive to intellectuals in the Soviet Bloc of nations . . . . A major intellectual development in world sociology is impending, and it will be accelerated to the extent that Marxism and Academic Sociology move into increasing contact and mutual dialogue.
    – Alvin W. Gouldner, *The Coming Crisis of Western Sociology*

Societal evolution . . . belongs to a movement in contemporary social science which aspires to emulate the Renaissance by doing more than reviving old ideas.
                  – Talcott Parsons, *The Evolution of Societies*

1. A kindly critique of Kingsley Davis

In his influential presidential address before the American Sociological Association, Kingsley Davis (1959) argued that because no important differences exist between functional analysis and sociological analysis generally, we should no longer speak of functional analysis as a special method unique among forms of sociological analysis. In essence, Davis claimed that every sociologist who is part of the mainstream of his or her discipline is doing the same sort of analysis that functionalists do and, therefore, that any distinction is unreal, a mere matter of semantics. He implied that if one were to select a number of social scientists who call themselves functionalists and compare them with a number who call themselves something other than functionalists, one would find no important distinctions between the two groups in methodology or in approaches to theory construction.

This chapter will show that Davis's famous presidential preachment, despite its apparently large impact on the field and wide acceptance among those who think and write about theory construction (Friedrichs, 1970:294; Gibbs, 1972:71; Hage, 1972:192,197; Ritzer, 1983: 221; Wallace, 1969:26; but cf. Martindale, 1960: 446–47), is untenable in all its essential points: It does not show that functionalism lacks uniqueness; it does not demonstrate an inexorable lapse into teleology; it does not persuade us of the presumed methodological weakness of functional analysis (cf. Turner and Maryanski, 1979:95–96). The intention of the present volume, in fact, is to elaborate a form of functional analysis that thoroughly repudiates Davis's argument, a form of functionalism with several unique operating premises, with no indulgence in "purposes" beyond what is empirically justifiable, with an appropriately demanding methodological armamentarium, and with a conception of social dynamics that compels the use of time-series data. A form of functional analysis, in other words, that merely updates the splendid efforts of Adam Smith, Malthus, Morgan, Marx, Spencer, Durkheim, Tylor, Pareto, Malinowski, and Radcliffe-Brown. (The works of several of these authors are discussed in detail in the appendix.)

At a certain level of abstraction one must concede, with Davis, that functionalists and nonfunctionalists have common concerns, and even common methodological approaches. However, showing that there are abstract similarities is not the same as showing that there are no important distinctions. The logical fallacy committed by Davis is that of argument from analogy: merely demonstrating that *some* characteristics are shared by the two types of approaches does not mean that *all* important characteristics are shared. Much of what Davis says about the customary activities of functionalists is intended to show that functionalists are not really *doing* anything unique. Perhaps not, but this charge may result solely from the fact that "functionalists" themselves often do not understand which aspects of functional analysis are indeed unique, and they may not consistently pursue the singular aspects of functional analysis in their research. As a result, Davis's attack is merely an assault against a straw man: One can criticize functionalists at will, but criticizing functionalists is not necessarily the same thing as criticizing functionalism.

According to Davis, the notion of functionalism as a separate method of analysis should be abandoned "because it rests on the false assumption that there is a special method or body of theory called functional analysis that can be distinguished from other methods or theories *within* sociology and social anthropology" (1959:757). Davis concedes in the same paragraph that excellent work has been done under the functionalist banner, but he believes nevertheless that such work has used an approach that has no special properties. "Functional analysis," says Davis, "is most commonly said to *do* two things: to relate the parts of society to the whole, and to relate one part to another" (1959:758). He continues, "it strikes me that the first two traits simply describe what *any* science does;" in other words, "every science describes and explains phenomena from the standpoint of a *system* in nature." While granting this claim, one could point out that there are various ways to handle the problem of the systemic character of nature: Although all scientists may share a holistic perspective, there are many ways of describing a natural or social system in operation.

For instance, one apparently unique feature of functional analysis is the practice of explaining social structures with reference to their consequences (cf. Merton, 1957: 32,36,51). According to Davis (1959:759),

. . . Merton's characterization offers a point of departure. He describes "the central orientation of functionalism" as "the practice of interpreting data by establishing their consequences for larger structures in which they are implicated." If "interpreting" here means "explanation," the sense of the statement can hardly be that in functionalism data are explained *solely* in terms of their consequences; for nothing is explained that way.

Perhaps not – although the point will certainly be debated in this book. But Merton here identifies one of the unique elements of functional analysis.

Continuing in the same paragraph, Davis inadvertently arrives at a clear definition of another distinctive aspect of functional analysis:

in science some kind of system is usually being dealt with, an analysis of the effect of one factor must always be made with the possibility in mind of a possible return effect ("feedback") on that factor itself. If, for example, the increase of fish (y) in a pond has the effect of increasing the toxicity (x) of the water, the growth of the fish population (y again) will eventually cease unless other factors intervene. This is not explaining things solely by their consequences, but rather by the way their consequences react upon them.

If feedback and circular causation are essential elements of functional analysis, and if, as I believe, these concepts are rarely used in social theory (Zeitlin, 1973:13–14), then it follows that functional analysis has been rarely undertaken. Inexplicably but revealingly, the ideas of feedback and circular causation receive no further elaboration in Davis's article; the possibility that the famous fishpond may have self-regulating (or self-destroying) properties for which there are interesting analogues in human societies is never pursued. In Davis's example any change in either y or x will generate consequences that eventually have a self-correcting impact on the original disturbance. That is, changes are explained with reference to their consequences, but we must go well beyond such "explanations" by invoking the concepts of feedback and self-regulation. A functional theory such as Tylor's explanation of the incest taboo, to be discussed later, involves precisely the same pattern of interaction among variables as that observed in Davis's hypothetical fishpond.[1]

1. Entanglements of teleology

This brings us to the sticky issue of "teleology." When we try to explain a social structure with reference to its consequences, it is sometimes tempting to say that the structure has the *purpose* or *goal* or *function* of producing a certain consequence, and such language implies directionality, a tropistic tendency, that allegedly cannot exist unless one anthropomorphizes social structures. In Davis's example it would be preposterous to suggest that the toxicity level of the water is increasing *for the purpose of* bringing about or *in order to* bring about an appropriate reduction of the fish population; there is no temptation (at least in contemporary Western culture) to anthropomorphize water or even fish. If we wish, however, there is no reason why we cannot assume a similar lack of direction, or "purposiveness," in our analysis of social structures. Social structures contain people who have "motivation," but the structures themselves do not have conscious volition.

Part of Davis's inability to resolve the issue of teleology arises from his erroneous belief that there is something illegitimate about explaining behavior, in part, with reference to an actor's intentions. Davis' conviction, of course, directly contravenes a central methodological device of Max Weber, the emphasis on intentionality (Zeitlin, 1973:19). In Davis's view (1959:759),

terms connoting moral obligation or censure, or indicating explanation by intent, are particularly unsuited for the description of causal relationships because the meanings they stand for are properly part of the *objects* rather than the *basis* of explanation.

In functional analysis, with its emphasis on circular causation, intentions are both objects and bases of explanation. Further on, in a discussion of manifest and latent functions, Davis restates the point:

the manifest–latent distinction is important. Ironically, however, the [functionalist] movement has fallen victim to what it sought to overcome. The inability to see purposes and sentiments as objects of explanation, the unwillingness to remain detached – these have joined the inherent discomfort of analysis from a societal rather than a psychological standpoint and have riddled the weak terminology of functionalism with criticism and confusion.

Clearly the manifest–latent distinction is designed to force the investigator to ask whether a given function, or presumed function, is part of the conscious awareness of social actors. In the case of manifest functions the social structures generating them may receive the active support of members of society insofar as the latter perceive the nexus between structure and function. Their behavior, then, may be said to be purposive, and their intentions, motivations, or needs (cf. Bredemeier, 1955:176) may legitimately be used as a partial explanation for the existence and persistence of the social structure in question. Certainly the author of *The*

Power Elite, with his fundamental belief that major historical events occur because powerful people want them to occur, would be very pleased
with this mode of explanation.

   If it is widely believed, for instance, that the stable nuclear family helps
to prevent juvenile delinquency or creates psychological health or trans-
mits a strong religious commitment, and if such connections were shown
to exist, then the connections are manifest functions and it would be
legitimate to try to explain the persistence of the nuclear family, at least
in part, with reference to the intentions of those who recognize such
functions. If the rich and the super-rich believe that an assortment of tax
loopholes and government subsidies helps to perpetuate their wealth, and
if such connections were shown to exist (Lundberg, 1969), then again it
would be appropriate to ask how the wealthy may try to preserve structures with manifest functions that serve their interests (cf. Stinchcombe,
1968:93–98). If the political elite of Mexico believe that migration from
rural areas to large cities has a politically *conservative* impact on urban
populations while providing a safety valve for rural discontent
(Taller . . . , 1982:213), and if such relationships were shown to exist,
then it would be appropriate to explain the institutionalization of urban
migration, in part, with reference to the intentions and actions of members of the political elite. If political leaders subscribe to balance-of-
power theory, believing that a rough equality of power among two or
more contending power centers tends to suppress violent conflict, and if
such a relationship were shown to exist, then it would be appropriate to
ask how political actors – Bismarck comes to mind (cf. Freund, 1968:107–
8) – may make decisions intended to preserve a balance of power. In fact,
the entire corpus of knowledge, belief, supposition, judgment, and prejudice that defines the field of "strategic doctrine" turns on a key distinction between *intention* and *capability,* terms that more or less substitute
for Merton's means–ends distinction and that create an inescapable concern about manifest functions. The same is true of the field of economics,
which is built largely on the concept of *utility,* a concept that carries
strong connotations of intentionality. (A *rational* human being – that be-
loved prime mover of the econometrician's free-market model – may be
defined as one for whom many functions are manifest, and who acts
effectively to create and preserve structures that generate valued consequences.) As a final set of examples, consider the fact that the most
compelling questions raised by students of nonmarital fertility (Furstenburg, 1976) have to do with the circumstances under which actors are
successful in translating their fertility *intentions* into fertility *behavior,*

that advocates of effective fertility control for third-world nations must constantly anguish over the question whether motivation already exists or is dependent on further social development (Demerath, 1976), and that the prospects of gun control as a way of reducing violence seem to turn largely on the extent to which violent behavior is intentional, deliberate, premeditated, and so forth (Wright et al., 1983: ch.10).

One item in the preceding paragraph deserves special consideration. The relationship between intention and capability in the military realm is highly volatile, due primarily to the high rate of change in military capabilities. In recent years strategic doctrine in the United States, and perhaps in the Soviet Union, apparently has undergone radical change as a result of the fact that nuclear warheads can now be delivered with pinpoint accuracy. In terms of its impact (or expected impact) on intentions, missile accuracy may be far more important than "throw weight," number of warheads available, location of missiles, and so forth, because highly accurate weapons may tempt governments to launch counterforce or first-strike attacks. If such changes of intention were to occur, they would be tantamount to the abandonment of the pure deterrence strategy of the last several decades, which has been based on the presumption that only second-strike capabilities are essential and that such retaliatory attacks would be made primarily against nonmilitary targets. Such a change of intentions by either side, whether real or imagined, would bring about similar changes on the other side, producing a dangerous escalation at the level of "intersubjectivity" (Ford, 1985a, b). Neither side, of course, trusts the other not to make use of whatever capabilities seem to exist, and we observe a most un-Parsonian process of "technological drivenness." Social researchers unwilling to deal directly with the interaction of intention and capability would have little chance of capturing these dynamics.

We must always be aware, of course, that intentions are inferred entirely from observable behavior. This is a maxim among military planners, and it should be a maxim among social scientists.

In the case of latent functions, explanation by intentionality is not possible unless one were willing to make the "Freudian" assumption that unconscious intentions are ascertainable and have an impact even while remaining unconscious (cf. Freund, 1968:115). The author is quite willing to entertain such an assumption in conformity with a host of social psychologists and cultural anthropologists who use it as their main operating premise. On the other hand, those who believe in Mayhew's (1980) brand of purely structural explanation – an approach that eschews psychological perspectives – must be prepared to abandon the manifest–latent distinction altogether, a tactic that would seem to give the quietus to a large part of Davis's argument and perhaps also to a large part of sociology. The risks involved in throwing out an important part of the discipline are plausibly set forth by DiTomaso (1982), who argues that "structure" and "action" – the latter understood as behavior by individuals who have a means–ends rational orientation – must always be linked.

In brief, there is nothing wrong with using Weberian intentionality as a partial explanation of the creation and perpetuation of social structures (cf. Zeitlin, 1973:123–30,251–6). To refuse to do so is to run the risk of committing one or the other of an opposing pair of fallacies: Either we act like Kant's deluded dove, assuming that the ease with which our minds soar through the air implies that it would be easier yet for them to fly through a vacuum, or we walk hand-in-glove with the more naive disciples of Karl Marx, assuming that the ability of the human mind to impose itself on a recalcitrant world is just beyond a nullity. Neither extreme makes for good sociology, and effective research involves a balanced view. When Skocpol (1979:17) says that "as far as the causes of historical social revolutions go, Wendell Phillips was quite correct when he once declared, 'Revolutions are not made; they come,' " she tilts toward the Marxian end of the spectrum. And when Kreps (1986) shows that the response of communities to natural disasters sometimes involves a smooth transition from intentions – what Kreps calls "domains" and "tasks" – to the organization of "resources" and "activities," he illustrates Weberian rationality. On the other hand, when activities begin more or less spontaneously but eventually produce a conscious sense of responsibility, we observe a sort of Marxian emergence of superstructure from substructure, a process in which Weberian rationality is stood on its head. As I read Kreps's work, I am reminded of a fundamental question often raised by students of human creativity: Do inventions tend to occur by "accident" (Koestler, 1964: ch. VIII), or, on the contrary, is "necessity the mother of invention?" Some years ago the claim was made that what is unique about the modern research-and-development department is that it has "invented the social organization of invention"; that is, it exemplifies Kreps's notion of Weberian rationality and is rarely surprised by anything. But the truth of this claim remains an open question.

Colin Campbell (1982) points out that, despite the fact that the manifest–latent distinction receives considerable praise in textbooks, it is rarely used by practicing sociologists. This reluctance is attributed by Campbell largely to the fact that the manifest–latent distinction, as developed by Merton, has at least four different meanings:

There is, first of all . . . the contrast between conscious intention and actual consequence. Secondly, . . . Merton himself comes to use the dichotomy to refer to the difference between commonsense knowledge . . . and sociological understanding. Thirdly, there is the usage which equates manifest with the formal and official aims of organizations and latent with the purposes fulfilled by unofficial or illegal ones. Finally, there is the suggestion that manifest and latent relate to different levels of understanding with the former equal to apparent or surface meaning while the latter concerns the deeper or underlying reality of the phenomenon in question.

Although these several definitions tend to overlap one another, I have no quarrel against the suggestion that a thoroughgoing functional analysis would pursue all conceivable aspects of the manifest–latent distinction. As suggested earlier, intentions may have a lot to do with the creation and persistence of given social structures. Furthermore, the manifest–latent distinction sensitizes us to the sorts of questions that form the central theme of the sociology of knowledge. When disparities exist between intentions and actual consequences, between commonsense understandings and sociological insight, between "official" and "unofficial" consequences of structural conditions, between "apparent" and "deeper" meanings of social behavior, these disparities must be described, analyzed, and explained in the usual fashion, and it is the task of the sociologist of knowledge to provide these services. On the other hand, exercises in the sociology of knowledge are not an essential task of functional analysis, because functional analysis is concerned primarily with the consequences of social structures for the survivorship of larger social entities or interests. We do not insist, with Radcliffe-Brown (1935:400), that "usages" of a society only "function" through their impact on thoughts, sentiments, and actions of individuals. Although there is usually some degree of public awareness of the interconnections discerned through functional analysis, especially when "interests" are at stake, it is entirely possible that such awareness may be highly tenuous or completely absent and that the structures in question may have little to do with fulfillment of the expressed intentions of any sentient being. Functional analysis would not be vitiated in the least if virtually all functions turned out to be latent; furthermore, the discovery of large numbers of latent functions would do much to enhance the credibility of sociology as a productive enterprise worthy of high levels of public support. "Cultural dopes" would benefit immensely, along with sociologists.

In short, although public opinion and public perceptions are interesting phenomena, they are not fundamental to the concerns of functionalism.[2]

In fact, I lean toward Mayhew's conviction (1983:169) that ". . . the study of individuals [their opinions and perceptions] is likely to tell us little or nothing about the structure and operation of social systems." On the other hand, Mayhew seems to me all too ready to expunge social psychology from the field of sociology, disregarding the enticing prospects of the Marxian social psychology outlined by Zeitlin (1973:243–9).

Colin Campbell argues (1982:37) erroneously that functionalism tends to treat all behavior as if it were "Zweckrational" – that is, motivated by means–ends perceptions – while ignoring the "Wertrational, Affectual, and Traditional forms." Because one could never prove this claim unless one were willing to devote copious efforts to the study of intentions, and because functionalism places only a small emphasis on intentions, it is not necessary to tarry over this issue. Nevertheless, one may cite Campbell's claim (1982:37) that

although items of social structure may be used by individuals or groups as the means to the attainment of their goals, just as the instrumental action of people may coincide with the maintenance of such structures, this does not preclude the possibility that noninstrumental action may also serve to maintain them.

And one may respond that functionalists willingly study "noninstrumental action" – the various "expressive" forms of behavior so strongly emphasized in the Parsonian tradition – with regard to its impact on the survivorship of organizations or the discernible interests of individuals. There is nothing *sui generis* about expressive forms of behavior. They are fundamental (Collins, 1985:141–179).

Campbell warns us (1982:37) that, insofar as functional analysis becomes concerned about public awareness and the intentions of actors, it will be difficult to identify the relevant parties. ". . . Manifest and latent functions can be made to appear and disappear with ease merely by changing the perspective from which the action is viewed or by focusing on the different purposes served by it;" Petersen (1979:212) provides an excellent illustration when he says that "among two of the largest social classes of India . . . it is in the economic interest of each person to have many children, even though the overall consequence of this breeding is disastrous." This is a valid point, but it is precisely the transitory winds and ripples of human perception that make life (and the sociology of knowledge) interesting. Let us welcome the challenge. In charting these shifts, we should meet head on Campbell's claim that

the introduction of functionality actually makes the discernment of manifest functions a more difficult task than it was before, for if it is peculiarly difficult to establish exactly who intended and recognized which consequences, it is doubly difficult to establish exactly who intended and recognized their functionality.

Those who intend functionality, claims Campbell (1982:39–40), necessarily have ". . . a quite sophisticated knowledge of causal processes." If that claim applies to the laity, it must apply even more forcefully to functionalists, and it implies that functionalism demands the most sophisticated methods of analysis.

Toward the end of his paper (1982:41), Campbell arrives at the reasonable conviction that, while the manifest–latent distinction has some utility, sociologists should not confine themselves to the study of manifest functions, that they ". . . should examine the objective consequences of behavior and not merely the subjective dispositions of actors," and that ". . . a thoroughgoing functional analysis has no need of such terms as manifest and latent. . . ." I consider this conclusion to be inescapable because I believe that many functions turn out to be latent; that is, we would never discern them if we had to rely on public opinion as our major source of insight. If it is true that the advance of civilization occurs insofar as we are able to do complicated tasks without thinking about them, and if these tasks are important in maintaining survivorship and in preserving basic interests, then functional analysis may find itself sharing the claim of ethnomethodology that everyday, habitual forms of social behavior are the paramount concern. Perhaps Merton was right when he suggested that spectacular disasters such as plane crashes are not nearly so interesting as recurring minidisasters such as the daily harvest of traffic deaths (Merton and Nisbet, 1961:712). In studying the latter we would do well to ask whether the structures known as "compulsory safety inspections" or "tougher drunk-driving laws" have any appreciable impact on the rate of traffic mortality or injury, and what the social forces are that create and maintain these structures. It is a virtual certainty that we could not get far in answering these questions by means of public opinion polling. In the words of Elman R. Service (1962:202), a given social structure ". . . does not need to be necessarily a conscious understanding and total plan by the people . . . , [so that] it is not relevant . . . to argue about whether the people understand precisely what they were doing. . . ."

In an excellent paper dealing with "selection by consequences," B. F. Skinner (1981) deftly dismisses the teleology argument:

Only past consequences figure in selection. . . . A particular species does not have eyes in order that its members may see better; it has them because certain members, undergoing variation, were able to see better and hence were more likely to transmit the variation. . . . The consequences of operant behavior are not what the behavior is now for; they are merely similar to the consequences which have shaped and maintained it. . . . People do not observe particular practices in order that the group will be more likely to survive; they observe them because groups which induced their members to do so survived and transmitted them.

Skinner may be faulted for a tendency to overgeneralize (from time to time people do know what is going on) but his basic stand on the matter of teleology seems to be unassailable. In any case my position on the issue of teleology is identical to that of Braithwaite (1955:324,328), who says that

there is one type of teleological explanation in which the reference to the future presents no difficulty, namely, explanations of an intentional human action in terms of a goal . . . . For my teleological answer to the question as to why I am staying in Cambridge all through August – that I am doing so in order to finish writing my book – would be regarded by my questioner as equivalent to an answer that I am doing so because I intend to finish writing my book, my staying in Cambridge being a means to fulfil that intention; and this answer would have been an explanation of the causal sort with my intention as cause preceding my stay in Cambridge as effect.

When Braithwaite then quotes with approval the notion that "teleological behavior becomes synonymous with behavior controlled by negative feedback" (cf. Hempel, 1959:298–9), he implies that we would do well to inquire as to how his past academic experiences have influenced his motivations for writing books. My position on this question is also identical to that of Alexander (1982,1983), who assures us that the tension of "instrumental structuralism" and "normative" theories that emphasize "individual control" would best be resolved if we were to concentrate on creating "multidimensional" theories integrating these two traditions. This strategy would have the additional virtue of enabling us to address classical problems such as "voluntarism" and "rationality."

If the preceding paragraphs make any sense at all, they must raise serious doubts about Levy and Cancian's claim (1968:24–25) that the concept of "nonfunction," in the sense of a structure that has neither "eufunctions" nor "dysfunctions," is "inutile." One can readily imagine structures that do not manifestly contribute to the survival value of any aspect of society, and do not have a recognized impact on vested interests. And if many structures are not clearly perceived by public opinion, it may be possible to eliminate these structures without offending power-

ful interests. When Levy and Cancian say (1968:41) that functional interconnections involve patterns that have "persistence . . . despite forces
that tend to destroy the pattern," they imply that there may be some
patterns that, by comparison, have little persistence in the face of pressure. The question should remain open; we cannot make the facile assumption, as did Malinowski (Garbarino, 1977:57), that every structure
has some identifiable function. If there are "vestigial" social structures
(survivals), it would be worthwhile to know about them.

2. Methodological inhibitions

Continuing his misdirected effort to show that functionalism is the common practice of virtually all social scientists, Davis (1959:769) argues that
any form of analysis claiming to be nonfunctionalist is either worthless or
outside the purview of sociology. Examining "that neglected concept,
'non-functional analysis,' " Davis says that

> this residual category seems, by implication, to include traits falling into one or
> the other of two classes: either they constitute some sort of reductionism and are
> therefore non-sociological in character, or they constitute some form of raw em-
> piricism or sheer data manipulation and are therefore non-theoretical. In other
> words, whatever falls outside the domain of sociological theory falls outside the
> realm of functionalism.

My response is twofold. First, I grant that functionalism is not mere
reductionism or raw empiricism; still, empirically based efforts to integrate biological, psychological, and sociological processes have an important role in functional analysis and should not unreflectingly be thought of
as alternatives to functionalism. The discussion of sex preselection of
children, presented later in this book, is a prime example. Any social
scientist operating on a holistic principle, examining relationships between parts and wholes, would necessarily view human behavior as involving a wide range of psychobiosocial considerations. Personality systems would be examined in relation to social systems, in relation to
biological systems, and so forth (cf. Alexander, 1982,1983), and empirical
data would be appropriate at all levels of analysis. Brilliant integrating
and generalizing investigations such as those of A. K. Cohen (1955) or
Yehudi Cohen (1964) would be forthcoming, one hopes, on a more or
less routine basis.

Second, there are respected forms of sociological explanation, neither
reductionist nor given to mere data manipulation, that do not exemplify in

any way Davis's claim that functional analysis involves feedback and self-regulation. Social scientists have developed theories of a highly abstract nature, parsimonious, involving elaborate causal mechanisms, founded on a mass of empirical data, holding forth the possibility of prediction and explanation, and such theories usually say nothing about circular causation, self-regulation, or the relative prospects of stationarity and change through time. If the latter properties are essential elements of functionalism, then such theories are nonfunctionalistic. And since they are often highly abstract and tend to explain social facts by means of other social facts, they cannot justly be said to exemplify either reductionism or mindless empiricism. Some examples would be recent theories about the intergenerational transmission of status, theories about crime causation, or theories about marital instability. In the concluding section of this volume I argue that, as a result of a sort of value-added process, such theories may *become* functionalistic, but at any given moment they may fall considerably short of what I call a *functionalist culmination,* a theoretical climax stage.

In *The Sociological Imagination* (1959) Mills argues that sophisticated research methods do not necessarily lead to sophisticated theories; in fact, he suggests, they may be an impediment. Critics of functional analysis have stood this thesis on its head, insisting that functional theory does not necessarily imply appropriate research strategies. In Davis's view, although functionalism "abounds in principles and categories," it cannot offer much in the way of verification; that is, it is methodologically weak. He then accepts this contention all too quickly, turning immediately to the question of *why* the charge is true. The answer, he claims, is that functionalism has an inordinate concern with goals and purposes, and data on such matters are inherently unreliable. It is difficult, however, to understand why we cannot study manifest functions – functions of which members of society have a conscious awareness – at least as satisfactorily as we can study latent functions. On the contrary, because manifest functions are widely recognized (by definition), they are amenable to analysis by means of standard research techniques such as questionnaires, interviews, and so on. It is precisely in the case of latent functions – those not involving conscious, goal-oriented behavior on the part of social actors – that the problem of data gathering becomes difficult, requiring all sorts of indirect approaches. Insofar as goal-directed behavior is a part of the structure-functional nexus, then, it would seem to make the methodological problems *more* manageable, not less so.

Elaborating on the alleged methodological shortcomings of functional analysis, Davis (1959:763) says that functionalism attempts to state the requisites for the existence of any society or to explain the universals of social organization. In such matters there can be no proof by co-variation, because, by definition, all actual societies exhibit the traits in question. Nor can functionalists create experimental societies to test the effect of omitting this or that ingredient.

This argument is crucial and, happily, it is wrong for several reasons. First, why can we not create experimental social entities to test the effects of omitting "this or that ingredient?" Creating whole societies may be impossible, but a wide range of functionalist hypotheses apply to smaller social entities – for example, an assortment of small groups such as families, work groups, or primary groups in the military – and such entities are readily observed in a natural setting or in the laboratory. Second, even structures that are thought to be "universals" are amenable to analysis by the method of covariation insofar as it is possible to study social entities other than "actual societies" through the use of historical records or even archaeological findings. For instance, it may be that virtually all existing small business firms of a given type meet certain universal functional prerequisites; however, agencies such as the Small Business Administration have records of countless businesses that failed presumably for lack of such prerequisites, and several other sources of information may be available (cf. Carroll, 1984). If Mayhew's inquiries were to take advantage of such information, they would avoid Davis's impasse of arguing for the universality – Mayhew calls it "widespread representation" (1983:208) – of hierarchies with unity of command and would search for evidence that hierarchies *lacking* this feature have little prospect of survival. Perhaps one could show, among other possibilities, that major corporations lacking unity of command (e.g., Getty Oil, ca. December 1983) are more likely to be taken over (i.e., absorbed) by other corporations.

It is interesting that Irving Zeitlin (1973:5,106) echoes Davis's argument about the inapplicability of "proof by covariation" in functional analysis and then contradicts himself by saying that one might try ". . . to show that certain empirical conditions contribute to a society's adaptive capacity and that their absence leads to its dissolution, conspicuous disadvantage, or the like" (1973:53), and that, in the process of "capital accumulation" and the "conflict among capitals," the losers are either "destroyed" or "absorbed" (1973:127). As we shall see, some functional theories – Tylor's theory of the incest taboo is an example – are stated at such a high level of abstraction, or refer to social processes that occurred so long ago, that they cannot be tested by the methods of covariation; for these instances Davis has a point. But such theories may turn out to be relatively infrequent in the entire corpus of functional analysis. In any case, we shall also see that for many types of social organizations it is possible to make life tables. A life table, by definition, must contain information about "death," and when we have organizations that "die" we are clearly able to invoke Davis's "proof by co-variation."

3. The languid logic of indispensability

In his discussion of functional indispensability, Davis wrongly accuses Merton of claiming that "certain cultural or social forms" are indispensable in fulfilling certain functions. Although I do not consider the indispensability question to be central to the functionalist endeavor in sociology, it is clear that many biologists recognize the strain toward indispensability, or universality, of highly adaptive structures:

The organisms of today are those that have succeeded in adapting and thus have survived the changes in their environment. The mechanisms that a biologist studies are *ipso facto* adaptations. Our study of these adaptations is merely our way of understanding the nature of the successful existence of organisms (Ruibal, 1967:1).

Notice that Ruibal is close to asserting a tautology: That which survives has apparent survival value, and that which has survival value tends to survive. Turner and Maryanski (1979:124), along with Chandler Morse (Alexander, 1983:189), consider such tautologies unacceptable. I would agree, unless one is willing to do what biological functionalism does routinely: compare surviving organisms with those that do not survive. Levy and Cancian (1968:31) repeat Turner and Maryanski's claim when they say that functional analysis has sometimes involved the following "vacuous" argument:

(1) Social patterns persist if and only if they are adaptive (or functional or fulfill needs);
(2) Pattern X is adaptive;

Therefore, pattern X has persisted.

This syllogism, as we shall see in a moment, would be vastly improved if the minor premise and conclusion were reversed, and if it were followed by a second syllogism involving a situation in which "pattern X has not persisted."

A universal, by definition, is a necessary condition for the fulfillment of a function. Those who seek out universals, again by definition, are using the method of "analytical induction" favored by a number of social scientists some years ago. This method, as explained by Robinson (1951), involves little more than the establishment of necessary conditions for the occurrence of a given phenomenon. It behooves us, then, to review the logic of necessary conditions.

In the classic logic of the syllogism we find the means of establishing both necessary and sufficient conditions. Consider the following syllogisms, in which the prime (') means negation (that is, absence) and the underline means "therefore":

Modus ponens:	*Modus tollens:*	
If C, then P	If C, then P	
C	P'	(1)
P	C'	
Assert the consequent:	*Deny the antecedent:*	
If C, then P	If C, then P	
P	C'	(2)
C	P'	

Either the modus ponens or the modus tollens establishes sufficient conditions, and either the argument asserting the consequent or that denying the antecedent establishes necessary conditions. It is often assumed in logic textbooks that one is primarily interested in establishing sufficient conditions, so that the last two forms of argument, in row (2), are considered fallacious. Although assertion of the consequent is the major form of proof used by analytic inductionists, denial of the antecedent could also be used. If C were an allegedly universal social structure fulfilling a certain function, then C could be established as a necessary condition by means of analytical induction (asserting the consequent) without observation of any instances in which C does not occur. This has been the basic strategy of functionalists making "requisite analyses." Denial of the antecedent would also establish C as a necessary condition without observation of any instances in which C is present. The denial-of-antecedent argument implies that in instances where a structure does not exist, one must observe a failure to survive in order to establish universality of the structure; but as Davis correctly points out, this strategy has never been popular among functionalists.

If one wishes to establish a condition as both necessary and sufficient for the occurrence of some phenomenon – a step that goes beyond a mere search for universals – the following approach may be used:

	Necessary (Indispensable)	Necessary'
Sufficient	Either form in row (1) and either in row (2)	Modus ponens or modus tollens
Sufficient'	Assert the consequent or deny the antecedent	None

Mill's method of difference involves the modus ponens combined with denial of the antecedent (the classic experiment) while holding background factors constant; the method of agreement involves the modus ponens only while allowing background factors to vary. Used together, Mill's methods are an attempt to identify conditions sufficient to create an effect under a variety of circumstances. If one were to design experiments that also denied the antecedent while allowing background factors to vary, one would be attempting to establish a necessary condition. But this is an uncommon procedure.

Other functionalist terms can be clarified with reference to the above cross-classification. If two or more structures are "functionally equivalent" in that they fulfill the same function, then each of the structures is a sufficient but not a necessary condition for the function and could be established as such either by the modus ponens or the modus tollens or both. Levy and Cancian (1968:32) use a stretched version of the modus ponens when they restate Kluckhohn's theory of witchcraft in syllogistic form:

(1) If a society survives (*A*), then hostility is managed (*B*);
(2) If hostility is managed (*B*), then witchcraft (*C*) or a functional equivalent (*D*) is present;
(3) The functional equivalents of witchcraft (*D*) are not present in Navaho society;
(4) Navaho society has survived (*A*);

Therefore, witchcraft is present in Navaho society (*C*).

Although I agree with Levy and Cancian's claim that this argument is highly sophisticated, it would be strengthened if (1) the first premise were stated in a way that mandates an effort to show that witchcraft, by way of hostility management, has a demonstrable impact on the survival of some aspect of society; (2) the matter of equivalents were not handled in the specious manner of the third premise. Such a strategy would begin by using, say, the modus ponens to establish witchcraft, S_1, as a sufficient condition for survival, SURV, over many societies:

> If S_1, then SURV;
> S_1;
> _____
> SURV

The prospect of an equivalent could then be assessed by testing whether S_1 were a necessary condition, perhaps by denying the antecedent:

> If S_1, then SURV;
> S_1';
> _____
> SURV'

If the minor premise were true, as observed, and the conclusion false, this would imply the existence of at least one alternative to witchcraft, S_2. We could then return to the modus ponens:

> If S_2, then SURV;
> S_2;
> _____
> SURV

S_2 cannot be a necessary condition for survival, because the sufficiency of witchcraft as a functional alternative has already been shown. This applies to all potential remaining equivalents. It should be made clear that lists of equivalents are not infinite as is sometimes alleged; they are limited by the same rules of closure that apply in any instance where we propose a multiple-causation hypothesis (cf. Hempel, 1959:284–5). Furthermore, when we speak of alternatives or equivalents, we are addressing the issue of equifinality in a way that avoids the usual confusion about human intentions and their teleological implications: Several structures may tend to produce the same results, and these tendencies, involving the classic model of multiple causation, may occur independently of human volition or awareness.

In the case of adaptation theories, discussed in Chapter 5, the use of one form of adaptation tends to eliminate other forms, so that adaptation mechanisms become "substitutable" (i.e., functionally equivalent) in the same way that, under the law of supply and demand, certain consumer items become substitutable for one another. It is important to remember, however, that the Aristotelian pitfalls – the false dilemmas (Babbie, 1983: 262–4) – of the above procedures are readily avoided. Powerful new methods for analyzing dichotomous (Aristotelian) and polytomous cross-tabulations, such as the log-linear model or FUNCAT in SAS (SAS User's Guide, 1979:221–36), say very little about necessary and/or sufficient conditions. The concept of "nested effects" implies that certain causal relationships occur only under certain conditions, so that the conditions could be regarded as necessary. But nested effects do not seem to occur often. In any case if we had dichotomous data about survival, presence or absence of, say, witchcraft, and presence or absence of possible equivalents of witchcraft, we would be far better off using log-linear methods rather than the above sort of syllogistic approach that has traditionally caused confusion. If we were to apply these methods in assessing ways in which Navaho society regulates hostility, we would learn far less about equivalents and far more about Navahos. And we shall see in Chapter 5 that, in situations where adaptation (e.g., survivorship) and various structural conditions are measured as continuous variables, it makes little sense to think in terms of the outmoded logic of indispensability. This logic has been the bane of functional analysis.

The final irony of Davis's article is his formulation of a quintessential functional theory to explain the historical rise of functional analysis – an early exercise in Alvin Gouldner's "reflexive sociology." In the latter part of the nineteenth century, according to Davis, social scientists throughout Europe and North America were struggling to find a safe niche in universities that were often less than enthusiastic about new and unimpressive disciplines. As in the fishpond example, these social scientists were trying to reduce the toxicity of the waters, and they soon realized that if they were to adopt a strange new language such as that of functionalism, they could at least create the impression if not the substance of having many new things to say. "A movement gains strength," says Davis (1959:768), "if it can rally under a special name." Although all this is no doubt true, my contention is that the special language of functional analysis and its claim of uniqueness had at least as much scientific substance as they had political impact; functional analysis, in other words, had both manifest and latent functions.

2. The incest taboo: social selection as a form of feedback

Leslie A. White (1948), a founder of neo-evolutionary anthropology (Garbarino, 1977:88), has provided a penetrating analysis of the social functions of the incest taboo, an analysis that affords us an opportunity to clarify the central functionalist concept, that of social survivorship. In the iconoclastic fashion of Emile Durkheim, White begins his lengthy disquisition by evaluating various theories: some essentially biological, some psychological, some sociological. He then explains convincingly why each of these theories is unsatisfactory as to logic, evidence, or range of explanatory power.[1] After mildly castigating his colleagues in sociology and social anthropology for eventually abandoning the effort to explain the incest taboo, White (1948:423) resurrects a nearly forgotten theory developed many decades ago by Edward B. Tylor:

Exogamy, enabling a growing tribe to keep itself compact by constant unions between its spreading clans, enables it to overmatch any number of small inter-marrying groups, isolated and helpless. Again and again in the world's history, savage tribes must have had plainly before their minds the simple practical alternative between marrying out and being killed out.

In a singularly perceptive series of paragraphs, White claims that alliances among small kinship bands are further strengthened by such practices as the levirate,[2] sororate,[3] bride-price, and dowry. The remainder of the article offers a series of trenchant speculations about the way in which severe economic deprivation might intensify competition among small food-gathering kinship bands, thus producing a need for larger fighting groups with reduced mortality from internecine war. An elaboration of this theory is found in a study by Service (1962: ch. 3), who discusses Julian H. Steward's concept of the "band level of sociocultural integration" in the same terms as White. A further elaboration, involving ritual slaughter of livestock (i.e., "intentional" creation of economic deprivation) as a way of forcing alliances, is discussed by Moran (1982:56). The central role of competition and scarcity in sociocultural evolution is discussed in Harris (1968, 1979).

Many theories of the functionalist genre have in common the fact that a given social structure – in this instance, the incest taboo – is being explained with reference either to its effects on population increase or its effects on the survivorship of a larger social structure. In the case of Tylor's theory it is readily apparent that a failure of population replacement, brought about by lack of success in an endless "deadly quarrel," would constitute a condition terminating the existence of a social organization (Aberle et al., 1950). Let us assume, with Tylor, that some bands are killed out, and let us thereby raise the formidable issue of social selection and the "mortality" of social organizations. After clarifying these matters, we shall return briefly to Tylor's theory.

What is death? To many the answer seems obvious, but in W. Ross Ashby's description (1968:297) of a cat killing a mouse, it is not at all obvious:

Suppose a mouse is trying to escape from a cat, so that the survival of the mouse is in question. As a dynamic system, the mouse can be in a variety of states; thus it can be in various postures, its head can be turned this way or that, its temperature can have various values, it may have two ears or none. These different states may occur during its attempt to escape and it may still be said to have survived. On the other hand if the mouse changes to the state in which it is in four separated pieces, or has lost its head, or has become a solution of amino-acids circulating in the cat's blood then we do not consider its arrival at one of these states as corresponding to "survival."

An agency of the United Nations has struggled for many years with the problem of establishing an internationally acceptable definition of death, and a few years ago an important study committee of the Harvard Medical School suggested "a new criterion for death" (Petersen, 1975:246) based on a cessation of brain activity. Clearly, the mortality of social organizations is at least as difficult to define as that of individuals; yet, despite this hardship, many responsible students of social organization believe with Marschak (1959:139) that "one empirically useful approach is to estimate the efficiency of an organizational form by taking as the goal a high chance of survival" – never mind the fact that the discipline has no recognized definition of the termination of social organizations. A similar argument was made many years ago by none other than Kingsley Davis (1949:144) regarding the survival value of consensus about the "ultimate ends" of a society:

. . . the possession of common-ultimate values by the members of different societies arose in the process of societal evolution. It resulted from the process of natural selection on a societal basis. In the struggle against nature and in the struggle between one human society and another, only those groups survived and perpetuated their culture which developed and held in common among their members a set of ultimate ends. The important thing was not so much the particular content of the ends but rather the fact of having ends in common. Viewed in this light the possession of common ends must be virtually as old as human society itself.

As we shall see, this sort of social selection is a form of negative feedback involving circular causation and "cybernetic control." Once again, Davis touches upon a unique aspect of functionalism, a form of analysis that he was later to criticize for arrogating a uniqueness that it did not have.

Accepting for the moment the notion that social organizations may cease to exist, we may wish to identify conditions that create high (or low) survival value among organizations. Many scholars have sought such conditions, and several noteworthy efforts are summarized in Table 2.1. The first three lists apparently were intended by their authors to define the "functional requisites" (Sztompka, 1974: ch. 8) of whole societies, that is, necessary conditions for the existence of societies. Hage's intention, apparently, was to indicate forms of social investment that bring about an increase in a number of "outputs" (Hage, 1972:128,132); because Hage deals with quantitative variations, it is inappropriate in his case to speak of necessary conditions or prerequisites, but the abandonment of that particular usage does not involve any real loss. In fact, Hage moves away from requisite analysis in the manner suggested by Chapter 1. Hage's analysis implies that the output of any social organization could become critically deficient, thereby threatening the continued existence of the organization (1972:164).

The lists in Table 2.1 are formal taxonomies; yet, none seems to comply entirely with the standard criteria of sound classification. It is unclear, for instance, whether the categories of each scheme are intended to be exhaustive; it is even less certain that they are mutually exclusive. And they are so abstract as to be almost meaningless. For instance, it is possible that (as Marxists imply) certain "economic systems" become dysfunctional at certain levels of social development, yet merely asserting that an economic system is a prerequisite would hardly encourage one to undertake the appropriate Marxian analysis.[4] Finally, and with the possible exception of Malinowski and Parsons (cf. Szymanski, 1972), these taxonomies are largely incommensurable with one another, indicating a lack

Table 2.1. *Conditions threatening the survivorship of social organizations*

==

Conditions	Definitions/ Indicators	Authority

----

1. Absence (or deficiency) of at least one prerequisite — Malinowski
   a. Economic system
   b. Political organization
   c. Social control
   d. Educational system

2. Absence (or deficiency) of at least one prerequisite — Parsons
   a. Adaptation — Economic sector
   b. Goal attainment — Political sector
   c. Integration — Symbolic, ritual activity
   d. Latency — Socialization, social control

3. Absence (or deficiency) of at least one prerequisite — Aberle et al. (1950)
   a. Provision for adequate relationship to the environment and for sexual recruitment
   b. Role differentiation and role assignment
   c. Communication
   d. Shared cognitive orientations
   e. A shared, articulated set of goals
   f. The normative regulation of means
   g. The regulation of affective expression
   h. Socialization
   i. The effective control of disruptive forms of behavior

4. Deficiency of at least one input — Hage (1972)
   a. Input of instrumental knowledge — Expenditure for education
   b. Input of expressive knowledge — Expenditure for art
   c. Input of instrumental power — Expenditure for military
   d. Input of expressive power — Family income
   e. Input of instrumental reward — Capital investment in industry
   f. Input of expressive reward — Expenditure for leisure time activities (sports, entertainment, vacations)
   g. Input of instrumental rights — Expenditure for health
   h. Input of expressive rights — Expenditure for religious activities

==

of consensus among social scientists as to conditions threatening survivorship of social entities.

I believe that such incommensurabilities will persist until we turn away from the problem of defining prerequisites (or quasi prerequisites as in Hage's case) and concentrate more fully on social selection processes thought to be influenced by our erstwhile prerequisites. An analysis of such linkages would force us to define prerequisites more carefully, perhaps even to abandon the notion of prerequisites altogether in favor of the reasonable conviction that certain quantifiable conditions have a measurable impact on quantifiable aspects of social survivorship. Such a perspective would necessarily lead us to adopt the "variation-and-selective-retention" model nicely described in a neglected article by Donald Campbell (1969) and elaborated more recently by Hannan and Freeman (1977), Langton (1979), Skinner (1981), Weick (1981), Freeman and Hannan (1983), and Carroll (1984). Theories of sociocultural evolution, claims Campbell, have shown an almost exclusive concern with the course, rather than the mechanisms, of social evolution. This misplaced emphasis has created such unfortunate aberrations as parallelism, or "unilinear progress theories," which usually imply that all human societies tend to evolve from simple to complex forms, with the latter best exemplified by modern societies, usually one's own. Campbell claims that parallelism has been slightly tainted by its strong association with a conservative political outlook, citing in this connection his own case study of A. G. Keller, a collaborator of William Graham Sumner (Campbell, 1969:71). Campbell seems to feel that the charge of conservative bias has been made unjustly against the evolutionary perspective; it is arguable, in fact, that certain brands of Marxism have a strong commitment to parallelism, albeit by other names. In any case our readiness to assign social thinkers to various political pigeonholes may be shaken by Harris's (1968:609) remark that "Keller was perfectly aware of the resemblance between [his and Sumner's] point of view and that of Marx." "Ideological" issues of this sort are discussed more fully in the appendix.

In Donald Campbell's view the *mechanisms* of social evolution have an abstract similarity to those of natural selection in Darwin's theory (Campbell, 1969:73):

The most exciting current contribution of Darwin is in his model for the achievement of purposive or ends-guided processes through a mechanism involving blind, stupid, unforsightful elements. [There is a] . . . formal parallel between natural selection in organic evolution and trial-and-error learning. The common analogy also has been recognized in many other loci, as in embryonic growth, wound healing, crystal formation, development of science, radar, echo-location, vision, creative thinking, etc.

The specific mechanisms of variation in social selection, however, are not at all similar to those of biological evolution, and social selection may be far more complex than the biologist's reproductive or lethal selection because of the difficulty of measuring the survival value of social organizations.

Campbell (1969:73) argues that variation in social behavior is continually taking place:

Such variations can be of several kinds: on the one hand, there can be variations between social groups, as in the form of social organization or some item of material culture. Equally relevant are internal variations such as differences between persons within a group in their execution of common custom. Also usable are variations across occasions, as in the execution of some collective organizational problem. Such variations provide adequate raw materials for selective systems to operate on, whether the variations are deliberate or haphazard.

Admittedly, this is a vague formulation. The advocates of social evolutionary theory are still assailed and confused by the problem of explaining the initial occurrence of structural forms such as, say, the incest taboo. As Sumner used to insist, social origins are often lost in obscurity – often, but not always.[5] In any case the search for origins (initial "variations") is only a small part of the variation-and-selective-retention approach; furthermore, as Langton (1979:288–9) has argued, contemporary social scientists

know . . . at least as much about innovation and enculturation as Darwin knew about heredity and variation; . . . they know at least as much about the struggle for reinforcement as Darwin knew about the struggle for existence; . . . they know at least as much about sociocultural selection as Darwin knew about natural selection; and . . . they know at least as much about the relationships among these components of sociocultural evolution as Darwin knew about the relationships among the components of organic evolution.

On the all-important matter of social selection, Campbell recognizes social survivorship (among other processes) as an essential mechanism (1969:74):

Because of the differences in the social preservation system, and because of the greater variety of integrational organizations compatible with effective collective action, human social organizations, unlike the organization of cells in the body and unlike the social organizations of insects, can be varied and eliminated and modified on a part-by-part basis. . . . Nonetheless it is conceivable that [various customs] became dominant through the extinction of total societies lacking these customs.

Clearly, then, social organizations may fail to survive, but their failure is far more complex (and perhaps more glorious) than that of Ashby's mouse slain by a cat.

A social organization, or even a whole society, may die in many ways. Up to now we have discussed the termination of social organizations only by the most obvious means, a failure of population replacement. In the literature of history and of the social sciences one finds a large assortment of circumstances allegedly bringing about the decline and fall, the collapse, disintegration, or termination of complex social forms. (A content analysis of this literature would be most edifying.) Unfortunately, we do not have the benefit of a consensus on the precise nature of such circumstances. If, for instance, a social organization is absorbed by another, has it ceased to exist? If an organization breaks up, or is partitioned (as in the case of Poland around 1795) by its enemies, at what point has it failed to survive? Can a society cease to exist through mass apathy? Can rates of social deviance become so high, or failures of social control so massive, that an organization thus afflicted may be said, at some point, to have terminated? These questions are not merely rhetorical: At least one scholar has answered each of them in the affirmative. For example:

The competition between societies was something very different from the Darwinian struggle for existence. The weaker did not get eliminated, but in all but a few cases, absorbed. The victors were usually content to let the institutions of the weaker people alone so long as they themselves controlled the government and collected the taxes. It was impossible to demonstrate any general Darwinian mechanism that would eliminate dysfunctional institutions (Homans, 1962: 27).[6]

[One] might wonder what the definition of survival is. This goes back to the definition of what a society is. The suggested definition . . . is that there is a production of eight outputs, one of which is sovereignty. As there is a decline in one or more of these outputs, the existence of the society becomes more and more in doubt. One contemporary [sic] example is the collapse of Poland at the end of the eighteenth century (Hage, 1972:164).

The realization of any of the following conditions terminates the existence of a society – the existence of the structure of action, though not necessarily the members.

    A. The biological extinction or dispersion of the members . . .
    B. Apathy of the members . . .
    C. The war of all against all . . .
    D. The absorption of the society into another society . . . (Aberle et al., 1950:103)

I must quarrel with all these formulations: They are vague (e.g., the "collapse" of Poland through partitioning, the war of all against all), they often refer to transitory events (e.g., military occupation), and they do not necessarily retain the imagery of an ending of a social form (e.g., mass apathy).

In short, of conditions terminating social organizations we have no measure. It is not surprising, therefore, to find scholars lamenting the fact that they cannot resolve critical issues such as the role of churches in creating social "fragmentation *versus* integration" for the obvious reason that we have "no metric for doing so" (Hammond, 1981). Until an adequate metric is made available, the fundamental Hobbesian questions about social cohesion cannot be approached. If such a metric were to take the form of life-table analysis, as advocated herein, we would quickly realize the advantages of studying large cohorts of small organizations rather than small cohorts of large organizations (Hannan and Freeman, 1977:933,960; Turner and Maryanski, 1979:77–78). The latter tend to get us caught up in idiographic explanations, when we should be seeking nomothetic levels of explanation. And despite the popular belief that large firms dominate modern economic systems, small firms remain ubiquitous and "bountiful" (Granovetter, 1984). In the next chapter we shall illustrate these points.

In the meantime we must agree with Irving Zeitlin (1973:24,53) that, in the absence of a consensus as to how social organizations die, the traditional functionalist jargon involving prerequisites, universals, and the like should be abandoned.

One of the referees of this volume believes that my emphasis on "large cohorts of small organizations" is a poor tactic. She accuses me of using ". . . micro-systems for convenience . . ." and of implying that ". . . macro-solutions will grow naturally out of micro-solutions." She adds that "the question that has to be answered has to do with what it means for institutions and social systems to die." The answer, she says, "will not come automatically from solving the question at the micro-level: No amount of knowledge about the life or death of particular families will answer the question of the life or death of marriage as an institution or society as a system." This critic is correct in insisting that social theory does not develop automatically and that the life or death of whole societies remains problematical. But I do not accept other parts of her argument for several reasons: First, I do not use microsystems "for convenience" but rather because the discipline has a degree of consensus about what constitutes the life or death of microsystems; second, survivorship is not always the dependent variable in functional analysis, and i-functions (those that serve particular interests rather than having an impact on survival) can be studied within any organization, large or small; third, I agree with Martindale's (1960: chs. 18,19) suggestion that microfunctionalists have tended to become macrofunctionalists, and perhaps vice versa; fourth, the macro/micro distinction does not, or should not, represent some frightening Rubicon that we all fear to cross: It is merely a dichotomization of organizational size, and size is just another variable among many; fifth, as I try to show in Chapter 3, if there is in the United States strong social selection, for instance, in favor of families headed by females, I believe that this change is tantamount to a change in the *institutions* of marriage and kinship. Institutions, in other words, are processes that take place within social organizations.

Assuming, then, that in many instances it will be possible to measure the survival value of organizations, we are ready to return to a consideration of Tylor's theory of the incest taboo. If we can imagine an extremely harsh environment in which large numbers of kinship bands are contending for available resources, what the Tylor theory tells us is that some of these bands, lacking the requirement of exogamy, are killed out by similar organizations in which the incest taboo is maintained; as the Nuer say, "they are our enemies, so we marry them." In Tylor's theory it is clear what the factors are that bring about the termination of kinship bands: Individual members are killed in an endless series of deadly quarrels. And it is equally clear that the reduced survivorship of nonexogamous kin groups acts as a cybernetic control device that holds the average practice of exogamy at a level that presumably maximizes survivorship, just as fish mortality in Davis's fishpond regulates the toxicity of the water, and vice versa. The Tylor theory, then, is a feedback theory about the maintenance of an organizational form or structure, and the theory has precisely the same elements as evolutionary theory in biology (Hardin, 1959). In the latter instance a disturbance (variation) raises or lowers the average development of some anatomical feature; if this disturbance is dysfunctional (as most genetic disturbances are), then natural selection tends to remove those individual organisms whose phenotypes (visible structural features) had the largest impact in raising or lowering the average development of the structure in question; the preceding optimal development of the structural feature is thereby reestablished. Levy and Cancian fail to recognize this process when they claim (1968:37) that ". . . the explanation of the incest taboo in terms of its function of creating alliances among families . . . does not involve reciprocal or self-regulating relationships."

One may object that social processes do not operate in the mechanistic way just suggested; but neither do biological processes, and this fact has never weakened the alacrity of evolutionary theorists in biology. One may also object that performing a pure "thought experiment" based on Tylor's theory is an exercise in the crassest form of "conjectural history," defined by Radcliffe-Brown as a futile search for distant social origins. If, however, our ideas about origins are recognized as nothing more than thought experiments, as metaphors, then they have utility.

We are now ready to attempt a definition of social survivorship. Because it appears that social organizations may be terminated in more than one way, our definition will be multidimensional; that is, several criteria must be met in order to establish the viability of a social organization. Certainly population replacement is one of these criteria, and the Tylor theory of the incest taboo provides an illustration. It is easy to find such illustrations: Many aboriginal tribal populations have been thoroughly depleted on coming into contact with European colonists (Petersen, 1975:380–6), and this process continues to the present day (Lernoux, 1977:A13). The size of human populations, however, is not merely a matter of fertility and mortality, because a population may also be depleted through emigration. Ancient Israel ceased to exist not because Jews were killed, but because they were dispersed; that is, they left a certain territory. And there is a clear lesson in this: Even an obvious condition terminating a social organization, such as a critical loss of population, may occur only in relation to a given territory, so that in defining social survivorship we must inevitably turn to a consideration of social "boundaries."[7]

In Sztompka's words (1974:60), "the assumption of boundary claims that the intensity of interrelations between the elements of the system is significantly stronger than the intensity of interrelations between the objects or variables not being considered as elements . . . ." If we accept this definition of boundaries, several consequences follow: First, population dispersal through migration terminates a social organization only insofar as such dispersal sharply reduces "intensity of interrelations;" in effect, we must reject the notion that, for instance, a polity *requires* territory by definition (Barnes, 1948: 89, 405, 428–30, 811, 875–8). (Territory, I believe, is significant only insofar as common possession of it facilitates "intensity of interrelations.") Secondly, partitioning and absorption terminate social organization only when they reduce "intensity of interrelations" to virtually nothing. Third, apathy and its obverse, "the war of all against all," both designated by Aberle et al. (1950) as conditions terminating society, are nothing of the sort unless they virtually terminate interaction. Turnbull's (1972) mountain people, in the clearest example of "the war of all against all" to be found in the literature, fight one another incessantly for the tiniest pieces of food; and yet, barring universal homicide, the society endures. Lernoux's Paraguayans (1977) are at far greater risk of failing to survive. Similarly, mass apathy terminates a society only if and when it reaches the extreme of universal catatonia, reducing social interaction to nought. Finally, the life-table studies cited herein, each involving some notion of a cessation of a social status or a social organization, ideally define statuses and organizations in interaction terms: One becomes a dropout when one ceases interacting (as a student) with schools, and a former congressman when one ceases interacting (as a congressman) with Congress; similarly, marriages end when partners cease interaction with one another.[8]

One further point: Although Sztompka speaks of the "intensity" of interaction, I prefer Edwin Sutherland's broader concept of differential association, emphasizing the frequency, duration, intensity, and priority of interaction as a multidimensional measure of social integration. A marriage, for instance, is terminated when the frequency, duration, intensity, and priority of interaction between husband and wife drop below a minimal level. It is for this reason that it is probably wise to regard separation as a better indicator of marital termination than divorce per se.

A surviving (viable) social organization, then, shall be defined as one that maintains an adequate population base (avoiding, among other catastrophes, universal homicide), and possesses boundaries clearly demarcated in terms of the frequency, duration, intensity, and priority of internal as opposed to external interrelationships, thereby avoiding partitioning, absorption, or a degree of apathy approaching universal catatonia or threatening population replacement (cf. Kreps, 1984). As noted in Table 2.2, functionalist jargon regarding the termination of social organization has much in common with politico-military jargon regarding the termination of organized resistance, an analogy that enables us to say, paradoxically, that the major function of military attack is to create dysfunctions (Shils and Janowitz, 1970) within military organizations of the enemy and, since the advent of total war, within many other large social entities of opposing societies. Perhaps the Pentagon would do well to learn that one does not win wars by propagandizing (cf. Shils and Janowitz, 1970) or killing people; one does so by destroying organizations. The Vietnam war was already lost by 1963 when the "strategic hamlet" program failed to displace organizations created by the enemy.

Finally, a few words about revolution. Defined as ". . . a cultural phe-

Table 2.2. *Comparison of functionalist and politico-military terminology regarding termination of social organization*

Functionalist Terminology	Politico-Military Terminology
1. Failure of population replacement	1. Genocide: high kill ratio
2. Emigration	2. Dispersal of the enemy
3. Universal homicide; war of all against all	3. Divide and conquer
4. Partition	4. Divide and conquer
5. Absorption	5. Annexation
6. Apathy	6. Pacification

nomenon involving fundamental changes in norms and values and in ways people experience the world, . . . accompanied by cognitive changes, changes in the very way that individuals perceive and experience reality, . . . a fundamental change of world view" (Kramnick, 1972: 31), revolution does not necessarily bring about the termination of a society (under our definition), although it is likely to destroy some of the organizations that constitute a society. Even an unsuccessful revolution, such as the American Civil War, may be important primarily for its ability to destroy social organizations such as those that defined the plantation-slavery system. Basically, revolutions realign the structures of a society in such a way as to make them serve interests, or appear to serve interests, neglected prior to the revolution. Those who resist (or make) revolution usually claim that the survival of society is at stake – e.g., that national security or national sovereignty is threatened – but such claims are ordinarily an attempt by the governing class (or their enemies) to persuade the masses that a limited set of vested interests are the interests of all. In assessing the effects of revolution, we must focus more on class interests than on the survivorship of social systems, a strategy that would surely please Irving Zeitlin (1973).

In any case social evolutionists who wish to understand revolution would do well to heed the words of Gould (1982) on "punctuationist" thinking in modern biology:

At issue is not the general idea that natural selection can act as a creative force; the basic argument, in principle, is a sound one. Primary doubts center on the subsidiary claims – gradualism and the adaptationist program. If most evolutionary changes, particularly large-scale trends, include major nonadaptive components as primary directing or channeling features, and if they proceed more in an episodic than a smoothly continuous fashion, then we inhabit a different world from the one Darwin envisioned.

We might also note that the geneticist Barbara McClintock, after many years of being ignored, finally has won a Nobel prize (1983) for her work on "jumping genes" in corn.

In sociological parlance we need to be on the alert for strictly expressive forms of behavior (Collins, 1985:141–79), we need to be attuned to the possibility that social change may be episodic rather than gradualist, and we need to realize that the major task of functional analysis is, first, to determine which structural features do have adaptive value and, second, to determine the circumstances under which social systems change explosively through, let us say, the wholesale destruction of particular forms of organization.

3. Exemplary exercises in survivorship

In this chapter we shall provide several examples, increasingly complex and instructive, of the use of life-table logic in the study of social statuses and social organizations. An SPSS (1983) subroutine called SURVIVAL will be used for part of this analysis, although in some instances it may be necessary to go beyond the current capabilities of that impressive program. For the final example, involving survivorship of marital units, it will be shown in some detail that what Davis calls the "method of covariation" is readily applied to questions about ways in which structural conditions influence the survivorship of social organizations.

1. Years in school

Stockwell and Nam (1963) have prepared a series of "double decrement" life tables to estimate life expectancies of young Americans in the role of student. Such tables show the impact of both mortality and the school dropout rate on enrollment expectations, and clearly reflect the substantial increase in the holding power of schools during the fifties. The average number of school years remaining to Americans alive at a given age is shown in Table 3.1. Stockwell and Nam (1963:1124) point out the utility of life-table methods in assessing the impact of various social characteristics on school enrollment expectations:

Important differences in school life expectancies may be observed by construction of separate school life tables for males and females, for various racial and ethnic groups, for groups of persons in different socioeconomic circumstances, and for groups from different regions, places, and urban and rural sectors of the country, and in different countries.

These remarks strongly imply, in contradistinction to a point made by Kingsley Davis, that separate life tables based on such characteristics would easily lend themselves to analysis by the method of covariation. Although Stockwell and Nam focus on the status of student and rates of

Table 3.1. *Expected years in school at each age, United States, 1950–2 and 1957–9*

Age x	Expected Years in School, e_x 1950–52	1957–59
5	12.85	13.76
6	12.34	13.19
7	11.39	12.23
8	10.41	11.24
9	9.42	10.25
10	8.43	9.26
11	7.44	8.27
12	6.46	7.28
13	5.47	6.29
14	4.49	5.30
15	3.53	4.32
16	2.58	3.36
17	1.78	2.48
18	1.13	1.74
19	0.78	1.32
20	0.57	1.03
21	0.40	0.80
22	0.28	0.64
23	0.21	0.53
24	0.14	0.45

...

termination thereof, a major task of the present work is to show that life-table logic is applicable to complex social organizations. The Stockwell–Nam example, dealing with status roles of individuals, may seem a little tangential to this task unless one is willing, as I am, to think of any status role, even if exemplified by a single individual, as a form of social organization.

2. Congressional tenure

It is a curious commentary on the sociology of knowledge that Edmund Halley is remembered primarily for the discovery of a comet that does nothing more than make a brief, routine, and inconsequential appearance every 76 years, when he must also be given much of the credit (along with John Graunt) for the invention of one of the most powerful analytical tools ever conceived – the life table. At present, the life table is used almost exclusively by demographers for academic studies of mortality and by life insurance companies to find out how many years a person of a given age is expected to live (i.e., how many premiums he can be expected to pay) before his beneficiaries collect. Actually the life table, as we shall see, can provide much information in addition to these simple life-expectancy figures. In fact, one of the unacknowledged virtues of the life table is that it can be applied to almost any collection of elements with properties analogous to human fertility and mortality: That is, there must be a clear way of getting into the collection, a way of measuring the length of one's membership in the collection, and a clear way of getting out of the collection. The powerful method that demographers have developed for analyzing such collectivities is sometimes called the population model. As outlined by Ryder (1964:448), this model involves

an abstract view of a universe of phenomena comprising recognizable individual elements. Although demography is concerned substantively with humans, it has formal affinity with the analysis of all such collectivities. The first contribution by Alfred J. Lotka, the man most responsible for modern demography, was a study of the "mode of growth of material aggregates." . . . the special contribution of the demographer to social analysis is focused on those items of individual information which can be thought of as defining quasi-populations, because they endure. Thus a characteristic [e.g., a status] may be viewed as an individual's residence over a period of time. The time interval has a beginning and an end for the individual – an entry into and an exit from that particular quasi-population – and within the interval the individual is exposed to the risk of occurrence of various events, in particular, that of departure from that quasi-population. It is at least operationally conceivable that not only an enumeration of the individuals within these quasi-populations at successive times can be obtained, but also a registration of entries and exits. Full utilization of the power of the population model would also require determination of the length of time each individual has spent within the quasi-population.

Unfortunately, there are not many instances in which entries into and exits from sociologically significant collectivities are carefully registered; this form of registration is probably the most essential desideratum of the type of functional analysis advocated herein.

Among the many quasi populations of sociological interest would be the following: marriages contracted during a given time interval, parolees placed on parole at a given time, entering college freshmen in a given year, all newly registered voters, recently arrived immigrants into a given area, newly appointed college professors, newly established academic departments, small businesses established during a given year, newly diagnosed mental disorders (Hollingshead and Redlich, 1958), teenagers who remain sexually inexperienced (Zelnik et al., 1979), and so forth. It cannot be emphasized too strongly, then, that *population* does not always refer to people; this is the clearest lesson to be drawn from Lotka's work. The term could refer to types of social structures (Chronicle of Higher Education, 1982), types of social behavior, types of cultural artifacts, populations consisting of nonsense syllables learned by rote (Ebbinghaus curves, identical to one of the life-table columns), populations of subatomic particles with their half-lives, citations to the scientific literature with their half-lives, and to many other such items. More specifically, any set or collection amenable to life-table analysis must have the following characteristics:

1. No individual element of the set survives longer than a certain number of years (or months, weeks, minutes, etc.).
2. Subsets can be distinguished on the basis of length of time in the set by our use of time intervals of any appropriate length.
3. A cohort of a given size enters the set at the beginning of a given time interval, forming at the time of entry a subset with a total accumulated tenure of zero.
4. A termination rate (the rate according to which elements may leave the set during each time interval) can be calculated in relation to each subset.
5. The termination rate is less than 1.0 for each subset except the oldest, for which it is arbitrarily set at 1.0.
6. Once a given element has terminated, it cannot reenter the set at a later date unless it reenters in some meaningful way as a member of a new cohort.

With this model in mind, we need merely seek out quasi populations of social structures having the characteristics essential to the model.

The small quasi population known as the House of Representatives appears to meet most of the criteria of a life-table population. On this point the following observations may be made:

1. Rarely, at least for recent Congresses, does a representative have a tenure of office of more than about 30 years (15 terms). For instance, of the 435 members of the seventy-fifth Congress, elected in 1936, only seven were reelected to the Ninetieth Congress in 1966.[1]

Table 3.2. *Tenure expectancy table, Seventy-fifth Congress, freshman members*

Term	Number Entering Term	Number Departing	Prob. of Termination	Stationary Population	Average Remaining Tenure
x	ℓ_x	d_x	q_x	L_x	T_x	e_x
1	92	34	.370	92	351	3.82
2	58	12	.207	58	259	4.46
3	46	15	.326	46	201	4.37
4	31	3	.097	31	155	5.00
5	28	6	.214	28	124	4.43
6	22	3	.136	22	96	4.36
7	19	4	.210	19	74	3.89
8	15	4	.267	15	55	3.67
9	11	2	.182	11	40	3.64
10	9	0	.000	9	29	3.22
11	9	1	.111	9	20	2.22
12	8	5	.625	8	11	1.38
13+	3	3	1.000	3	3	1.00

2. It is relatively easy to distinguish subsets of representatives according to length of time as members of Congress, making use of the assumption that (a) with each general election a cohort of determinable size enters the House of Representatives, forming at the time of entry a subset with a total accumulated tenure of office of zero; (b) any congressman who obtains his office by appointment or by a special election is a member of the cohort created by the general election immediately following his assumption of the office, if he retains the office at that time; (c) similarly, for any congressman who dies or resigns before the end of his term of office, it is assumed that his tenure of office extends to the following general election. Thus, entering and exiting from Congress are not regarded as continuous processes, but rather as discrete events that always occur at intervals divisible by two. Table 3.2 has been calibrated according to these rules.

3. Termination rates can be derived longitudinally by following cohorts

of congressmen on a term-by-term basis to the point where all or nearly all members of the original cohort have exited the quasi population, either through loss of an election, death, resignation, failure to receive renomination, or failure to run for reelection. It should be mentioned that, as an alternative to the longitudinal method, it is possible in many cases to use concurrent census and registration data to obtain termination rates cross-sectionally. In the cross-sectional approach, the termination rate for a given age refers only to the membership of a single, unique cohort who have arrived at that age.

4. It may be assumed, probably wrongly but with little cost, that the oldest cohort (i.e., the one with the greatest seniority) in a given Congress will not be members of the Congress created by the next general election; their probability of termination, in other words, will be set at 1.0. (This procedure conforms to that of SURVIVAL in SPSS.)

5. It is appropriate to assume that if a congressman's tenure of office is terminated at some point and he later reenters Congress he should be regarded as a member of the newly arrived cohort with which he reenters.

Table 3.2 is a tenure table for all freshman members of the Seventy-fifth Congress, elected in 1936. Examining the q_x column, we see that the termination rates are relatively high for the early terms, relatively low for the middle terms, and begin to increase consistently at about the tenth term. (Curiously, this pattern more or less characterizes human mortality, where there is a comparable "liability of newness.") If the numbers in the q_x and l_x columns were to remain constant for about 30 years, the resultant stationary population would total $T_1 = 351$ and would have the seniority structure given in the L_x column. Under existing norms, however, such an outcome is not permitted. Because, by law, the House of Representatives at any given time contains 435 members, it is possible to predict on the basis of this table that, prior to the time of termination of the last member of the cohort, either some of the termination rates must be reduced, or future cohorts must become larger in size, or both of these changes must occur. In other words, over time the value T_1 is subject to cybernetic regulation in a way typical of many functionalist processes, and it would be fascinating to see how much fluctuation occurs over time around the "equifinal" value $T_1 = 435$. (Once again: If this be teleology, then let us make the most of it!) This particular property of the life table has many uses. If, for example, cross-sectional tenure tables were constructed separately for the two major parties at a given historical moment, the Republican stationary population as a percentage of the Democratic stationary population could be taken as a sensitive measure of the relative strength of the parties in Congress, and many fascinating time-series analyses of this variable could be made. Again, however, these studies would only be possible if the measurement processes were repeated at frequent intervals.

The e_x column of Table 3.2 shows that, upon entering the House of Representatives, congressmen who were first elected to the Seventy-fifth Congress had an average tenure expectancy of 3.82 terms of office, and that the average remaining tenure for this cohort increased to a maximum of 5.00 terms at the start of the fourth term, declining steadily thereafter. Because this pattern is similar to the pattern found in human populations with high infant mortality rates, it is apparent that only "vigorous" congressmen survive beyond a few terms.

The results of this preliminary inquiry show that there is considerable merit in the idea of using the population model in the analysis of a variety of quasi populations. Additional studies of the House of Representatives are needed in which an effort would be made to analyze causes of termination along with various individual and structural factors that may influence tenure expectancies. A number of theoretically important problems occur. Is it true, for instance, that Congress is a "rich man's club" in the sense that high-SES representatives have greater tenure expectancies than their lower-SES colleagues? Does a party man have greater tenure expectancies than a renegade or otherwise nonconforming member of a party? Are there symbiotic ties among members of voting blocs that tend to enhance the tenure expectancies of such congressmen? What are the regional and temporal variations in tenure expectancies and in the various properties (e.g., the seniority structure) of the stationary population of congressmen? The possibilities appear to be virtually inexhaustible; again, the existence of many of these possibilities would seem to vitiate Davis's claim that the method of covariation cannot be used to test functionalist hypotheses.

3. Duration of marriage

One of the more persistent popular fallacies, perpetuated in good part by social scientists, is the notion that the stability of marriages can be assessed by examining either the divorce rate per se or the ratio of the divorce rate to the marriage rate. Just as the crude death rate is a poor indicator of average life expectancies in a population, so the divorce rate (number of divorces registered per thousand population per year) is a poor indicator of the viability of marriages. The clear secular trend toward increasing divorce rates in the United States (National Center, 1973:22) may reflect increasing marital instability, but the data do not compel such an inference any more than Mexico's relatively low crude death rate, as compared with that of the United States, compels the belief that Mexicans enjoy higher life expectancies than other North Americans. They do not.

The crude rates, because they do not take into account the length of time marriages have existed before ending in divorce, are much easier to obtain than survivorship rates, and this is one of the chief reasons for their frequent use. Despite the relative ease of data collection, the United States in recent years does not have a complete divorce registration system, with only about 30 states (National Center for Health Statistics, 1979:24–25) supplying divorce statistics. A number of special studies, however, have been conducted. In the latter part of the nineteenth century and at various times in this century, surveys have been undertaken by such agencies as the Department(s) of Labor and Commerce, the Census Bureau, and the National Office of Vital Statistics, and occasionally these surveys provide data amenable to life-table analysis. In 1907, for instance, at the instigation of President Theodore Roosevelt, Congress authorized the Census Bureau to collect and publish marriage and divorce statistics for the period 1887–1906. Using divorce court records for the entire nation, they obtained the following information (National Center, 1973:5):

1. State and county of divorce
2. State and county in which marriage took place
3. Date of marriage
4. Date of separation
5. Date of filing petition
6. Who was the libelant?
7. How was notice served?
8. Was the case contested?
9. Was decree granted?
10. Date of decree or judgment
11. Number of years married
12. Cause for which divorced
13. If not a direct cause, was intemperance an indirect cause?
14. Kind of divorce (absolute, interlocutory, etc.)
15. Number of children
16. Was alimony asked?

17. Was alimony granted?
18. Occupation of parties to divorce
19. Residence of libelee

Item 11 provides data that enable us to make duration of marriage tables for all marriages *destined to end in divorce* during the period covered by the survey. (It would be preferable to develop such tables for all marriages regardless of their reasons for termination, but the necessary data are not readily available from government sources.) Duration of marriage tables for such marriages provide only an indirect measure of the viability of all marriages; what these tables do tell us is the length of time marriages persist when they are destined to be broken by divorce and, potentially, how the duration of such marriages is influenced by legal factors (items 6, 7, and 8 in the foregoing list), by cause of divorce (12, 13), the presence of children (15), financial factors (16, 17), and so forth.

Again the method of covariation is potentially applicable, and one can easily imagine hypotheses linking structural factors to the survivability of marriages ending in divorce. Cherlin (1978, 1981), for instance, suggests that the low survivorship of second and subsequent marriages may be due to a lack of clear norms governing stepparent–stepchild and in-law relationships. Table 3.3, based on all divorces granted during the 20-year period 1887–1906 for which information was available on length of marriage, shows that divorces were granted, on the average, after 8.74 years of marriage. If, however, a given marriage survived the first three years, it would be expected to endure another 7.52 years, for a total of 10.52 years. Similarly, marriages surviving the first 10 years endured an average of 10 + 5.98 or 15.98 years; those surviving the first 15 years endured 15 + 4.02 years or 19.02 years, and so on.[2] In a moment we shall show that if separate tables were prepared based on cause of divorce, number of children, occupation, and so forth, the method of covariation could readily be used to test hypotheses about the impact of these factors on the survivability of marriages at any point in their development.

Along with the data providing the basis for Table 3.3, the National Center for Health Statistics (1973) has collated the 1887–1906 findings on length of time between marriages and separations. It was stated earlier that separation may be a better indicator of marital instability than divorce; with this possibility in mind, we used the SPSS subroutine SURVIVAL in order to compare separation and divorce as factors terminating marriages. Results are found in Figure 3.1. As one would expect, marital survivorship is greatly foreshortened when separation is the basis for

Table 3.3. *Duration of marriage for representative cohort of 1,000 marriages ending in divorce, United States, 1887–1906 (based on 900,584 cases)*

Years	Number Surviving	Number Terminating	Prob. of Termination	Stationary Population		Average Remaining Years
x	ℓ_x	d_x	q_x	L_x	T_x	e_x
1 or less	1000	52	.0520	974	8743	8.74
2	948	68	.0717	914	7769	8.19
3	880	81	.0920	840	6855	7.78
4	799	82	.1026	758	6015	7.52
5	717	76	.1059	679	5257	7.33
6	641.	70	.1092	606	4578	7.14
7	571	63	.1103	540	3972	6.95
8	508	56	.1102	480	3432	6.75
9	452	49	.1084	428	2952	6.53
10	403	45	.1116	380	2524	6.26
11	358	40	.1117	338	2144	5.98
12	318	36	.1132	300	1806	5.67
13	282	31	.1099	266	1506	5.34
14	251	28	.1115	237	1240	4.94
15	223	26	.1165	210	1003	4.49
16	197	22	.1116	186	793	4.02
17	175	20	.1142	165	607	3.46
18	155	18	.1161	146	442	2.85
19	137	16	.1167	129	296	2.16
20	121	15	.1239	114	167	1.38
21 or more	106	106	1.000	53	53	.50

classifying a marriage as having ended. In Figure 3.1, providing survivorship curves, we see that at the point on the ordinate where half of all marriages have been terminated, the separation curve (designated by the number 2) shows a median life expectancy of 4.73 years, and the divorce curve (designated by the number 1) shows a median life expectancy of 8.15 years. Notice, also, that the two survivorship curves seem to converge over time, a pattern suggesting that the transition from separation to divorce is made more rapidly among those couples who have deferred

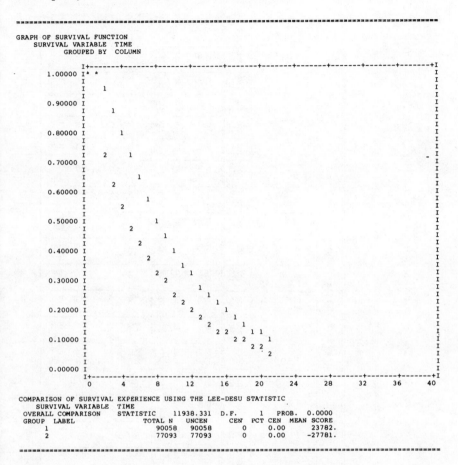

Figure 3.1. Comparison of survival rates for separation and divorce, United States, 1887–1906 (based on 900,584 cases)

marital dissolution for the longest time. Social psychologists must have a theory that accounts for this pattern.

Our most convincing illustration, however, of the uses of life-table logic in functional analysis is based on detailed state-by-state data taken from the Census Bureau's huge survey of 1887–1906 (1908:Table 8). Table 3.4 shows a small part of the data gathered by this mammoth early exercise in survey research. In other parts of the census volume, the data for this single state are broken down on a yearly basis, and similar data are provided for all other states and territories: The data, therefore, extend

Table 3.4. Divorces by classified cause, libelant, and duration of marriage, by states and territories, 1887–1906 (single years)
Source: Bureau of the Census (1908: 208)

ALABAMA.

CAUSE AND TO WHICH PARTY GRANTED.	Total.	NUMBER OF YEARS MARRIED. 1887 to 1906																					Un-known.
		1 or less.	2	3	4	5	6	7	8	9	10	11	12	13	14	15	16	17	18	19	20	21 and over.	
All causes:																							
Husband	13,093	446	503	980	1,108	1,058	1,049	936	831	684	710	522	437	369	298	295	254	199	159	155	149	895	966
Wife	9,714	382	483	800	873	804	790	699	625	532	546	403	315	277	226	236	162	129	113	111	121	467	620
Adultery:																							
Husband	3,990	335	368	350	353	271	325	277	226	199	182	134	114	97	64	60	57	36	37	33	25	151	257
Wife	804	88	80	85	68	58	67	52	52	35	41	34	24	19	9	15	8	11	8	10	10	34	47
Cruelty:																							
Husband	44	8	4	3			1	1		2	4			2			1					3	4
Wife	1,839	191	192	197	155	149	126	105	92	82	81	68	39	43	37	32	24	19	16	13	21	70	87
Desertion:																							
Husband	8,530	25	170	595	722	757	697	637	578	472	503	378	308	268	220	216	180	155	118	119	122	734	547
Wife	6,057	35	122	447	590	539	524	471	443	364	392	266	227	190	161	164	119	88	77	77	70	323	350
Drunkenness:																							
Husband	60	6	3	5	3	3	3	1	7	2	3	1	4		4	4	2	2	2	2		2	3
Wife	498	47	58	40	27	36	31	34	18	29	17	10	12	18	11	14	4	6	9	4	7	19	26
Neglect to provide:																							
Husband																							
Wife																							
Combinations of preceding causes, etc.:																							
Husband	173	5	9	12	12	10	17	15	17	9	14	5	6	2	6	6	4	4	1	1	1	5	6
Wife	296	11	14	28	19	14	33	30	17	15	13	13	12	5	3	8	7	4	6	3	3	19	9
All other causes:																							
Husband	326	67	39	15	13	8	6	5	3		4	4	4	3	3	3	1	1	1	2	2		149
Wife	182	10	8	3	5	8	9	7	3	7	2	3	1		5			1		1	1	2	101

widely through time and space, and such data are essential to the functionalist undertaking. Using SPSS SURVIVAL, it is relatively easy to generate survivorship curves and hypothesis tests for various combinations of states and years, and then to correlate these survivorship functions with various structural features according to the method of covariation.

For instance, suppose we wished to develop an index of male dominance using the sort of data found in Table 3.4, and to assess the impact of this variable on marital stability. One possible indicator of male dominance is based on the presumption that in any state where male dominance prevails, a relatively large proportion of divorces based on adultery will be awarded to husbands rather than wives. We note that this proportion, which is $3960/(3960+864)$ = .821 for the state of Alabama, varies substantially among states; what is left for us now is to develop a measure of survivorship that can be correlated with our rough measure of male dominance.

Arkansas, Iowa, and Massachusetts have been selected for this demonstration. For the period 1887–1906, these three states had male dominance scores of .756, .530, and .505, respectively. Their marital survivorship curves are shown in Figure 3.2, with the Arkansas curve designated by 1, the Iowa curve by 2, and the Massachusetts curve by 3. Because the median survival years for the three states are 6.26, 7.83, and 11.37, respectively, the data suggest that high levels of male dominance tend to reduce the survivability of those marriages ending in divorce. Clearly, however, these results are not definitive, and they are not definitive for a host of reasons: First, in the best of all possible worlds we would have data on all marriages, not merely those destined to end in divorce; second, data for many additional ecological units, not a mere triad of states, need to be brought into the analysis; third, temporal variations in male dominance and survivorship must be assessed if we are to determine whether, for instance, there is social selection against those marital units in which male dominance prevails; finally, because the social selection hypothesis involves causation, many extraneous factors would have to be controlled in such a way that the life table, in effect, would merely provide a small number of the variables to be used in multivariate analyses.

None of these needs should be regarded as a mere trifling point. Consider the need for more extensive data. For those interested in evaluating functionalism as a way of explaining social change, an important difference exists between the Stockwell–Nam tables of school life expectancy and our own tables of congressional tenure and marital survivorship: The former is cross-sectional, and the latter are longitudinal. That is, Stock-

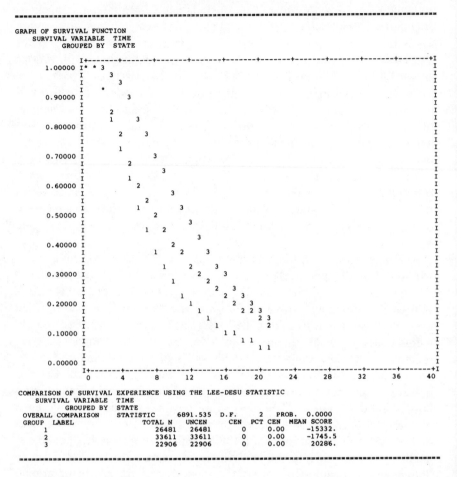

Figure 3.2. Comparison of marital survival rates for Arkansas, Iowa, and Massachusetts, 1887–1906

well and Nam used life-table values and school enrollment data for two points in time, the early and late fifties. In contrast, the congressional tenure table was based on data gathered by following careers of congressmen through time until those careers ended. Similarly, the marital duration tables were based on respondents' answers (in divorce courts) to questions about the duration of their marriages, so that in effect the longitudinal experiences of cohort members are being reported from memory – a reliable source when dealing with highly salient characteristics such as marital status. The fundamental problem in our reliance on the longitudinal approach is that it more or less rules out any attempt to assess the survivorship of those marriages that will end through causes other than divorce, such as the death of one of the spouses. It is for this reason that all survivorship tables presented in this section speak only to the experiences of those married couples who were destined to be divorced. If, on the other hand, divorces (and other ways of ending marriages) were registered as efficiently as births and deaths are registered, and if data were available on the age of all currently existing marriages, then it would be possible to create cross-sectional life tables, for marital units, that would have all the properties of standard life tables: Data would be as up-to-date as possible, they would pertain to a given point in time, and it would be much easier to obtain survivorship measures for all marital units, not merely for those ending in divorce. Note, however, that none of these remarks rules out the possibility of following marital cohorts through life, just as we now follow birth cohorts through life in the preparation of longitudinal life tables. The current deficiency resides in the fact that following divorce cohorts (retrospectively) is not the same thing as following marriage cohorts.

As we shall see later, in testing social survivorship hypotheses it is preferable to have a *series* of *cross-sectional* life tables – a way of retaining the best of both the synchronic and diachronic worlds, that is, in a more dialectical sense, a way of synthesizing social statics and social dynamics. A series of cross-sectional life tables for small business firms, for instance, would be invaluable (Churchill, 1955; Carroll, 1984).

In selecting appropriate ecological units (nations, states, counties, cities, census tracts, etc.) for survivorship analysis, one has to remember the many caveats that apply to situations in which observations are aggregated into ecological areas or other categories. In the above example, data on marital units were aggregated by state, and an attempt was made to show how one would test the hypothesis that a given structural feature measured at the state level – that is, male dominance – may have an impact on marital survivorship. One possible interpretation of the apparent association between male dominance and relatively low marital survivorship is that social selection operates, at a state level, against marital units that exemplify male dominance. If this were the case, any state that moved in an upward direction on male dominance (the structural feature) would be acted upon by the social selection process and brought back to its optimal level. There are many reasons, however, why this interpretation may be wrong. For one thing a given state may have a high male dominance score, or even an increasing male dominance score, because male dominance is part of the folkways of that particular state. If that were the case, social selection presumably would not countervail against the force of changing folkways and would probably be discernible only in instances where the impact of social selection could be separated from that of a strong contrary secular trend. The appropriate methods have been used by econometricians for many years (Croxton et al., 1967) and will be discussed later in detail.

If we have to become wary of trends, we may as well do so with a degree of sophistication. If we harken back to the variation-and-selective-retention model, we recall that in the writings of Donald Campbell and others on this topic, little attention is devoted to the process of variation, whereas much attention is devoted to social selection. This is unfortunate, because it is arguable that the social selection approach is of little utility unless there is a substantial amount of variation, at a given ecological level, in the structural feature thought to have an impact on the survivorship of some kind of organization. If levels of male dominance, for instance, remain fixed over time with small variance, then it is probably futile to ask whether the level of male dominance is influenced at all by social selection, either reproductive or lethal selection. Yet, it is precisely this sort of question, among many others, that functional analysis must ask.

The real question, then, has to do with how we decide whether a given set of ecological units or other aggregations provides enough variation to be challenging to the variation-and-selective-retention model. And the best way to answer this question is to treat ecological units as panels (with relatively low dropout rates!), obtain mean scores on structural features of organizations within these ecological panels, and then determine whether the structural features provide sufficient variation over time. In approaching this question it is well to remember that variations over time in an array of scores may be due either to measurement unreliability or to genuine change, and that it is desirable to have at least three data points in order to separate unreliability from real change (Heise, 1969; Wiley and Wiley, 1970). In conclusion, then, we must pay much more attention to the tasks of gathering time-series data on the structural features of organizations within those ecological units where the most interesting variations seem to take place. Simultaneously, data on the survivorship of the same organizations should be obtained.

The appropriate ecological level would then be defined as that which provides the most promising results in terms of both variation and the clear operation of selective retention.

Suppose, for instance, that we wish to examine structural factors that might influence the survivorship of Great Books study groups (Davis, 1957). Suppose, further, that data are aggregated in a way that facilitates preparation of life tables for a number of ecological units. The literature suggests (Lippitt and White, 1958) that small groups operating more or less democratically have a higher problem-solving ability and higher morale than small groups that operate on a laissez-faire or autocratic principle. In assessing the survivability of Great Books study groups, one might hypothesize that a democratic leadership style would make for relatively high survivorship, whereas the alternative leadership styles would tend to reduce survivorship. Only if there were sufficient variation in both these variables across areas and over time would it be possible to test this hypothesis. If leadership styles were stable over time, and if apparent changes were only a result of unreliability, then it would be inappropriate to attempt a test of variation-and-selective-retention hypotheses. One would merely be able to point to a situation dominated by powerful, rigid social norms.

It should be noted tangentially that if leadership styles were conceptualized as a continuous variable ranging from, say, high to low "intensity of social control," then we would expect a curvilinear relationship between the structural variable (leadership style) and the survivorship of organizations (study groups). In any instance where a structural feature can be either overdeveloped or underdeveloped – and there are many such instances – we must be alert for curvilinear relationships. The functionalist emphasis on equilibrium and optimal values suggests that curvilinearity (with its special methodological demands) may be a common feature of functional analyses. When Durkheim (1951) hypothesized that both low social cohesion and high social cohesion tend to raise the suicide rate, he was proposing precisely this sort of curvilinearity.

Let us briefly return to a consideration of marital units and ask how one might apply the social selection model to marital endogamy. The literature suggests that, in general, marriages that are endogamous as to age, race, social class, religion, and so forth, have greater survivability than marriages exogamous on these characteristics (Udry, 1966:ch.12). If that is true, then it follows that if we were able to identify an ecological level (e.g., states or counties) in which there were sufficient variance and time-series instability in marital endogamy, we could readily correlate the rates of endogamous marriage with the survivability of marriages. (A fascinating analysis by Matras [1973:277–91] suggests that in any given national population demographic changes inevitably create transformations in the "mate-selection and marriage regime.") Our hypothesis suggests that, ceteris paribus, high endogamy would make for high marital survivability. As in the case of male dominance, we would have to be attuned to the possibility that social selection processes may be obscured by strong secular trends toward, in this instance, decreasing marital endogamy. In other words, the operation of selection against exogamy does not rule out the possibility that the practice of exogamous mate selection may be increasing over time, and there is every possibility that the social selection process may be totally dominated by a strong secular trend.

Skeptics may ask why the social selection hypothesis is superior to the more traditional approach in which, to return to our last example, one merely asks whether "happily married" couples differ from divorced couples in the proportion of all marriages involving endogamy (Locke, 1951). The answer is that we pursue the social selection methodology for the same reason that epidemiologists employ ecological correlations to identify general environmental factors that make for high disease rates. An emphasis on epidemiological studies does not rule out surveys and experimental studies of individuals who may have various diseases; on the contrary, epidemiological studies *supplement* those studies that operate on the level of individual patients, and the latter provide a host of hypotheses for use in epidemiological research. The Locke-type inquiry may tell us something about the prospects of a given marriage; the epidemiological approach, emphasizing social selection, tells us something about large ecological variations in important structural features, such as exogamy, and something about the ways in which such variations may influence the survivorship of large cohorts of organizations such as marital units. In addition, we may learn something about the composition, growth rates, and so forth, of the quasi population consisting of marital units. Note, too, that virtually all ecological variables, typically rates, are defined at the quantitative (interval) level, whereas the individual traits from which these variables are derived may well be qualitative in nature. I do not imply that quantitative measurement is ipso facto superior; I do imply that generalizations applicable over several levels of measurement, as well as several units of analysis, are indeed superior.

What is being advocated herein is nothing more than the methodology of Durkheim's *Suicide*. Just as Durkheim examined ecological variations in social facts that may impinge on the suicide rate, so the present inquiry recommends a focus on ecological variations of factors that influence the survivability of organizations. In Durkheim's study, such factors also were shown to vary among taxonomic categories, for example, religious groupings. This comparison is enhanced by the fact that suicide, if we believe Durkheim, is a form of social selection.

In any study that is essentially epidemiological, one must raise questions as to whether explanatory factors inhere in the objects under study or in the "environment" in which these objects exist, as in Durkheim's case (cf. McKelvey, 1982:105–37). A major advantage of epidemiological methods is that they facilitate use of the latter kind of variable. Again, we may take hints from biology. When animal ecologists try to explain variations in survivorship among several subpopulations of a species, they examine both the anatomical characteristics of the animals in question and the general environmental conditions that may impinge on a given ecological niche and thereby affect the survivorship of animals occupying it. Similarly, when social scientists apply the social selection hypothesis they would do well to examine characteristics of the surrounding social context as well as characteristics inhering in the organizations occupying these contexts (Boyd and Iversen, 1979). In the example of Great Books study groups, we asked whether the prevailing leadership structures of these groups – an internal characteristic – had any appreciable impact on survivorship. One could ask also whether the organizational environment – say, the presence of a university within the area (an external characteristic) – has any impact either in the sense that such an institution would stimulate demand for special study groups or would tend to fulfill the demand, thereby making special study groups superfluous. One could ask whether a "global" feature of the environment, such as population heterogeneity, has any measurable impact on the survivability of organizations such as Great Books study groups. Population heterogeneity, along with many other demographic measures, is an environmental characteristic that is external to any given type of social organization. It is a macrosociological feature; in Mayhew's words (1983:155), ". . . the fundamental problems of system survival are located in macrostructural interaction," a point made some years ago by Levy (1952:120) when he distinguished between a "unit" and its "setting."

The same considerations apply to marital endogamy. Because endogamy is definable for single marital units, it is an internal characteristic. It is appropriate, as we have shown, to relate such characteristics to the survivability of marital units. On the other hand, many external environmental features, some defined at the global level and characterizing an entire ecological unit, may well have an impact on the survival value of marriages. Examples include rates of geographical mobility, the racial, religious, and class composition of the surrounding population, and so forth. An excellent paper by Blau (1977) suggests in a logically consistent fashion the many ways in which the demographic composition of ecological areas (and communities) may influence organizations within these contexts. Blau's paper derives over a dozen theorems about the impact of compositional features on the proportions of various segments of a population who intermarry (or have another exclusive association, such as mutual best friends), on the mean number of intergroup associations, and on the mean amount of time spent in intergroup associations (Blau, 1977:35). Several of these theorems derive entirely from deterministic mathematical properties: for instance, a theorem stating that "the more a majority discriminates in social intercourse against a minority, the smaller is the difference between the majority's lower and the minority's higher rate of intergroup associations" (Blau, 1977:37). In other words, the more a majority discriminates, the greater is the similarity of associational experience for majority and minority members. If, for instance, a community has 10 intermarital ties between a majority of 50 persons and a minority of 20 persons, the majority's rate of intergroup association is $10/50 = 0.2$, and the minority's is $10/20 = 0.5$, for a difference of -0.3. If the community practiced discrimination more strongly so that only 5 intermarital ties existed, then the two fractions would become 5/50 and 5/20, with a difference of $0.1 - 0.25 = -0.15$. Therefore, the rates of association would have become more alike. The paradoxical character of this insight is fascinating, but it is less fascinating than the notion that variables with trend may deterministically create trend in other variables, a process of great significance for functional analysis. Several other fascinating properties of Blau's work will be developed in Chapter 5.

Because many of Blau's theorems deal with structural factors that influence the *establishment* of intergroup ties, they tend to focus more on variation than on selective retention. This is no serious flaw, however, because it turns out that many of Blau's propositions make good sense when restated in terms of social survivorship. Take, for instance, the following theorems, all of which invoke large structural factors that inhere in social environments and not within the social entities occupying these environments (Blau, 1977):

1. People in middle as well as in high strata in a pyramid probably associate more with others below them than with others above them in status (p.43).

2. Increasing heterogeneity increases the probability of intergroup relations (p.44).
3. Strongly correlated parameters consolidate status and group differences and thereby impede intergroup relations (p.45).
4. The more society's inequality results from inequality within rather than among communities, the more probable are social associations [sic] both among different strata and among different communities (p.48).

On the assumption that the most probable forms of association would have the highest survival value, that is, that there is a strong correlation between reproductive and lethal selection, one could hypothesize that for people in middle strata, downward associations have higher survival value than upward associations; that for people in heterogeneous communities, as opposed to homogeneous communities, associations such as exogamous marriage have high survival value; that in communities where status differences are strongly correlated or, as E. A. Ross used to say, where "lines of cleavage coincide," associations such as exogamous marriages have low survival value; that when inequality resides within rather than between communities, associations across strata and communities have high survival value. Research inspired by such hypotheses would be functionalist research employing the methods of social epidemiology.

If we take the advice of Hannan and Freeman (1977:933, 1984; cf. McKelvey, 1982:3) and adopt an ". . . explicit focus on populations of organizations" that emphasizes the survival of organizations, we shall probably find ourselves using life tables and testing hypotheses similar to those proposed by Hannan and Freeman: for example, the hypothesis that "niche width" (the degree of "diversity" among organizations of a given type) may have an impact on survival prospects, or that "excess capacity" may have such an impact. In using life tables, we must take full advantage of the deductive powers of this model, recognizing that any given life table is derived solely from length-of-life data for individual persons, organizations, or other entities. The aggregated data – survivorship curves, stationary and stable population properties, age composition, life expectancy, vigor, and so forth – must be meaningful within some theoretical context lest the entire exercise become mere sound and fury signifying nothing. In subsequent chapters these theoretical contexts will be explored.

4. The nature, determinants, and consequences of time-series processes

This chapter proposes that the major goal of any functionalist inquiry is to clarify the nature, determinants, and consequences of a given time-series process. It begins by arguing that, although social scientists tend to state generalizations in linear form, it is likely that the most important time-series processes are nonlinear. Therefore we must develop a taxonomy of time series: We must be able to classify a given variable as having stationarity through time – a constant mean, constant variance, and no autocorrelation – or as departing from stationarity in any of a large number of linear and nonlinear patterns; next, we must examine the structural determinants and consequences of any given pattern, stationary or otherwise. The chapter then provides an extended discussion of Malthus's theory of population in which it is shown that the original version of this theory would have been applicable only to societies in which the basic demographic processes were more or less stationary through time, and that the efforts of recent neo-Malthusians have been directed, appropriately, toward explaining departures from stationarity in these same processes. Throughout this chapter there is an implicit recognition that the form of a time series provides clues as to the sort of theoretical explanation that would be appropriate: In general, stationary series require stability models, and nonstationary series require growth models (cf. Kasarda, 1974).

A major deficiency of social theory is its tendency to neglect relationships that depart from rectilinearity. In Hage's words (1972:92), ". . . sociology has generally relied upon linear or straight-line operational linkages," although recent work shows an increasing willingness to search for nonlinear relationships, of which Hage notes several examples. A large proportion of theories involving curvilinearity have time – often extremely long historical periods – as a causal factor in relation to some social process; the latter varies nonlinearly with time. Theories of this sort I prefer to call *process* theories, conforming to Fararo's usage (1973: ch. 8).[1] The following list contains both familiar and lesser known examples:

56

1. Growth models: for example, the Pearl–Reed logistic curve depicting the growth of the U.S. population; the theory of demographic transition, showing the historical pattern in which human populations have gained a modicum of control over mortality and fertility, and the effects of such control on natural increase, migration, economic growth, and so forth (Petersen, 1975:8–15); and Lenski's (1966) argument that the relationship between economic development and inequality is generally positive, with inequality increasing rapidly at low levels of development and becoming nearly stable at higher levels of development. Nonlinear aspects of growth are incisively discussed in Kasarda (1974).
2. Diffusion models: for example, the Coleman et al. (1966) model of the diffusion of medical innovations, often involving an S-shaped pattern similar to the Pearl–Reed growth curve – a pattern with the extraordinary property that it is predictable on the basis of a theory.
3. A theory defining social problems as social movements and depicting the latter as evolving through stages such as incipiency, coalescence, institutionalization, fragmentation, and demise (Mauss, 1975:61–66; cf. Smelser, 1962: 18–19,111–12; cf. Kreps, 1984:315); a similar theory envisioning revolution as a series of distinct stages (Brinton, 1965).
4. Ecological models: for example, invasion-succession-dominance processes in urban growth, often involving displacement of one racial-ethnic group by another (Hawley, 1950:400).
5. Cybernetic control processes: for example, Taagepera's (n.d.: Fig. 2) example of the stability of the cube-root law relating the size of the U.S. "active" population to the size of the House of Representatives for the entire period from 1790 to 1970.

For some of these instances it is easy to imagine that variables changing through time could achieve stability at some point. Growth models are often conceived as generating a population or structure that eventually varies around an optimal value, provided that environmental conditions remain more or less constant. Diffusion of innovations is readily conceived as a form of growth having this property. Although social movements may meet their demise eventually, their "institutionalized" bequests may be preserved over a long period of time. Finally, Taagepera argues, albeit not too convincingly, that the cube-root relationship is maintained by a cybernetic control process in which rapidly growing constituencies, imposing too many communication channels on a given legislator, necessitate an increase in the size of a legislative body. Taagepera's work is fascinating in that it provides for an optimal (in this case, minimal) number of communication channels around which the actual number, for the average congressman, tends to oscillate; the model is similar to that discussed earlier, involving the oscillation of a "stationary population" around some preestablished value – an instance of "equifinality" that has no demonstrable bearing either on anybody's intentions or on organizational survival. Taagepera's model works, however, only because the number of communication channels is arrived at somewhat arbitrarily.

1. Patterns of change within stability

Oscillation: that is the essential process. In Tylor's theory of the incest taboo it is clear that each variable, if not unduly disturbed, would tend to oscillate within limits. Dysfunctional deviations from incest restrictions might grow large for a time due to variation; however, these very deviations, through the operation of social selection, would eventually be self-correcting. All intervening variables would describe the same oscillations. If one could observe such oscillations over a long period of time, one could learn something about their frequency (the number of cycles or completed alternations, per unit of time, of a wave or oscillation) and their amplitude (the value of the maximum displacement from a mean value during one period of an oscillation: in Tylor's theory the maximum deviation of the practice of exogamy from its average over time). Such information, as we shall see, would be of great value in showing the proper time calibration for testing hypotheses having the form of Tylor's theory of the incest taboo.[2] Although Ashby (1968:298) argues that cybernetic control devices such as automatic pilots are efficient insofar as amplitudes remain small enough to be imperceptible (thereby providing "no information" about outside disturbances), we shall make no such assumption about oscillations in social behavior. Despite the fact that it is difficult to identify sources of variation for use in the variation-and-selective-retention model, human social life seems inherently to offer a much bumpier ride than a Boeing 747. Schlesinger (1949), for instance, produced a noteworthy study in which he charted the frequency of left-to-right political swings in American national government; they are highly perceptible. In another instance George Stigler recently won a Nobel prize in economics for showing, among many other fascinating things, that the cost of obtaining price information creates more price variability (higher amplitude) for cheap commodities than for expensive ones; price variations for expensive items appear to be noisier, but this illusion is only due to our sharper focus. A similar pattern may occur in several Latin American economies based on one or two major crops: Dependence on a limited product (a narrow niche width) creates wild fluctuations in level of living that do not escape anyone's attention (Stycos, 1974:24). Finally, classic simulations with queueing show that if we follow the U.S. Postal Service's practice of having a single queue for many windows, waiting time gets flattened out as a cross-sectional variable, although it continues to vary over time (something we all love to complain about).

All these examples involve "cycles" (Lofland, 1984:106–107). And, contrary to Zeitlin's claim (1973:14), they all have a "history."

Frequency and amplitude, of great use in defining the amount of lag in a causal process, may also be presumptive indicators of the presence of powerful social forces; as Kuhn says (1974:31), "the amplitude of the oscillation will vary inversely with the speed and sensitivity with which the negative feedback operates." Imagine, for instance, a ratio-scale variable (one with a meaningful zero point and no negative values) with high frequency and high amplitude. Perhaps we could measure frequency (F) by counting the number of peaks per year, where a peak is defined as a maximum (perhaps a *relative* maximum, as mathematicians say) at least one standard deviation above the mean (for a year) of all the daily means. Amplitude would have to be defined to control the effects of the scale of measurement; taking our inspiration from the "coefficient of variation" (Blalock, 1979:84), we shall define amplitude (A) as the average of all peaks (as defined above) divided by the yearly mean of all the daily means. Then, employing Ashby's (1968:298) concept of disturbances or noise (N), we shall hypothesize that $N = FA$.

Hawley (1950:301–4), for instance, shows the pattern of daily variation in volume of traffic flow into and out of a central business district by hours of the day. There appear to be two peaks per day on the average weekday (with a steadier pattern on weekends), although some apparent peaks may not be counted under the foregoing criterion as to what constitutes a peak. Assuming, then, about 200 peaks per year, with an amplitude guessed to be about 1.3 for Hawley's data,

$$N = 200 \times 1.3 = 260$$

and this expression can be considered a measure of noise that would permit comparisons, say, of several traffic arteries. Examining the consequences of frequency and amplitude, we shall hypothesize that the absorption of high levels of noise involves high costs (C), or that

$C = a + b(\text{FA})$

Costs, in other words, are assumed to be a linear function of the product of frequency and amplitude. It is now generally recognized that the day–night cycle, with its associated patterns of traffic flow, imposes exorbitant costs on society. Some effort is now under way to integrate living and working activities so that they occur in more limited spaces, to reduce the social impact of the day–night cycle and seasonal variations, and so forth (Toffler, 1980). The latter possibility is illustrated by the widespread use of air conditioning (the controlled environment concept cherished by architects), closed shopping malls, and so on; the former, by the "back to the city" movement. We also hypothesize that, in any instance where high noise levels threaten survival or threaten strong vested interests, a major human endeavor is that of reducing it (Klapp, 1978) or developing an excess capacity for dealing with it (Hannan and Freeman, 1977:949). Several illustrations occur: (1) the steady decline in *FA* for human crude mortality, throughout the historical process known as the demographic transition; (2) the decline in *FA* associated with seasonal or daily variations in temperature within the typical human ecological niche; (3) the decline of *FA* in the human diet (cf. Stinchcombe, 1983:87–88); (4) West-off and Rindfuss's claim (1974) that when sex preselection of offspring is introduced into the American population an initial series of wide fluctuations in the sex ratio at birth will eventually be dampened–a prospect discussed in detail in a later chapter (cf. Figure 5.2, showing a stable population projection of the U.S. 1967 population); (5) an apparently unremitting effort (as during the fall of 1985) by governments to minimize fluctuations in international currency exchange rates. On the other hand, total noise abatement is tantamount to the termination of organization through apathy, and if human ingenuity does not create enough noise, then nature, as Marxists say, will do so.

What we must do, then, is to gather vast amounts of time-series data on all aspects of human social behavior, we must learn to model these time series using techniques such as ARIMA or LISREL or spectral analysis (Mayer and Arney, 1974), and we must seek out mechanisms by which social organizations try to control high levels of noise (that is, those engendering high costs) or low levels of noise (that is, those engendering ennui). If nonoptimal levels of noise tend to generate adaptive efforts, and if adaptive efforts serve to optimize noise, then we are back at Kingsley Davis's fishpond. Ecological anthropologists have found many instances (Moran, 1982: 50–51) in which the threat of natural disasters such as localized famine is mitigated by requirements of sharing (cf. casualty insurance) or by practices such as that found among pastoralists who ". . . aim at converting their agricultural surplus into cattle, which are less subject to climatic vagaries and can reproduce themselves. . . ." It is also possible in this type of economy to make ". . . cyclical shifts between pastoralism and agriculture." All such efforts, again, involve noise reduction.

In any instance where dynamic functional analysis is undertaken, an important preliminary task is that of deciding whether enough noise exists to justify an attempt to explain it sociologically; universal ennui, tantamount to the termination of social organization through apathy (Aberle et al., 1950), is not by definition a sociological phenomenon. A similar challenge occurred earlier when we discussed marital endogamy, male dominance, and so forth; insufficient amounts of variance and temporal instability at any given ecological level tend to rule out application of the social selection model. This is the classic problem, of course, of trying to decide which social variables are worthy of study and which are not. In making this decision with respect to time-series data, we now have standard procedures (e.g., Cook and Campbell, 1979; Markus, 1979; SAS User's Guide, 1979:381–8; Roberts, 1981) for separating unreliability from real temporal instability, for assessing the ways in which time series may be interrupted by social change, for correlating two or more variables over time, and so forth. All of these methods are indispensable for functional analysis.

2. The stabilities and instabilities of Malthus and Marx

One is able to gain a preliminary insight into the importance of temporal patterns by considering the Malthusian theory of population in its original formulation and as it has evolved at the hands of a host of neo-Malthusians. The Malthusian theory of population, as set forth by Malthus in the first edition of his famous work, is a theory that has the essential properties of self-regulation as found in the Davis fishpond example or in the Coleman formula in note 1 of Chapter 1: It is a functionalist theory par excellence. Malthus argued that population growth produces pressure on the means of subsistence, that pressure on the means of subsistence eventually brings into operation the positive checks (famine, disease, and war), that the positive checks bring about an increase in mortality, that an increase in mortality (due to the constancy of fertility, according to one of Malthus's postulates) brings about a reduction in the rate of natural increase, and that a reduction in natural increase acts as a check against further population growth (cf. Petersen, 1979:ch. 3). In other words, increasing population growth, due to the fact that the algebraic product of the Malthusian causal loop is negative, tends to bring about a decrease in population growth, so that a Malthusian population remains in a state of stability, with the variables composing it perhaps approaching stationarity. One must remember that this theory was substantially modified by Malthus himself in the preparation of his second edition in 1803. In effect, he gave a larger role to human volition.

The earlier formulation of the Malthusian theory recalls a famous speculation of Darwin about a self-regulating process that works as follows: A large "spinster" population has acquired a large number of cats. Because the cats often feed on field mice, any increase in the cat population would tend to reduce the field mouse population. Because the mice feed on the larvae of bumble bees, a reduction of the field mouse population would make for an increase in bumble bees, and the latter would soon become active in pollinating the local cash crop, clover. As the clover harvest begins coming in, the farmers in the area become rich and soon find themselves marrying members of the potential spinster population at a dizzyingly high rate. On marrying, the women tend to get rid of their cats by any of 101 methods, whereupon all the causal impulses reverse themselves, the farmers eventually go bankrupt, the divorce rate increases, the cats return, and so forth. Babbie (1983:53–55) provides a similar example involving "a Rube Goldberg ecosystem." Without any disturbance, these kinds of systems would go on forever.

The trouble is that much of the time human societies do not seem to work this way, as Malthus discovered in the preparation of his second edition: There are too many sources of disturbance, too many instances in which a social transformation – for example, the invention of effective fertility control – disrupts a self-regulating system that otherwise might have retained considerable stability over time. It is noteworthy, however, that despite the discrediting of Malthus's original formulation, modern Malthusians still hold to the argument that, eventually, human populations will have the self-regulating properties that Malthus insisted upon. Consider, for instance, a recent demography textbook by Weller and Bouvier (1981:47):

The earth is finite. Prolonged growth *at any rate* will eventually fill this finite space. . . . Obviously there are limits to growth. When they are reached, the earth's population will have to stop growing. . . .

These comments do not mean that at some point in the distant future the population will suddenly stop growing and never again increase in size. More likely, the rate of population growth will gradually approach zero and the size of the population will fluctuate. Increases will be followed by decreases, and vice versa. [That is, populations will produce noise.] However, the *average* rate of growth will, of necessity, be zero. This demographic situation would be very similar to the one in prehistoric times, except that the absolute number of people involved would be much larger.

When this day arrives it will be time to dust off our ancient copies of Malthus, for the world's population will have returned to the self-regulating stability that he described so compellingly and so eloquently (cf. Frejka, 1973).

On the other hand, it may well be that during the centuries intervening between the original Malthusian stability and a future Malthusian stability, the world will experience the series of catastrophes envisioned by the Club of Rome and its famous world model (Forrester, 1971; Meadows et al., 1974). The world model, which has gone through about as many editions as did Malthus's theory, departs substantially from the stable negative feedback model that so often seems to be the delight of functionalists. But just as there is no reason why stability should delight us, there is no reason why we should regard the catastrophism of the Club of Rome (and other neo-Malthusians) as any more alien to the functionalist traditions than biological catastrophism is alien to the functionalist traditions of Darwinism. In Gould's view (1982), Darwinian functionalism will readily incorporate the new catastrophist hypotheses of molecular biology. And Gould's view would be considered a major advance by J.B.S. Haldane (1969), who never had any trouble integrating his Marxian–Hegelianism with his commitment to Darwinian functionalism, or Barbara McClintock, who realized that her work on "jumping genes" had long ago made her worthy of a Nobel Prize despite the fact that she did not receive it until 1983.

The Club of Rome world model is nothing more than a sophisticated form of Malthusianism, and it is readily comprehended under the functionalist rubric despite the fact that it seems to lead to catastrophe. It elaborates on Malthusianism in a number of ways. First, it contains many more variables than the Malthusian theory did, some of which have to do with population, but several of which involve measures of pollution, capital formation, agricultural production, utilization of various resources, and so forth. In its typical formulation, the world model contains seven or eight times as many variables as the Malthusian model. Furthermore, the relationships among these variables are far more complex than what one finds in the Malthusian theory. In the world model, many relationships are curvilinear in the sense that X may influence Y at certain levels of X, but not at others; in the Malthusian model, by contrast, most relationships are linear. The world model contemplates many more instances of multiple causation than did Malthus, and its authors are not nearly so cavalier about the introduction of constants (such as the "passion between the sexes"). Finally, and most importantly, the world model contains a large number of causal loops compared with the singular Malthusian loop described above, and given the nonlinearity of causal relationships in the world model it is more difficult to determine whether a given causal loop has a positive or a negative algebraic product. The world model is a system theory par excellence, and it is a little surprising that a major two-volume tome containing pure Parsonian sociology should have no index entries for the Club of Rome or any of its major authors (Loubser et al., 1976).

In short, the world model must be run on large computers. When it is, it usually shows that catastrophe occurs inevitably around the middle of the next century, *catastrophe* referring to such phenomena as a nearly total extinction of the human population, a nearly total depletion of nonrenewable resources, or a nearly total saturation of the earth's surface with pollution. Through various manipulations of the program it is possible to head off catastrophe, and these manipulations are analogous to fundamental social changes of the sort that we shall soon be referring to as adaptation processes.

In a sense, then, the Club of Rome world model may be a social theory that is expected to self-destruct; as it does so, we may learn something about forms of adaptation that will restore the stability conditions promised by Weller and Bouvier. On the other hand, if Marxian catastrophism prevails, the transformations that lead to a new stability may occur more rapidly and violently than we expect. Eventually, however, we shall catch our breath and begin to understand the structure and functioning of the new synthesis.

There is indeed a strong prospect that theories such as the Club of Rome world model will self-destruct by acting as self-destroying prophecies, and it would be profitable to contemplate the way in which this outcome could occur. Those who read carefully the formulations and findings of the Club of Rome project cannot fail to realize that the authors intend their theory to act as a warning: They hope that the human race will see catastrophe approaching and will do whatever is necessary and practicable to ward it off;[3] in general, the strategies must be of a "revolutionary" nature, and piecemeal attacks on specific problems, such as high fertility, are ineffective. The authors of the world model want their audiences to invent and implement structural changes that would act as adaptive mechanisms (having manifest functions) by reducing the likelihood of the assorted disasters projected by the model. Forrester, the Meadows, and their collaborators have always been highly optimistic about this prospect and have always implied that the explosive variables of the world model could be brought under control (i.e., stabilized) by appropriately strenuous effort. Stabilization will necessitate the forms of surveillance over various environments and the forms of effective adaptation that seem to be taken for granted in books like Sanders's *Computers in Society* (1981), which provides numerous illustrations of ways in which imminent eco-catastrophes may be (or are being) headed off.

In fact, there is no appreciable difference between the catastrophism of the Club of Rome and the catastrophism of Marxism (Serrón, 1980), despite the fact that neo-Malthusians and Marxists are constantly brawling all over the world – the 1984 World Population Conference in Mexico City is merely the latest outburst. It is a form of catastrophism worthy of the Club of Rome to argue that as capital becomes more and more "concentrated" (Zeitlin, 1973: 130–36), the large firms thereby created must pursue radical new policies designed to enhance and perpetuate themselves (Galbraith, 1971, 170–2,174–5). And listen to two noted Marxists as they go to work to show us how contradictions accumulate in modern capitalism (Baran and Sweezy, 1966:81):

Not only surplus . . . but also the investment-seeking part of surplus tends to rise as a proportion of total income. Whether this tendency will be realized, however, is another question. In attempting to answer it, we must first determine whether the system normally provides investment outlets large enough to absorb a rising share of a rising surplus.

The logic of the situation is as follows: If total income grows at an accelerating rate, then a larger and larger share has to be devoted to investment; and, conversely, if a larger and larger share is devoted to investment, total income must grow at an accelerating rate. What this implies, however, is nonsensical from an economic standpoint. It means that a larger and larger volume of producer goods would have to be turned out for the sole purpose of producing a still larger and larger volume of producer goods in the future. Consumption would be a diminishing proportion of output, and the growth of the capital stock would have no relation to the actual or potential expansion of consumption.

Baran and Sweezy are here describing a number of variables in a process of explosion due to the same sort of positive feedback that characterizes the Club of Rome model. Baran and Sweezy will never apply to be included in Sanders's book, however, because as Marxists they believe that while surveillance is possible – that is, they can tell us about the gathering storm – there is nothing we can do to head off catastrophe, and in fact we ought to contribute whatever we can to an inevitable revolution. In short, they do not expect their theory to self-destruct. Because the Marxian catastrophism may well be correct, and because I have never encountered anybody who knew how to predict the precise contours of a new Hegelian synthesis, I am willing to concede that true Marxian– Hegelian catastrophes cannot be predicted, explained, or understood by functionalist sociology or any other brand of sociology with the possible exception of sociology-as-art-form (Bierstedt, 1960; Nisbet, 1966:18–20). As Crane Brinton used to say, social scientists may be able to describe the wave of the future, but only artists can anticipate sea changes. Social scientists (functionalists and otherwise) do not focus on social stability because they deem it more important than social change; they do so because stability is easier to predict and explain. And even Marxists, with their promising premise that the basic contours of a given social system are always implicit in preceding systems, have achieved little success in predicting fundamental social changes.

The "bottom line," however, is that there is almost nothing in Marxian theory that cannot be incorporated into dynamic functionalism.

Part II. Adaptive structures and social processes

We have yet to experience the impact that *thinking about processes in time* will have on the way research is designed.
   −John M. Gottman, *Time-Series Analysis: A Comprehensive Introduction for Social Scientists*

. . . there is no substitute for macro-theory founded on detailed diachronic and synchronic causal-functional analysis of specific cases.
   −Marvin Harris, *The Rise of Anthropological Theory*

5. Patterns of adaptation

In a discussion of "the logic of functional explanation," Stinchcombe (1968:87–91) shows that theories such as Malinowski's theory of magic involve reciprocal interaction between a "structure" and a "homeostatic variable." In Malinowski's theory, as depicted by Stinchcombe (Figure 5.1), the structure (S) to be explained is the recurrent practice of magic as an elaborate social ritual, and the homeostatic variable (H) is "anxiety." Anxiety is continuously produced by "objective uncertainty" (T), an apparent measure of environmental hazard (cf. Goldschmidt, 1966:35). Paying close attention to the sign of each relationship, we note that any increase in environmental hazard reduces homeostasis (by raising anxiety); reduced homeostasis leads to increased resort to magic; the latter presumably serves to restore homeostasis. Malinowski's theory of magic belongs to a large class of theories that I propose to call *adaptation theories*; that is, it is a theory showing how changes in one sector of a social organization, herein to be called adaptations, help to resolve problems in another sector. Problems (departures from homeostasis) tend to *increase* adaptive efforts, whereas adaptations (when they are effective) tend to *reduce* problems – a pattern that, as we shall see, has a host of theoretical and methodological consequences. For the present it suffices to say that adaptation theories are an essential part of all contemporary sciences.

Consider, for instance, the physical and biological sciences. Clerk Maxwell's theory of the steam boiler regulator explains essentially how a valve, controlled by a servomechanism, corrects boiler pressure disturbances: Disturbances activate the valve, and an activated valve reduces disturbances. In modern societies the physical environment is abundantly supplied with "engineered systems" (Henshel, 1976:26–32) that control everything from refrigerator temperatures to airline flight paths, from carburetor fuel–air mixtures to automatic elevator doors, from household water pressure to freeway traffic flow. Unaltered natural phenomena in the physicochemical realm often exemplify the cyclical properties of engineered systems: reversible chemical reactions such as the Haber process

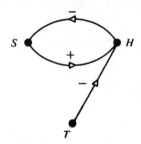

Figure 5.1. The elementary causal structure of a complete functional explanation
Source: Stinchcombe (1968: 89)

are good examples, the nitrogen and phosphorous cycles of the earth's biosphere are excellent examples, and the carbon cycle and proton–proton cycle of thermonuclear reactions are stellar examples. In biology, natural selection involves self-regulation through elimination of genetic deviance, and physiology, at least since the days of Claude Bernard and Walter B. Cannon, has been dominated by the principle of homeostasis, with many Nobel prizes nowadays awarded to scholars who have discovered the various electrical and chemical mechanisms ("spark" and "soup" processes) whereby the body regulates itself (cf. Schmidt-Nielsen, 1979). (Biofeedback advocates attempt to make volition a more prominent part of these mechanisms; this takes us back again to processes of expansion and contraction in the "role of the actor.") In animal and plant ecology the balance of nature represents the essential homeostatic theme. It is ironic that Kingsley Davis, arguing wrongly that there is nothing unique about functionalism, illustrated the subject of his critique with a fishpond example involving all the unique elements of Figure 5.1.

Indeed, no important distinction exists between Stinchcombe's model of functional explanation, Davis's fishpond example, and Durkheim's famous speculations about the dynamics of deviance and social control (1938:95–96):

> When . . . *the explanation of a social phenomenon is undertaken, we must seek separately the efficient cause which produces it and the function it fulfills.* We use the word "function," in preference to "end" or "purpose," precisely because social phenomena do not generally exist for the useful results they produce. *We must determine whether there is a correspondence between the fact under consideration and the general needs of the social organism, and in what this correspondence consists, without occupying ourselves with whether it has been intentional or not.* All these questions of intention are too subjective to allow of scientific treatment.

Not only must these two types of problems be separated, but it is proper, in general, to treat the former before the latter. This sequence, indeed, corresponds to that of experience. It is natural to seek the causes of a phenomenon before trying to determine its effects. This method is all the more logical since the first question, once answered, will often help to answer the second. Indeed, the bond which unites the cause to the effect is reciprocal to an extent which has not been sufficiently recognized. The effect can doubtless not exist without its cause; but the latter, in turn, needs its effect. It is from the cause that the effect draws its energy; but it also restores it to the cause on occasion, and consequently it cannot disappear without the cause showing the effects of its disappearance.

For example, the social reaction that we call "punishment" is due to the intensity of the collective sentiments which the crime offends; but, from another angle, it has the useful function of maintaining these sentiments at the same degree of intensity, for they would soon diminish if offenses against them were not punished.

Furthermore, it is arguable that the study technique known as "evaluation research" (Rossi et al., 1979) consists primarily of the testing of adaptation hypotheses. The major virtue of evaluation research is that it forces us to specify and measure the functions, goals, or aims of social action programs (Babbie, 1983: ch. 12), to assess whether desired outcomes are actually being attained, and to explain why ineffectual programs (survivals?) so often seem to persist.

Adaptation theories abound in the psychological and sociological realms. In the bygone era of social Darwinism it was widely believed that social entities evolved through a process of birth, growth, maturation, decay, and death, and that social selection therefore had a role similar to that of natural selection. Although social Darwinism is said to have taken its inspiration from biology, it should be remembered that, on the contrary, both Darwin and Wallace gained important insights from Malthus (Petersen, 1979:219), a social scientist par excellence whose theory of population (first edition) is most assuredly a theory of adaptation (sans intentionality) and cybernetic control. The same is true of Adam Smith's theory of the free market, an important antecedent of the Malthusian theory (Parsons, 1933). In the words of Himmelfarb (1960:xxiii):

The logic of Malthus was the logic of Adam Smith, and there was nothing in the principle of population that was not implied in the now "classical" principles of political economy. Wages, Smith had said, and Malthus agreed, tend naturally to hover about the subsistence level; if they rise above this level, the population increases until the increased demand for jobs once more drives them down to that level. Malthus only made more dramatic what Smith had earlier insisted upon: that men were as much subject to the laws of supply and demand as were commodities – that they were, indeed, in the free market-place, nothing more than commodities.

If Adam Smith, a fine sociologist, inspired Thomas Robert Malthus, another fine sociologist, and if the latter was a major inspiration for Darwin and Wallace, both fine biologists, and if all the major theories formulated by these men involved the essential functionalist imagery of feedback and self-regulation, then it is appropriate for biology to thank sociology for what has become its major theoretical model, and it is inappropriate for sociologists to continue flagellating themselves with the conviction that they rely too heavily on biology. In Harris's words (1968:122–3), ". . . Darwin's principles were an application of social science concepts to biology." When sociologists realize that biological evolutionism is a form of functional analysis (Hardin, 1959), they will dismiss contentions about the incompatibility of functionalism and evolutionism and will realize further that this apparent incompatibility was merely a by-product of the historical accident that functionalism in the social sciences became prominent as a reaction – perhaps an overreaction – against misapplications of evolutionary theory. These matters are discussed more thoroughly in the appendix.

Nineteenth-century balance-of-power theories follow the basic functionalist imagery (Dougherty and Pfaltzgraff, 1971:30–36), and the utilitarianism of the Benthamites urged the belief that all social control processes involve the manipulation of pleasure and pain as adaptive mechanisms, an idea that remains with us, for instance, in the form of deterrence theory (Gibbs, 1975). The Freudian version of the "hydraulic hypothesis," positing a range of adjustment mechanisms that enable one to adapt to the tension of id and superego, involves all the imagery of self-regulation and homeostasis. And finally, the same processes of circular causation are an essential part of modern learning theory.

1. The subtleties of circularity

An appreciation of the form of an adaptation process goes far toward clarifying theories that might otherwise remain obscure. In a famous article, for instance, George Homans (1941) attempted a "reconciliation" of Malinowski's and Radcliffe-Brown's theories of magic. With the adaptation model in mind, however, we shall see that the two formulations remain irreconcilable primarily because they imply different patterns of causation between magic and anxiety.

In Malinowski's theory of magic it is proposed that high levels of anxiety make for increased use of magic and that magic in turn serves to reduce anxiety. The alternative hypothesis proposed by Radcliffe-Brown holds that the relationship between anxiety and magic is precisely *opposite* to that posited by Malinowski. In the words of Radcliffe-Brown, as quoted by Homans (1941:169):

I think that for certain rites it would be easy to maintain with equal plausibility . . . that *if it were not for the existence of the rite and the beliefs associated with it the individual would feel no anxiety, and that the psychological effect of the rite is to create in him a sense of insecurity or danger.* It seems very unlikely that an Andaman Islander would think that it is dangerous to eat dugong or pork or turtle meat if it were not for the existence of a specific body of ritual the ostensible purpose of which is to protect him from those dangers. Many hundreds of similar instances could be mentioned from all over the world. [Italics added.]

Clearly, Radcliffe-Brown is arguing that the performance of magical rites *creates* anxiety. He seems to align himself with the strict behaviorists of the twenties and thirties, who believed that a man runs not because he is frightened but becomes frightened because he is running. In reformulating Radcliffe-Brown's theory from a functionalist standpoint, we must ask when it would become imperative that anxiety be intensified in a society, if ever; that is, what is the nature of the objective threat? High anxiety, one presumes, gives rise to an assortment of adaptive efforts: for example, more thorough preparation for childbirth, for warfare, hunting, shelter construction, and so forth. Radcliffe-Brown, realizing that this question must be answered, remarks that

the Andamanese taboos relating to childbirth are the obligatory recognition . . . of the significance and importance of the event to the parents and to the community at large. . . . Similarly I have argued in another place that the Andamanese taboos relating to the animals and plants used for food are means of affixing a definite social value to food . . . . The *social* importance of food is not that it satisfies hunger, but that in such a community as an Andamanese camp or village an enormously large proportion of the activities are concerned with getting and consuming of food, and that in these activities, with their daily instances of collaboration and mutual aid, there continuously occur those inter-relations of interests which bind the individual men, women and children into a society (1952:150–1).

Homans, however, in his effort to reconcile these many ideas, completely misinterprets Radcliffe-Brown's theory and thus provides a spurious logical basis for a reconciliation of two theories that remain sharply at variance with one another. In Homans's words (1941:169–70):

This attack [by Radcliffe-Brown] on Malinowski's theory appears at first glance to be devastating. But let us examine it a little more closely. Put in simpler language, what Radcliffe-Brown is saying is that the Andaman mother and father do not apparently feel anxiety at the fact of approaching childbirth. *They feel anxiety only*

when the ritual of childbirth is not properly performed. There is no doubt that
similar observations could be made of backward people all over the world. It is true
that their techniques do not allow them to control completely the natural forces on
which their lives depend. Nevertheless when they have done their practical work as
well as they know how and have performed the proper rituals, they display little
overt anxiety. If anxiety is present, it remains latent. [Italics added]

If the magical rites are not properly performed, says Homans, the Andaman parents feel anxiety. If you do not scratch, in other words, you
continue to itch, and with appropriate lag time there would be a negative
correlation between these two variables. Radcliffe-Brown, on the contrary, believes that scratching causes itching, a condition that would make
for a positive correlation between the two variables.

  If magic is an adaptive effort, it is brought about by some threatening
disturbance of a homeostatic variable, and magic in turn has a measurable
impact in reducing that disturbance. A functionalist would tend not to
assume that anxiety is created as an expressive exercise; in fact, a functionalist following Mayhew's (1980) prescriptions would not include anxiety as an object of study and would be content to focus solely on the
magical rites and their relationship with "techniques . . . to control . . .
natural forces." In any case the major problem in reconciling Malinowski
and Radcliffe-Brown is to decide which variable is the disturbance term
(*H*), which is the adaptation (*S*), and whether these variables interact
through time in the way suggested by one or the other (or neither) of
these two scholars.

  In a similar vein, Petersen (1979:79,83,89) raises several issues deriving
from the Malthusian tradition and essentially involving questions as to
direction of causation. Does subsistence regulate population, or does
population regulate subsistence? In agrarian societies do grain prices determine rent of agricultural land, or does rent determine prices? Does
supply create demand and thereby stimulate an unlimited expansion of
human voracity, or does demand call forth a supply that satiates finite
human needs, which is the essential question on which Malthus took issue
with Jean Baptiste Say and his followers. Precisely the same theme occurs
in a study of firearms by Wright et al. (1983) in which an attempt is made
to determine whether crime causes people to acquire weaponry, whether
the availability of weaponry causes crime, and/or whether private weaponry deters crime. Similar questions are raised by McCarthy and Hoge
(1984) regarding the interaction of delinquency and self-esteem and by
Thornberry and Christenson (1984) regarding the interaction of crime and
unemployment. The latter study begins with the comment that

When causal relationships are reciprocal . . . unidirectional models are misspecified and impede an accurate understanding of the causal processes at work . . . . The empirical consequence of such misspecification is that results . . . can be incomplete and misleading. Conceivably, . . . tests could indicate a unidirectional relationship between two variables when the actual relationship [is reciprocal or reversed] (Thornberry and Christenson, 1984:399).

In dynamic functional analysis these sorts of questions are ubiquitous.

In a classic study of academic freedom in the United States, Lazarsfeld and Thielens (1958) made the surprising discovery that those professors who felt the greatest apprehensiveness about threats to free speech were far more likely than their colleagues to exercise free speech, to defend unpopular beliefs in public. The authors, however, do not make clear the nature of any causal dynamics between apprehensiveness and the exercise of uninhibited speech. If we interpret their work from the standpoint of the Stinchcombe diagram, however, we see immediately that Lazarsfeld and Thielens are grappling with a problem that is precisely the same as that encountered by Malinowski, Radcliffe-Brown, and Homans. If one assumes that apprehensiveness is an adequate index of objective threats to free speech and that threats represent an adaptive effort on the part of those who wish to suppress free speech, the Stinchcombe diagram may be an appropriate way to represent the causal interrelationships of the two variables: Free speech stimulates threats, and threats suppress free speech. The first of these causal impulses may be strong enough to sustain the positive correlation observed by Lazarsfeld and Thielens. On the other hand it is entirely possible – as Radcliffe-Brown might warn us – that the observed positive correlation between apprehensiveness and free speech arises from a tendency for threats to academic freedom to *stimulate* the uninhibited speech they seek to suppress. Again, the signs and directions of causal impulses can hardly be ascertained through cross-sectional data analysis. And as an exercise in logical possibilities, we should contemplate two additional hypotheses: that high levels of anxiety may suppress the practice of magic, and that uninhibited speech may suppress threats to academic freedom.

The Stinchcombe diagram, then, although it appears to be relatively uncomplicated, raises questions that are not readily answered. Moreover, when we consider the T term, a type of risk factor, we encounter an entirely new problem. During the horrendous winter of 1977 I heard a TV interviewer ask the admissions director of a hospital in International Falls, Minnesota, how the hospital handles the many cases of frostbite that must occur during severe winter weather. The admissions director answered that he could not remember the last time he had seen a case of frostbite and that one could probably find many more cases in a place like Louisiana. Avoiding frostbite, he implied, is part of the culture of his community. Ever since hearing this interview, I have referred to the tendency to overadapt to clearly perceived threats as the "International Falls effect."

On taking another look at the Stinchcombe diagram, we realize that the International Falls effect is capable of disguising an important causal relationship. If a strong causal arrow with a positive sign were to go from threat (T) to social structure (S), representing an impulse toward adaptive over-compensation, then it would be entirely possible for the $T \rightarrow S \rightarrow H$ (positive) mechanism to cancel out the $T \rightarrow H$ (negative) mechanism, and vice versa, thereby leading to the erroneous impression that risks are not really risks, or that adaptive efforts do not count for much, or both. Wyer and Conrad (1984), for instance, may be correct in surmising that academic inbreeding has no deleterious impact on scholarly productivity, but I should like to examine this relationship within institutions having different proportions of inbred faculty members; I would take a low proportion as an indicator of high perceived threat. My hypothesis is that those institutions with few inbred professors are probably "overprotecting" themselves against the perceived risks of faculty inbreeding, that inbred professors at such institutions are probably excellent scholars, and that the traditional stigmatization of inbreeding is probably accounted for mainly by those institutions that do a lot of it. This would be an instance of the epidemiological research discussed in Chapter 3.

2. An almanac of adaptations, with helps

Theories of natural and social selection, the free market, the balance of power, personality dynamics, and deviance–social control are highly abstract and general theories, each of which is applicable to a wide range of social phenomena. When we examine the social science literature dealing with adaptation, we find many instances in which a specific structure allegedly increases the survivorship (among other possible outcomes) of a social entity; a specific exchange process allegedly creates a sense of justice fulfilled; a specific psychological adjustment mechanism is thought to reduce frustration or enhance one's self-image; a specific form of threat is presumed to act as a deterrent; a specific strategy is held to maximize rewards. In Table 5.1, several such theories are listed. For each example a homeostatic variable – a condition to be maintained – is indicated, followed by a proposed adaptation. In some cases, due to authors' preferences, a problem or disturbance of a homeostatic variable is indicated in lieu of the homeostatic variable itself, but the distinction is unimportant. A similar table, involving ". . . vital sequences incorporated in all cultures," is found in Turner and Maryanski (1979:49).

All theories listed in Table 5.1 have in common the distinctive features of adaptation theories; therefore, they all illustrate the basic model of Figure 5.1. Aside from these common features, the theories are disparate in many ways. Some of them, for instance, seem to have a time dimension, whereas others do not. Although one must be wary of putting words into the mouths of theorists, it would appear that Durkheim's theory of the division of labor, Kamen's hypothesis on the creation of "membership categories," Chambliss's hypothesis on traffic citations as a means of social control, Ehrlich's hypothesis on the deterrent effects of capital punishment, or the Malthusian theory of population – all such theories and hypotheses seem to place a strong emphasis on temporal variations, on the dynamics of social processes through time. One readily imagines, for instance, cyclical variations in economic deprivation that, over time, may have brought about similar variations in the lynching rate. Other adaptation theories, at least as initially formulated, appear to be far more static: Weber does not ask, for instance, whether there are temporal variations in the motivation of capitalist entrepreneurship (cf., however, Hammond and Williams, 1976), with commensurate adjustments in the form of a reaffirmation of the Protestant ethic. Nor does the famous Davis–Moore theory ask whether leaps and lags in work motivation are associated over time with appropriate adaptations in the form of social differentiation (cf., however, Hagstrom, 1965). Similarly, Sorokin and Merton (1937) do not envision periodic disruptions of social coordination with resultant adaptations in the form of increasing resort to standardized time measurement. Finally, Merton does not assume repeated disruptions of a community's sense of gemeinschaft, for which there is a compensating upsurge of machine politics. Although such possibilities could be explored, the theorists in question appear to be more concerned with explaining social origins (e.g., the *establishment* of astronomical time measurement or capitalist entrepreneurship) than with accounting for continuous social processes subject to periodic disruptions or variations (cf. Bredemeier 1955:175). Accordingly, the theories are episodic; many of them, perhaps, are testable by methods appropriate for "interrupted time series" (Cook and Campbell, 1979). In the imagery of Figure 5.1, these theories do not clearly envision periodic disturbances (*T*) that cre-

Table 5.1. *Adaptation theories and hypotheses: some illustrations*

Homeostatic Variable or Problem (H)	Adaptation (S)	Source	Date
Maintenance of population equilibrium	Positive checks	Malthus	
Stability of price and supply of food grains	"Corn laws"	Malthus	
Maintenance of bourgeois class interests	Bourgeois democracy	Marx	
Motivation of capitalist entrepreneurship	Protestant ethic (inner-worldly asceticism)	Weber	
Maintenance of competitive advantage	Division of labor	Durkheim	
Economic insecurity	Fertility control	Dumont	1890
		Banks	1954
		Easterlin	1980
Maintenance of social coordination	Astronomical time measurement	Sorokin and Merton	1937
Economic deprivation	Lynching	Dollard et al.	1939
Economic stagnation	Emigration	Stouffer	1940
Maintenance of motivation	Social differentiation	Davis and Moore	1945
Anxiety	Magic	Malinowski	1948
Advantage in internecine warfare	Incest taboo	White	1948
Maintenance of family legitimacy	Social stigmatization of alternatives	Davis	1949
Political integration	Alternating power structures (gumsa and gumlao)	Leach	1951
Maintenance of social boundaries	Social conflict	Coser	1955
Maintenance of Gemeinschaft	Political machines	Merton	1957
Group cohesion	Deviance	Dentler and Erikson	1959
Expectation-achievement discrepancy	Revolution	Brinton	1965
Sex-role stabilization	Male initiation rites	Young	1965
Parking violations	Citations and fines	Chambliss	1966
Economic scarcity	Potlatch	Piddocke	1969

Table 5.1. *(cont.)*

Homeostatic Variable or Problem (H)	Adaptation (S)	Source	Date
Various "positive" functions	Poverty	Gans	1972
Information overload	Legislature size	Taagepera	c.1974
Maintenance of balance of power	Midterm elections	Tufte	1974
Homicide	Capital punishment	Ehrlich Black and Orsagh	1975 1978
Criminal court overload	Plea bargaining	Church	1976
Profit maximization	Racial and sexual discrimination	Szymanski	1976
Maintenance of bureau-cratic legitimacy	Creation of membership categories	Kamens	1977
Maintenance of equity	Social norms	Walster et al.	1978
Crime victimization	Reduced exposure	Balkin	1979
Erosion control	Horticulture norms	Berry	1981
Population replacement	Pronatalist norms	Hoff and Abelson	1982
Control over bequests under high mortality	Non-kin/kin ratio among heirs	Smith	1982
Survival of imperatively coordinated organizations	Unity of command	Mayhew	1983
Civil disorder	"Welfare explosion"	Schram and Turbett	1983

ate departures from homeostasis (*H*). One can hardly think of a more pertinent question for the Davis–Moore theory, however, than whether modern societies, or the separate bureaucracies found within them, are assailed by occasional crises of work motivation (breakdowns of worker morale) to which they may adapt, as the Davis–Moore theory implies, by means of a further elaboration of social differentiation.[1] Similar questions could be raised about any adaptation theory.

Among the theories listed in Table 5.1 several do indeed have a time dimension, but this dimension pertains primarily to life-cycle variations in the experiences of individuals. Although a nexus may exist between a young man's experience of initiation rites and his sense of being a man, such a nexus would tell us little or nothing about whether severe disruptions of sex-role stabilization ever occur, and whether such disruptions bring about an increased resort to intense and prolonged initiation practices. Similarly, one could ask whether the Dumont–Banks hypothesis, which assumes a nexus between individual fertility and economic insecurity, is generalizable to a "systemic" level where it would imply variations in general fertility rates in response to fluctuations in the business cycle (Easterlin, 1980). (Among demographic theories, Stouffer's theory of migration as a response to economic opportunity often has been tested with time-series data at a system level.) As we shall see, adaptation processes that operate at the individual level of analysis do not necessarily operate at the organizational level or the systemic level, and vice versa. Assumptions to the contrary violate either the "Robinson rule" – that organizational- or system-level generalizations (aggregate generalizations) do not necessarily apply to individuals – or the "Nosnibor rule," which is the Robinson rule in reverse. On the other hand, epidemiological and other aggregate-level studies are often inspired by individual-level findings, and vice versa.

Regarding the Sorokin–Merton theory of solar time measurement, recent incisive work by Zerubavel (1982) affords a fine opportunity for showing how dynamic functionalism would address contemporary patterns of stability and change in the international standard-time-zone system, that is, how the functionalist perspective would enable us to move beyond the sociohistorical level of understanding justifiably claimed by Zerubavel.

Zerubavel argues, in keeping with Sorokin and Merton, that national and international standard time became necessary as complex societies with modern transportation and communication began to understand that coordinated interrelationships would become either "inefficient" or "dangerous" (Zerubavel's claims) in the absence of a consensus as to what time it is at any given geographical point. Significantly, the first attempts at devising a standard-time system were made by British railroad companies early in the nineteenth century; these efforts created Greenwich mean time as a standard that eventually achieved much wider use. Zerubavel discusses the International Meridian Conference of 1884, an elaborate and extraordinary exercise in the "social construction of reality" at an international level that created the modern time-zone system in its essential outlines. Over the last century this arrangement has undergone a rapid diffusion and is now used in most parts of the world, although there are still many communities and some nations that resist the use of Greenwich time to one degree or another. Finally, Zerubavel explains that the time-zone system involves a social construction that transforms continuous solar time into a series of 24 discrete intervals, each an hour in width. He points out that this interval could easily have turned out to be less than one hour, or perhaps even more than one hour. The width of the interval, of course, is crucial in determining how large a discrepancy in solar time will be permitted between two communities that regard themselves as having the same standard time. We encounter here a fascinating platonic dialectic involving difference-within-identity and identity-within-difference.

It is clear that in Zerubavel's sociohistorical theory the most important events are the invention of the clock (or sundial) with its arbitrary unit of one hour, the invention of modern forms of transportation and communication, the invention of Greenwich mean time and its complement (180 degrees longitude away) the International Date Line, and so forth. These are the objective realities that serve as the basis for standard time as a social construction. (They may not be as objective as, say, the solar system, but they are at least as objective as Sumner's famous "dead hand of the past.") One is tempted therefore to take the standard time system as a social construction that is to be explained idiographically as a unique cluster of historical events; this is the essence of the Sorokin–Merton theory. Yet, as Zerubavel implies, the system apparently has many interesting instabilities (time series variations) that persist up to the present moment and will continue indefinitely.

First, there are many aspects of time measurement that are not yet standardized; daylight-saving time, for instance, is a relatively anomic practice both domestically and (especially) internationally. The conditions under which a given community or nation decides to adopt (or to reject) daylight-saving time are of paramount concern to dynamic functionalism.

Second, the lines separating time zones are not simply arbitrary meridian lines but tend to follow natural contours such as rivers and mountain crestlines, political boundaries, perhaps the boundaries of communication and transportation systems, and so forth. A community that is close to a time-zone boundary often has the option of joining the zone to its east or the zone to its west. Dynamic functionalism asks how often these decisions are made, under what circumstances, and what the socioeconomic factors are that influence them in addition to the sanctions provided under laws similar to the 1966 U.S. Standard Time Act. As for the latter, we have an instance in which we could invoke the delict–sanction model.

Third, logic dictates that as nation-states continue to become more interdependent, the time zones should become wider; after all, this process began with a mosaic of many thousands of small areas that had local time. Zerubavel claims that the historical dominance of the eastern United States has tended to push the zone line separating eastern time from central time in a westerly direction. If, as Zerubavel suggests (1982:20,21), the standard time system *promotes* interdependence as it also *reflects* interdependence, then we may be in the presence of reciprocal interaction involving positive feedback and leading to wider time zones in the future: The survival of wider time zones would provide a compelling instance of Campbell's (1969) change through social selection. Zerubavel describes (1982:21) the Soviet Union's attempt to impose Moscow time on airports and railroads across 11 standard time zones, but he does not seem to recognize that this practice may turn out to be the wave of the future, especially if people continue to pay less and less attention to the position of the sun. (Anybody who has not discerned the ways in which the U.S. airlines, along with Ma Bell, are making space disappear as a socially meaningful construct through flat fees that have almost nothing to do with distance has not been observing carefully and has not been reading Toffler (1980).) As Bartky (1984:1422) points out, the possibility of a single standard of time for the United States has been seriously considered.

Fourth, on the matter of affiliation with or opposition to the international standard-time system, it is not helpful to assert, as does Zerubavel (1982:18), that a community or nation may wish to "accentuate its separateness" by rejecting the standard-time system, and that such behavior may be "a symbolic act of actual defiance" (1982:19). As Mayhew (1980) would say, these are instances in which people are said to behave in a certain way *because they wish to do so*, and this is not always an adequate explanation. For dynamic functionalism the questions are (1) What are the conditions concerning interdependence (primarily) that may lead communities to reject or disaffiliate from the standard-time system? (2) Is it possible for a community actually to reduce interdependence by such rejection or disaffiliation?

Let us turn to another example: Several authors, among them Westoff and Rindfuss (1974), have tried to spell out the implications of the wide-

spread use of sex preselection of offspring. Here we have another instance in which we ignore human volition at our peril: Once again, we
reject Mayhew's (1980) disparagement of human intentions as a partial
explanation, pointing to an instance in which the most important questions pertain to "what people want to do." I have carried out a number
of simulations of the sex preselection process in which the variables have
included (1) the degree to which the sex of offspring is controllable, (2)
the proportion of husbands and wives who wish to control the sex of
their first-born child, with various ways of reconciling disagreements, (3)
comparable proportions for higher parities as influenced by the sex of
children born earlier, and (4) the size distribution of completed families
in a population. In simulations involving what might be called a worst-
case scenario – one in which there is a strong preference for boys at the
earlier parities (especially) and in which completed families remain
small – it is possible to raise the sex ratio at birth from its usual level of
105 (boys per hundred girls) to more than 115.[2] Such an increase in the
sex ratio at birth would probably have a profound social impact, constituting a serious and unprecedented disruption of a homeostatic variable.
What sorts of social consequences would follow, and what are the adaptive processes that would be invoked in order to restore the sex ratio at
birth to some new optimal level? Would there be an occasional bounty
on girl babies? Would there be an increasing practice of bachelorhood
on the part of males? Would polyandry occur? Would sex preselection
be made illegal? These adaptive processes, of course, should be traced
carefully over time.

Although we have as yet no answer for these questions, they are clearly
the sorts of questions that will be raised by dynamic functionalism if and
when the time arrives. The example of sex preselection involves a classic
illustration of a nearly stationary series, controlled largely by nature and
therefore not yet worthy of inclusion in Table 5.1, interrupted by technology and volitional human action, and then presumably subject to feedback establishing a new equilibrium. Adherents of Harris's (1968:4)
"techno-environmental" and "techno-economic" brand of social anthropology would delight in this sort of problem, and so would devotees of
Parsonian voluntarism.

A first rule for testing adaptation theories, then, is that any theory that
purports primarily to account for social origins, to explain an interrupted
time series, should be tested for its applicability to continuous time variations. In the language of ecological anthropology (Moran, 1982:7), we

must ascertain whether "developmental responses," although they appear
to be "not reversible," may have sufficient flexibility to become "regula-
tory" or "acclimatory" responses. It is the general lack of such a tactic
that has earned functionalism a reputation for failing to pay proper attention to temporal dynamics. In the Schram–Turbett (1983) study of social
welfare, a highly instructive example, we encounter not merely an attempt to discern the sociohistorical origins of the welfare state but also an
impressive effort to test the hypothesis that ". . . the historical role of
public welfare has been one of expansion and contraction in response to
the alternating needs of the state for political stability and acceptance of
low-wage work by the poor," a vastly more dynamic (and interesting)
formulation. The appropriate data for this study are time-series data, the
appropriate methods are highly sophisticated, and the results do indeed
suggest that public welfare policies respond to political instability and
probably influence it in turn.

3. Evolving taxonomies

Some adaptation processes, as described in the literature (and in Table
5.1), are far more general or abstract than others. The relationship between economic deprivation and the lynching rate, for instance, is merely
one among scores of instances subsumed under the frustration–aggression
hypothesis. The relationship between criminal court overload and plea
bargaining is a specific instance of more general queuing processes, and
there are many specific instances of deviance–conformity theories. Other
homeostatic or problem variables – among them the achievement of competitive advantage, maintenance of motivation, maintenance of bureau-
cratic legitimacy, information overload, maintenance of social boundaries – are highly abstract, and under such abstractions one hopes to place
myriad instances.

   These extreme variations in levels of abstraction suggest that the social science disciplines would benefit immensely if more attention were
given to the creation of systematic taxonomies; one welcomes a modicum of guidance as one moves about on the ladder of abstraction. And
in creating taxonomies it is well to bear in mind that social processes
involving a similar time dynamic – for example, the time dynamic of the
typical adaptation theory – are relatively more likely to have close taxonomic relationships. Male initiation rites, traffic citations, lynching,
magic, revolution, and warfare, for instance, may all be specific in-

stances of a general relationship between frustration and aggression. Such general adaptive forms are the sociological counterpart of "biomes" in animal and plant ecology.

The most effective way of discerning these abstract patterns is to make good use of a highly developed taxonomy. In their classic textbook on research methods, Goode and Hatt (1952:58) provide excellent examples, of which I have selected one:

Principle: Rather extensive, but relatively unsystematized, data show that members of the upper occupational-class strata experience less unhappiness and worry and are subject to more formal controls than members of the lower strata.

Deduction: Our hypothesis would then predict that this comparison also applies to the marital relationships of members of these strata and would predict that such differential pressures could be observed through divorce rates. There should be an inverse correlation between class position and divorce rates.

Berelson and Steiner (1964) have compiled a lengthy collection of abstract principles similar to that cited by Goode and Hatt, and it is an edifying exercise to try to deduce from these principles a range of specific hypotheses. Similarly, one is able to read just about any contemporary journal article presenting specific findings and to derive abstract generalizations from these specifications; the process, in other words, works both ways (M.R. Cohen, 1959:124). In functional analysis a highly abstract assertion that "Y is functional with respect to X" presumably would be applicable to a wide range of structures of type Y and organizations of type X. For instance we now have in the literature highly abstract generalizations about the ability of deterrence to bring about conformity (Gibbs, 1975). For another instance, we turn to an excellent paper by Bredemeier (1955:174):

We can . . . be more rigorous methodologically by reformulating the incest hypothesis as follows: Certain status relationships are comprised (by cultural definition) of rights and obligations and sentiments which are psychologically incompatible with certain sentiments that might be associated with sexual relations. For example, the employer–secretary, professor–student, father–daughter, priest–parishioner relationships are conventionally defined in our society so as to make sexual relationships (as *they* are conventionally defined) inconsistent with performance of the defined responsibilities. We understand the incest taboo, then, as one of a class of taboos, existing *because* the role players *have been trained* into responses incompatible with the sexual response.

Equally edifying discussions of the value of systematic taxonomies are found in Blau (1980), McKelvey (1982), and Stapleton et al. (1982).

Reading Blau's paper I became convinced that the American Sociological Association should establish immediately a continuing committee on social science taxonomy. Although initially upset when this suggestion was called "childlike," I now agree with the characterization, but with the proviso that (1) we are all children, and (2) we all have an equally compelling need for this particular source of nurturance.

Another way of exploiting taxonomies would involve perusal of existing adaptation theories to determine whether any given homeostatic variable or any given adaptation variable appears in a large number of instances. If so, we may be in the presence of functional or structural equivalence. For instance, Szymanski's (1976) suggestion that racial and sexual discrimination are alternative means of economic exploitation is a hypothesis involving at least three variables; multivariate methods therefore are mandatory, and those who ignore such methodological imperatives run the usual risks of turning up spurious results. Suppose, with Szymanski, that both racial and sexual discrimination by employers serve the interests of (I gather) profit maximization, but that they do so alternatively, as structural equivalents.[3] By the usual definition structural equivalency means that the presence of one structural feature is associated with the absence of the other, and vice versa, implying a negative correlation between the two structural features and implying also that neither structural feature is indispensable. For racial and sexual discrimination (although his measures are unsatisfactory) this is precisely what Szymanski finds, and he dangerously adduces this finding to support the notion that racial and sexual discrimination are structural alternatives. If, however, one were to attempt to tie either form of discrimination to some measure of profit maximization, one would be forced to deal with the fact that, if a structure S_1 were *positively* associated with such a homeostatic variable (H) and *negatively* associated with another structure S_2, then the association between S_2 and H would tend to disappear or to become negative. Social structures acting as alternatives, in other words, tend to obscure one another.

We encountered in Chapter 1 exactly such a situation, involving Navaho witchcraft. In that instance we considered the hypothesis that, although witchcraft may contribute to "hostility management," other structures may have a similar impact and may also be functional alternatives. If we test the multiple-causation hypothesis that hostility management is a positive function of both witchcraft and some alternative structure, while constraining witchcraft and the alternative to be negatively related to one another, we encounter a sort of dead end that was pointed out some years ago by Duncan (1963:452): If the value of two correlations is highly positive, it is likely (within limits stipulated by Duncan) that the third will also be positive. It makes little sense to define functional alternatives as structural conditions that are inversely related to each other; this practice merely imposes an arbitrary restriction on the data. In any instance, then, in which one is testing a theory about structural or functional equivalents, it is essential that all such equivalents be identified, that each of them be assessed with the others held constant, that potential interaction effects of equivalents be evaluated, and that equivalency be understood to mean "rough equality of effects," rather than "substitutability." In other words, the methodological complexities of the situation must be taken into account. And it goes without saying that whenever we do encounter alternatives that tend to substitute for one another, we must try to account for *selection* among them. This occurs when economists speak of the substitutability of commodities, when psychologists speak of the substitutability of symptoms of mental disorder, and when sociologists speak of the substitutability of lethal weapons (Wright et al., 1983: 189).

As depicted in Figure 5.1, adaptation theories involve both a positive and a negative relationship between a homeostatic or problem variable (*H*) and an adaptive process (*S*). Because these relationships are of opposite sign, it is likely that any instantaneous or cross-sectional correlation between *H* and *S* will be close to zero. The two elements of this kind of reciprocal causal relationship tend to cancel one another, and negative results such as those obtained by Szymanski (1973) and Garofalo (1977) are potentially explainable precisely on this basis. In addition to experimental or simultaneous-equation methods, reciprocal causation may be assessed through use of lagged endogenous variables, and because the introduction of lag is tantamount to introducing time-series data, we conclude that "the logic of functional explanation," as shown in Stinchcombe's diagram, involves a nearly inescapable commitment to the use of time-series data. Because only those time-series variables that actually vary substantially over time are likely to play an important role in social research, we conclude that *functional analysis is inherently dynamic* in the sense of focusing on social variables that change (i.e., have temporal instability). According to the typical adaptation theory, a social problem (i.e., a disruption of a homeostatic variable) produces adaptive responses; the latter, in turn, diminish the initial problem or disruption. The phrase "in turn" alludes to the appropriate lag time, and the major burden of any test of an adaptation theory is to demonstrate the pattern of a positive relationship followed by a negative relationship, that is, to demonstrate circular causation with negative feedback. Most of the "theories" in Table 5.1, then, should properly be called hypotheses, because most have never been appropriately tested.

In brief, if functionalism deals with social structure and if structure is defined as "recurring process" (Radcliffe-Brown, 1935:396), then by definition structures and their consequences can only be observed through time. And functionalism, also by definition, can only be applied to time-series data or to data amenable to special methods such as two-stage least squares, in which we try to reconstruct time-series processes. The erroneous notion that "structure refers to an aspect of empirical phenomena that can be divorced from time" (Levy and Cancian, 1968:22) must be abandoned; this notion did not serve early functionalists well (Garbarino, 1977:58,97–98), and it will not serve contemporaries.

4. Positive feedback and social catastrophism

Table 5.1 lists only a small proportion of the many theories and hypotheses that exemplify Stinchcombe's concept of "a complete functionalist explanation" with its emphasis on circular causation and negative feedback. If we entertain the possibility that circular causation may create positive feedback as well as negative feedback (cf. Toffler, 1980:288–91), we encounter an exotic new set of theories and hypotheses having to do with "vicious" or "benign" circles. When Hauser and Duncan (1959:ch. 28) tell us that the broad field of human ecology focuses primarily on the interaction of population, organization, environment, and technology (the renowned POET paradigm), it is only a short step to the realization that there must be thousands of circular causation processes among these four large sets of variables, processes fulfilling every conceivable possibility for positive and negative feedback, nonlinearity, qualitative change of system states, and so forth (Duncan, 1961). Even *within* each of the four areas we sometimes find highly developed theories that meet the conditions of the Stinchcombe diagram: Demographers, for instance, routinely speak of mortality as a *cause* of changes in age composition (the stable population model) and as an *effect* of such changes (differential mortality); that is, mortality rates and age composition interact in a way that involves circular causation. What is fascinating about this particular interaction is that it is possible to show by means of stable population analysis (the theoretical basis of the life table) that, given a constant set of age-

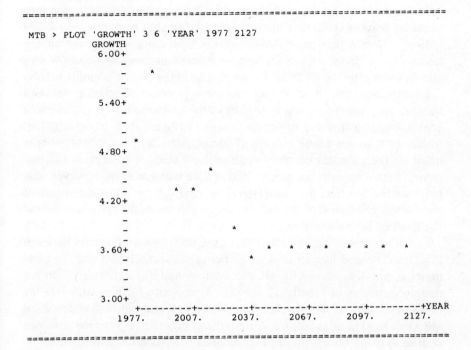

```
MTB > PLOT 'GROWTH' 3 6 'YEAR' 1977 2127
         GROWTH
         6.00+
            -
            -     *
            -
            -
         5.40+
            -
            -
            -
            -   *
         4.80+
            -
            -          *
            -
            -       *   *
         4.20+
            -
            -
            -                *
            -
         3.60+          *    *    *    *    *    *    *    *
            -              *
            -
            -
         3.00+
            +---------+---------+---------+---------+---------+YEAR
           1977.     2007.     2037.     2067.     2097.     2127.
```

Figure 5.2. Projection of U.S. population toward a stable five-year growth rate, 1977 to 2127

specific birth and death rates, age composition and crude mortality rates interact in predictable ways for about a century, after which time they both become constants (Figure 5.2). If such a process were actually to occur, all interesting noise pertaining to mortality and age composition would disappear, and there would be nothing left to explain.

Fortunately, such processes are only approximated in the real world because even though the stable population model is deterministic – appropriate for a "closed system" – the real world is filled with "open systems" in which equilibrium-seeking processes are subject to noise. Models assuming closed systems, taken too seriously, invariably go the way of the Malthusian theory (first edition). On the other hand, the stable population model, for all its determinacy, has been realistic enough that it served a few years ago as the basis on which President Nixon's population commission recommended that the United States not strive for "immediate ZPG" but merely wait for its rate of population growth to become

zero (or less) as a result of stable population processes. New (or old)
forms of noise may disrupt these processes, but such a contingency seems
unlikely. Notice that most demographers now seem to believe that the
famous baby boom was not a very significant instance of noise (Weller
and Bouvier, 1981: 57). In this example, as in the earlier example involving sex preselection of offspring, we see a constant alternation between
stability and disruption that is not unlike the extraordinary alternations of
continuous and discrete radiation processes observed by physicists. Unfortunately, at least one influential sociologist (Zeitlin, 1973:115–18) is
upset by the prospect of "two metatheories" that try to capture the dialectic of stability and disruption. In dynamic functionalism, however, stability and disruption are understood as arising from the same types of
underlying processes, as we saw in comparing the Malthusian theory and
the Club of Rome world model.

I wish to state explicitly, then, that I see no substantial tension between
functionalism and human ecology or between functionalism and "cultural
materialism" (Harris, 1979): Human ecology and cultural materialism are
merely instances of functional analysis. I recognize further, with Hawley
(1984) and Harris (1979), that human ecology and cultural materialism
are closely akin to Marxism. From these premises I suppose one can
deduce that the best form of functionalism is Marxian functionalism.

In addition to the POET paradigm there are abstract theories such as
Merton's self-fulfilling prophecy (1957:ch. xi) or the labelling perspective
in deviant behavior research (Gove, 1975) in which circular causation is
invoked as a more or less explicit hypothesis. In both instances there is a
strong presumption that vicious circles can be transformed into negative
feedback processes, as in the case of the Club of Rome world model
outlined earlier. It is hoped, in other words, that self-fulfilling prophecies
will have a charming capacity to self-destruct; in any instance where that
capacity does materialize we have a need to formulate a new theory, one
clearly exemplifying the Stinchcombe diagram. Theories about interrupted self-fulfilling prophecies are the meat and potatoes of evaluative
research. When a sociology professor tries to persuade students that they
are not constitutionally incapable of understanding statistics, he or she is
attempting to interrupt a self-fulfilling prophecy.

On the other hand, Henshel (1976) raises a number of intriguing inquiries within the arcane tradition of "reflexive sociology" – a form of
sociology that by definition is given to the use of circular causal models –
and ends by suggesting that social scientists take advantage of an alleged
"prestige loop" in which successful social predictions, by adding to the
prestige of the discipline and affording opportunities to create "engi-

neered" social systems, would make possible ever more impressive social predictions. He ends, in other words, with a positive feedback theory of the benign circle variety and also gives a contemporary twist to Kingsley Davis's hypothesis, mentioned in Chapter 1, about ways in which social scientists have tried to enhance the credibility of their discipline. Among sociologists of science there is a famous hypothesis of Mertonian origins, similar to Henshel's, about "accumulative advantage" in science (e.g., Allison et al., 1982; Schober, 1984), a process in which high scientific productivity gives rise to enhanced prestige, prestige increases access to research resources, better resources give rise to still higher levels of productivity, and so forth. Other forms of productivity, for example, the production of marital happiness, may be caught up in similar processes of accumulative advantage.

Returning to a consideration of Blau's "macrosocial" models, we see that fascinating transformations of these models occur when they are viewed from the perspectives of dynamic functionalism. Blau's efforts, for all their immense value, are seen to fall short of what could have been accomplished if time-series, feedback, and social selection processes had been included as part of the research strategy. In the following Minitab program, Blau's deterministic principle (discussed in Chapter 3) about the relationship between discrimination and associational differences is simulated with several new twists. The program begins by creating a constant, 1000, that will be taken as the size of each of 40 different communities varying on characteristics emphasized by Blau. Next, we create a variable representing the size of the majority segment of the population, having a mean of 0.75 and a standard deviation of 0.09; it is called MAJPROP and is drawn from a normal distribution. We then obtain the minority proportion of the population through subtraction; this is called MINPROP. Next, we create a variable for the proportion of the minority population that is married exogamously with members of the majority population; this variable is called MINEXOG, and is drawn from a normal distribution. When MINEXOG is subtracted from 1 the result is taken as an index of discrimination (DISCRIM). The number of minority individuals exogamously married is then calculated, and this number is also used as the number of majority individuals who are exogamously married. We then obtain the proportion of the minority population who associate (through marriage) with members of the majority (MINASS), and the same calculation is made for the majority (MAJASS). Finally, we obtain the minority–majority associational difference (DIFF), and subsequent lines request a correlation matrix, a regression equation showing the impact of MAJPROP and DISCRIM on DIFF, and a partial listing of the data:

```
MTB > NOTE : CREATE COMMUNITY SIZE CONSTANT
MTB > LET K1 = 1000
MTB > NOTE : CREATE MAJORITY PROPORTION OF POPULATION VARIABLE
MTB > NOPRINT
MTB > NRAN 40 .75 .09 C1
MTB > NAME C1 'MAJPROP'
MTB > NOTE : COMPUTE MINORITY PROPORTION OF POPULATION VARIABLE
MTB > LET C2 = 1 - 'MAJPROP'
MTB > NAME C2 'MINPROP'
MTB > NOTE : CREATE MINORITY EXOGAMOUS MARRIAGE PROPORTION VARIABLE
MTB > NOPRINT
MTB > NRAN 40 .25 .09 C12
MTB > NAME C12 'MINEXOG'
MTB > NOTE : CREATE DISCRIMINATION INDEX
MTB > LET C3 = 1 - C12
MTB > NAME C3 'DISCRIM'
MTB > NOTE : GENERATE NUMBER MINORITY EXOGAMOUS MARRIAGES
MTB > LET C11 = 'MINEXOG'*'MINPROP'*K1
MTB > ROUND C11 INTO C4
MTB > NAME C4 'NMINEXO'
MTB > NOTE : OBTAIN MINORITY ASSOCIATIONAL INDEX
MTB > LET C5 = 'NMINEXO'/('MINPROP'*K1)
MTB > NAME C5 'MINASS'
MTB > NOTE : OBTAIN MAJORITY ASSOCIATIONAL INDEX
MTB > LET C6 = 'NMINEXO'/('MAJPROP'*K1)
MTB > NAME C6 'MAJASS'
MTB > NOTE : OBTAIN MINORITY-MAJORITY ASSOCIATIONAL DIFFERENCE
MTB > LET C7 = 'MINASS' - 'MAJASS'
MTB > NAME C7 'DIFF'

MTB > CORR C1-C7


          MAJPROP MINPROP DISCRIM NMINEXO  MINASS  MAJASS
MINPROP   -1.000
DISCRIM    0.127  -0.127
NMINEXO   -0.757   0.757  -0.716
MINASS    -0.122   0.122  -1.000   0.713
MAJASS    -0.822   0.822  -0.613   0.986   0.611
DIFF       0.495  -0.495  -0.779   0.123   0.781  -0.017

MTB > REGR 'DIFF' 2 'MAJPROP' 'DISCRIM'

THE REGRESSION EQUATION IS
DIFF = 0.314 + 0.468 MAJPROP - 0.673 DISCRIM

                            ST. DEV.    T-RATIO =
COLUMN       COEFFICIENT    OF COEF.    COEF/S.D.
              0.31386       0.02386       13.16
MAJPROP       0.46843       0.02403       19.50
DISCRIM      -0.67307       0.02436      -27.63

MTB > PRINT C2-C7
```

ROW	MINPROP	DISCRIM	NMINEXO	MINASS	MAJASS	DIFF
1	0.351092	0.803241	69	0.196530	0.106333	0.090197
2	0.359969	0.565645	156	0.433371	0.243738	0.189633
3	0.135286	0.716184	38	0.280886	0.043945	0.236941
4	0.409534	0.762000	97	0.236855	0.164277	0.072578
5	0.410100	0.739884	107	0.260912	0.181387	0.079525
6	0.316426	0.772951	72	0.227542	0.105329	0.122213
.	.	.	.	.	.	.
.	.	.	.	.	.	.
.	.	.	.	.	.	.

The regression equation shows that, as Blau predicts, higher rates of discrimination tend to reduce the size of associational differences between majority and minority segments of a population. The equation also suggests that as the majority segment of a population gets larger, associational differences will be enhanced. Although these relationships are no longer deterministic as in Blau's formulation, the results suggest that population composition and discrimination account for most of the variance in the associational differences.

Examining the strongly negative correlation between DISCRIM and MAJASS, we would surely be tempted to entertain the venerable hypothesis that a high rate of majority association with minority members of the population would tend to reduce prejudice and discrimination–the "prejudice-interaction" hypothesis. The correlation of $-.613$ between these two variables tells us that the majority's rate of association accounts for 38 percent of the variance in discrimination. In examining the correlation matrix, however, we see that there is potential feedback from DISCRIM to MAJASS: In particular, DISCRIM may influence MAJASS by way of NMINEXO and MININT. It seems plausible that reduced discrimination would tend to raise the number of minority individuals who marry exogamously, that these increased numbers would increase the minority's rate of association with the majority, and that the latter change would increase the majority's rate of association with the minority. In other words, a high rate of association by a majority may reduce discrimination, and reduced discrimination may tend to increase the majority's rate of association. Here again we have an instance of positive feedback involving a benign circle, but the assumed causal dynamic is not testable with cross-sectional data of the sort used in this simulation; the various coefficients cannot be properly estimated.

Many of the preceding pages provide examples of the myriad ways in which "systems in general," to use Kuhn's phrase (1974:ch.2), may manifest themselves. What Kuhn calls "a controlled, or cybernetic, system," and defines as ". . . any acting system whose components and their interactions maintain at least one system variable within some specified range or return it to within that range if the variable goes beyond it . . . ," is nicely illustrated by theories of the incest taboo, the Malthusian theory, Durkheim's delict–sanction model, or theories of price regulation under perfect competition. These theories assume that "equilibrium" occurs when a system ". . . is subject to negative feedback, negative meaning opposite, corrective, or compensating" (Kuhn, 1974:31). In the case of the Club of Rome world model, however, we have (in part) a positive feedback theory. Although such theories usually imply explosion and ultimate catastrophe, this theory may turn out to be an instance of Kuhn's equilibrium through positive feedback (cf. Hawley, 1984:911), which occurs ". . . if there exists an asymptotic limit on at least one variable . . . . For example, . . . temperature and rate of combustion may . . . reach an upper limit determined by the rate of availability of fuel or oxygen." One hopes that such limitations will impinge on the oxygen-consuming circular causal process described by Sigelman and Bookheimer (1983). These several ways in which variables interact will be discussed more systematically in the next chapter.

6. Processes, simulations, and investigations

This chapter begins with a brief introduction to time-series analysis, a method essential to the forms of functional analysis advocated in this book. Included in this introduction are computer simulations of time-series processes, presented solely for their didactic and heuristic value. Several published works are cited in order to illustrate various degrees of success and failure in studies of social dynamics, and it is concluded that powerful forms of functional analysis will be forthcoming when survivorship variables are incorporated into adaptation hypotheses tested by means of modern methods of time-series analysis.

1. A primer on time-series analysis

Suppose that in a multivariate causal model we have n variables of which k are endogenous, meaning that they are determined by other variables in the model. In addition there are $n - k$ exogenous variables, defined as those taken as "givens" of the model because they are not explained with reference to other variables included in the model. The several explanatory variables found in any equation may be correlated with each other, but as long as they are not highly correlated we usually do not have to worry about this feature.

In designing complex causal models, it is important that we make the equations representing them amenable to solution. Multivariate causal models, often consisting of several interrelated equations, cannot be solved unless they are "identifiable." A necessary condition for identification, a condition that must be met if the important coefficients of a model are to be meaningfully estimated, is that in the equation for any endogenous variable the number of variables excluded from the equation must at least be equal to $k - 1$. Stated differently, the number of endogenous variables in a given equation cannot be greater than one plus the number of exogenous variables left out of the equation (Blalock, 1969: 59–66).

When these conditions are not met, the solution is to simplify the model, invoke additional exogenous variables, or give up.

When we test functional theories, we often encounter the hypothesis that a structure (X) gives rise to a certain consequence (Y) and that this consequence feeds back in such a way as to counteract disturbances of the structure (see Figure 5.1). In algebraic form,

$$Y = a + bX + e$$

and

$$X = a - bY + e$$

These equations, however, cannot properly be estimated because they violate the necessary conditions for identification stated above: There are no exogenous variables to be excluded from either equation. Again, we solve this dilemma by either simplifying the model – abandoning the feedback notion crucial to functional theory – or by invoking exogenous variables. Because the former tactic is tantamount to abandoning one of our basic theoretical forms, we shall avoid it. Notice, however, that in the system

$$Y = a + bX + cI + e$$

$$X = a - bY + cJ + e$$

we have met a necessary condition for identifiability, although it might be difficult to locate two "instrumental" variables that behave as helpfully as I and J. Ideally, the correlation of I and J would be close to zero.

When we have time-series data, even for a panel that we have observed only at two points in time, some new opportunities arise. Suppose we wish to explain changes in a variable Y with reference to X, allowing $t1$, $t2$, and so on, to represent data points in time:

$$\Delta Y = Y_{t2} - Y_{t1} = a + bX_{t1} + e$$

That is, *changes* in Y are produced by initial values of X; in functionalist terms we might hypothesize, say, that the higher the supply of some commodity (among states) at a given time, the greater will be reductions in demand for the commodity over the succeeding year. This equation appears to be reasonable until we rewrite it in a way that reveals an arbitrary restriction:

$$Y_{t2} = a + Y_{t1} + bX_{t1} + e$$

There is no reason for constraining the coefficient associated with Y_{t1} to be 1.0, and it is therefore more appropriate to test the following model:

$$Y_{t2} = a + b_1 Y_{t1} + b_2 X_{t1} + e$$

Among other things, this equation allows for the possibility that unusually high or low Y_{t1} values may tend to regress toward the mean, independently of X. It would be a worthwhile exercise to try to diagram these equations and to determine whether they appear to be identifiable. Observe that if the error terms for Y_{t1} are correlated with those for Y_{t2}, we have a possible distortion due to autocorrelation, a topic to which we now turn.

Suppose we have time-series data with which to test reciprocal interaction hypotheses. It should be noted that lagged terms such as Y_{t1} are called *lagged endogenous* variables, and what is especially useful about them is that they can be treated as exogenous variables. If we were dealing with a functionalist theory about the interaction of delicts (D) and sanctions (S), we might hypothesize that

$$S_{t2} = a_1 + b_1 D_{t1} + e_1 \tag{1}$$

and that

$$D_{t2} = a_2 - b_2 S_{t1} + e_2 \tag{2}$$

In other words, high rates of deviance tend, with some lag, to give rise to more severe sanctions, and the latter tend to bring about eventual reductions of deviance, a typical functionalist formulation. The basic problem here is that the error terms for a given dependent variable at two different points in time may be correlated, and this condition distorts our estimates of the model. The problem, again, is autocorrelation.

Equation (1) contains an expression for D_{t1}. Notice that we can rewrite Eq. (2) so that it applies to the preceding point in time and contains the term D_{t1}:

$$D_{t1} = a_2 - b_2 S_{t0} + e_2$$

By substitution we can write

$$S_{t2} = a_1 + b_1(a_2 - b_2 S_{t0} + e_2) + e_1$$

or

$$S_{t2} = a_1 + b_1 a_2 - b_1 b_2 S_{t0} + b_1 e_2 + e_1 \ .$$

When we collect constants and error terms under single expressions, this equation simplifies to

$$S_{t2} = A - b_1 b_2 S_{t0} + E$$

and tells us that, under a number of fairly strong assumptions about the behavior of error terms for sanctions at various time points, sanctions at time 2 are inversely related to sanctions at time 0, with the strength of the relationship reflecting the product $b_1 b_2$; this would be precisely the outcome anticipated under the functionalist hypothesis. There remains a problem, however, because the autocorrelation of sanctions – the tendency for sanctions to have continuity independent of any interaction with delicts – is likely to be strong, especially over relatively short lags. And since the size of lags is often implied by our theories, it is not always possible to manipulate the situation at will. (In addition, the equation for S_{t2} requires observations over three data points, a costly proposition.) In any case the autocorrelation terms for the two equations should eventually be included, as follows:

$$S_{t2} = a_1 + b_1 D_{t1} + c_1 S_{t1} + e_1 \tag{3}$$

and

$$D_{t2} = a_2 + b_2 S_{t1} + c_2 D_{t1} + e_2 \tag{4}$$

In arriving at Eqs. (3) and (4) we have encountered the typical causal patterns of two-wave panel studies (Heise, 1970). In Eq. (4), of course, we could have placed a minus sign in front of the S term, thereby retaining the hypothesis that sanctions tend to suppress deviance. Notice, too, that the only serious drawback of this model is that it rules out any instantaneous causal relationships, a restriction that may violate reality in the manner of José Arcadio Buendía, the mad scientist of *One Hundred Years of Solitude*, before his wife had him chained to a chestnut tree.

Although it was once fashionable to test the final model developed above by using cross-correlations, it has been demonstrated by several authors (e.g., Cook and Campbell, 1979: 309–21; Markus, 1979) that this method is unsatisfactory, especially when one is trying to determine whether the causal flow between two variables is predominantly in one direction. In most instances involving functional analysis, there is an interest in reciprocal interaction with a presumption that neither variable is predominant as a causal agent. It is still wise, however, to heed the cautions of the authors cited earlier; what they recommend is the use of path coefficients instead of correlation coefficients.

Consider now a statement from Cook and Campbell (1979: 317), which

I take to be an impassioned cry for better *theoretical* work as opposed to more clever methodological machinations:

In unpublished and published studies, several dozen sets of data involving some hundred pairs of variables have been explored for cross-lagged correlation differentials. It is our overall experience that statistically significant differences and differences of interesting magnitude are very rare.

To a functionalist, cross-correlation *differentials* are unimportant; what matters is to show significant reciprocal interaction between variables selected on the basis of functional theory, and to show that these interactions involve negative feedback in instances (e.g., the delict–sanction example) where functional theory predicts negative feedback. The disappointing findings reported by Cook and Campbell, then, do not lead me to question the functionalist belief that many social variables interact in ways that involve negative feedback. It is worth noting, however, that Cook and Campbell do cite several studies (Atkin et al., 1977; Jessor, 1977; Lave and Seskin, 1977) in which the major objective is to measure cross-lagged causal differentials, whatever the theoretical rationale may be.

Up to now we have discussed the type of study that involves a panel observed at only a few points in time. In many studies involving time-series data, however, there is a single case that is observed over many points in time. A paper by Roberts (1981), for instance, discusses a classic conundrum involving the high correlation of the death rate with the proportion of all marriages performed by the Church of England over a period of many years. In this example the data pertain only to a single case (a nation), but the two variables may be paired for many points in time. In this kind of investigation it is crucial to remove trend and autocorrelation from the data, because either condition tends to create spurious results. The high correlation between mortality and Church of England marriages is eliminated when both variables are detrended and adjusted for autocorrelation. In Roberts's approach, each of the two variables is expressed as a function of time, time squared, and itself lagged one year. When the two sets of residuals derived from this process are then correlated (allowing for various cross-lags), the result turns out to be nonsignificant. This procedure could readily be applied to the testing of functionalist hypotheses such as that involving the interaction of delicts and sanctions within a single social entity (e.g., a county, state, or nation). When we have data for a large number of cases observed over many points in time (e.g., a long-term panel study), we have a unique opportunity that demands unique methods (Hannan and Young, 1977).

Another way of eliminating autocorrelation, trend, and "random shock" from a single-case time series is to impose on the data an ARIMA (Auto-Regressive, Integrated, Moving Average) process that filters out undesirable patterns. In effect, relationships are assessed through use of residuals that have undergone a "prewhitening" process; that is, trend, autocorrelation, and random shock have been removed from the data. In developing ARIMA models, it is possible (see the Minitab handbook) for one to specify autocorrelation terms that assume that a given variable may be influenced by several of its own past values, to "difference" the series, to control for random shocks of considerable duration, and to control for seasonal variations. For most time series of sociological interest, however, autocorrelation typically involves only a single lag (Gottman, 1981:256–7), and it is sufficient to take only the first differences of the series in order to remove a linear trend. On the other hand, there are probably few social variables for which it is advisable to ignore the possibility of a significant ARIMA process. Incidentally, ARIMA concepts and terminology may provide a basis for the taxonomy of time series recommended earlier.

As we become familiar with the behavior of time series, program packages such as Minitab can be used to contrive fascinating experiments. Note that Minitab and other time-series programs often begin by providing graphic representations of autocorrelations, partial autocorrelations, and so on, and that it is of the utmost importance that one learn to recognize the autocorrelation "signature" of, say, an upward trend. As one experiment, one could obtain the Roberts data discussed above, subject them to ARIMA processes, and arrive at essentially the same results obtained by Roberts.

In Cook and Campbell (1979) a strong emphasis is placed on the sort of evaluative research in which one tries to assess the impact of a sudden change – say, a new law – on some time series such as the arrest rate for drunk driving. This type of investigation is fundamental to functional theory in that it is designed to determine whether a social system is capable of regulating a time series that shows signs of becoming dysfunctional, that is, whether effective negative feedback is likely to occur. A time series such as the arrest rate for drunk driving will probably present all the standard hazards of autocorrelation, trend, and so forth, but it will typically be possible to address these problems through ARIMA modeling and similar approaches. It is both paradoxical and problematical, however, that evaluative research often examines time series that appear to have been interrupted at a given point in time: paradoxical because the assumption that interruptions occur at discrete points in time seems to vitiate the value of time-series data, and problematical because in my experience ARIMA processes are easily distorted by large interruptions in time-series data, and the residuals from these processes often seem to provide misleading estimates of the impact of some discrete event, such as a new law.

Examine, for instance, the following Minitab program with explanatory notes:

```
NOPRINT
NOTE : CREATE INTEGERS 1 TO 100 IN STEPS OF 2, INTO COL 1:
GENE 1 2 100 C1
NOTE : CREATE INTEGERS 31 TO 130 IN STEPS OF 2, INTO COL 2:
GENE 31 2 130 C2
NOTE : JOIN COL 2 TO END OF COL 1, INTO COL 3:
JOIN C2 C1 C3
NOTE : CREATE 100 RANDOM NORMAL SCORES,
NOTE : MEAN 0, SD 10 OR MORE,
NOTE : INTO COL 4:
NRAN 100 0 15 C4
LET C5 = C3 + C4
NOTE : THIS IS AN INTERRUPTED TIME SERIES, WITH BRIEF
NOTE : RANDOM SHOCKS:
NAME C5 'INTTS'
NOTE : LIST CONTENTS OF EACH COL:
INFO
NOTE : SHOW TIME SERIES PLOT OF THE DATA:
TSPLOT 'INTTS'
NOTE : PROVIDE DESCRIPTIVE STATISTICS FOR THE DATA:
DESCRIBE 'INTTS'
NOTE : PROVIDE AUTOCORRELATIONS OF THE DATA FOR INCREASING
NOTE : LAGS, UP TO 10 TIME UNITS:
ACF 10 'INTTS'
NOTE : PROVIDE PARTIAL AUTOCORRELATIONS OF THE DATA FOR
NOTE : INCREASING LAGS, UP TO 10 TIME UNITS:
PACF 10 'INTTS'
NOTE : CREATE A VARIABLE REPRESENTING TIME, PLACING
NOTE : INTEGERS 1 TO 100 IN STEPS OF 1, INTO COL 6:
GENE 1 1 100 C6
NAME C6 'TIME'
INFO
NOTE : TEST AN ARIMA MODEL INVOLVING SINGLE AUTOREGRESSION TE
RM,
NOTE : FIRST DIFFERENCES OF SCORES,
NOTE : NO MOVING AVERAGE PROCESS,
NOTE : WITH RESIDUALS IN COL 17, PREDICTED SCORES IN
NOTE : COL 18, AND AUTOREGRESSION COEFFICIENTS IN COL 19:
ARIMA 1 1 0 'INTTS' C17 C18 C19;
START 'INTTS'.
NOTE : TEST ARIMA MODEL WITH SECOND DIFFERENCES:
ARIMA 1 2 0 'INTTS' C20 C21 C22;
START 'INTTS'.
NOTE : TEST ARIMA MODEL WITH TWO AUTOREGRESSION TERMS,
NOTE : FIRST DIFFERENCES, SECOND DIFFERENCES, ETC. :
ARIMA 2 1 0 'INTTS' C23 C24 C25;
START 'INTTS'.
ARIMA 2 2 0 'INTTS' C26 C27 C28;
START 'INTTS'.
```

```
NOTE : OBTAIN ARIMA PROCESS FOR FIRST FIFTY CASES:
PICK 1 50 'INTTS' C30
ARIMA 1 1 0 C30;
START C30.
NOTE : EXAMINE RESIDUALS IN VARIOUS COLUMNS FOR TREND, ETC. :
ACF 10 C17
PACF 10 C17
TSPLOT C17
ACF 10 C20
PACF 10 C20
TSPLOT C20
ACF 10 C23
PACF 10 C23
TSPLOT C23
ACF 10 C26
PACF 10 C26
TSPLOT C26
NOTE : CREATE A DUMMY VARIABLE FOR TIME,
NOTE : WITH PRE-INTERVENTION TIME POINTS
NOTE : CODED ZERO AND POST-INTERVENTION
NOTE : TIME POINTS CODED 1; AND A SPIKE
NOTE : VARIABLE WITH ALL TIME POINTS CODED
NOTE : ZERO EXCEPT FOR THE FIFTY-FIRST:
SET C41
50(0) 50(1)
END
NAME C41 'DUMMY'
SET C42
50(0) 1 49(0)
END
NAME C42 'SPIKE'
BRIEF
NOTE : WRITE AN EQUATION GIVING THE ARIMA RESIDUALS
NOTE : AS A FUNCTION OF THE DUMMY AND SPIKE VARIABLES:
REGR C17 1 'DUMMY'
REGR C20 1 'DUMMY'
REGR C23 1 'DUMMY'
REGR C26 1 'DUMMY'
REGR C17 1 'SPIKE'
REGR C20 1 'SPIKE'
REGR C23 1 'SPIKE'
REGR C26 1 'SPIKE'
NOTE : WRITE AN EQUATION GIVING THE INTERRUPTED TIME SERIES
NOTE : AS A FUNCTION OF TIME, THE DUMMY VARIABLE, AND
NOTE : AN AUTOCORRELATION TERM:
LAG 1 'INTTS' C9
REGR 'INTTS' 1 C9
REGR 'INTTS' 1 'TIME'
REGR 'INTTS' 1 'DUMMY'
REGR 'INTTS' 2 C9 'TIME'
REGR 'INTTS' 2 C9 'DUMMY'
REGR 'INTTS' 2 'TIME' 'DUMMY'
REGR 'INTTS' 3 C9 'TIME' 'DUMMY'
INFO
STOP
```

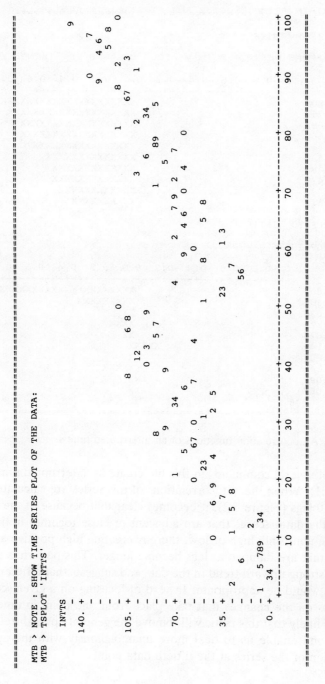

Figure 6.1. Illustration of an interrupted time series

```
============================================================================

MTB > ACF 10 'INTTS'

    ACF OF INTTS

            -1.0 -0.8 -0.6 -0.4 -0.2  0.0  0.2  0.4  0.6  0.8  1.0
             +----+----+----+----+----+----+----+----+----+----+
     1   0.808                         XXXXXXXXXXXXXXXXXXXXX
     2   0.759                         XXXXXXXXXXXXXXXXXXXX
     3   0.682                         XXXXXXXXXXXXXXXXXX
     4   0.660                         XXXXXXXXXXXXXXXXX
     5   0.613                         XXXXXXXXXXXXXXXX
     6   0.530                         XXXXXXXXXXXXXX
     7   0.483                         XXXXXXXXXXXXX
     8   0.479                         XXXXXXXXXXXXX
     9   0.421                         XXXXXXXXXXXX
    10   0.371                         XXXXXXXXXX

MTB > PACF 10 'INTTS'

    PACF OF INTTS

            -1.0 -0.8 -0.6 -0.4 -0.2  0.0  0.2  0.4  0.6  0.8  1.0
             +----+----+----+----+----+----+----+----+----+----+
     1   0.808                         XXXXXXXXXXXXXXXXXXXXX
     2   0.307                         XXXXXXXXX
     3   0.028                         XX
     4   0.129                         XXXX
     5   0.024                         XX
     6  -0.149                     XXXXX
     7  -0.003                         X
     8   0.148                         XXXXX
     9  -0.099                      XXX
    10  -0.067                      XXX

============================================================================
```

Figure 6.2. Autocorrelation functions of an interrupted time series

The first several commands in this file create an interrupted time series (Figure 6.1). When the autocorrelations of this series are calculated over the first 10 lags (Figure 6.2), it becomes clear that because of the secular trend of the data, scores that are adjacent or close together in time will tend to be uniformly high or low, thereby creating high positive autocorrelations that are damped as lags become longer. This pattern is an indication of strong upward trend in the data and suggests that differencing of the series would be appropriate: Instead of focusing on a given score, we shall focus on the changes that take place from one point in time to the next. It is likely that this tactic will remove the general upward trend from the data and enable us to deal more unambiguously with the apparent interruption of the series at the fiftieth data point.

Table 6.1. *ARIMA process for an interrupted time series, single autoregression term*

```
================================================================

MTB > ARIMA 1 1 0 'INTTS' C17 C18 C19;
MTB > START 'INTTS'.

ESTIMATES AT EACH ITERATION
ITERATION      SSE      PARAMETERS
    0        45933.8      0.100
    1        40210.5     -0.050
    2        36291.6     -0.200
    3        34177.3     -0.350
    4        33772.4     -0.443
    5        33770.3     -0.450
    6        33770.2     -0.451
    7        33770.2     -0.451
RELATIVE CHANGE IN EACH ESTIMATE LESS THAN   0.0010


FINAL ESTIMATES OF PARAMETERS
NUMBER      TYPE      ESTIMATE      ST. DEV.    T-RATIO
    1      AR 1       -0.4507       0.0920      -4.90

DIFFERENCING.  1 REGULAR
RESIDUALS.      SS =          33702.8   (BACKFORECASTS EXCLUDED)
                DF =    98  MS =         343.9
NO. OF OBS.    ORIGINAL SERIES   100    AFTER DIFFERENCING    99

================================================================
```

The several ARIMA patterns imposed on the series make adjustments for trend and autocorrelation. In the ARIMA 1,1,0 model (Table 6.1), for instance, the first differences control for trend, and these differences are then expressed as a function of themselves at the immediately preceding point in time as a control for autocorrelation. As is typically true of difference scores, these scores exemplify regression effects in the sense that large positive differences tend to be followed by negative differences, and vice versa, so that in the absence of any influences from other variables the autoregression term turns out to be negative. When the first differences are expressed as a function of the *two* preceding differences, as in Table 6.2, the second autoregressive influence is also nearly significant, so that the residuals from this ARIMA process have a good prospect of being free of unwanted trend and autocorrelation. Indeed, the autocorrelations remaining in the residuals are generally small (Figure 6.3), and the time-series plot (Figure 6.4) for these nicely filtered scores now seems to have little patterning except for the spike at the fiftieth data point, the only indication that this time series has been interrupted in any significant way.

Table 6.2. *ARIMA process for an interrupted time series, two autoregression terms*

```
=================================================================

MTB > ARIMA 2 1 0 'INTTS' C23 C24 C25;
MTB > START 'INTTS'.

ESTIMATES AT EACH ITERATION
ITERATION        SSE      PARAMETERS
    0         45375.4     0.100     0.100
    1         40092.4    -0.050     0.041
    2         36296.2    -0.200    -0.019
    3         33986.6    -0.350    -0.078
    4         33164.4    -0.499    -0.136
    5         33161.6    -0.507    -0.138
    6         33161.6    -0.508    -0.138
RELATIVE CHANGE IN EACH ESTIMATE LESS THAN   0.0010


FINAL ESTIMATES OF PARAMETERS
NUMBER      TYPE      ESTIMATE     ST. DEV.   T-RATIO
    1      AR  1      -0.5079       0.1016     -5.00
    2      AR  2      -0.1381       0.1024     -1.35

DIFFERENCING.  1 REGULAR
RESIDUALS.     SS =        33118.9  (BACKFORECASTS EXCLUDED)
               DF =   97  MS =         341.4
NO. OF OBS.    ORIGINAL SERIES   100    AFTER DIFFERENCING    99

=================================================================
```

Following the advice of Cook and Campbell (1979: 276), we estimate the size of the spike by creating a dummy variable for time in which all time points are coded zero except for the fifty-first, which is coded 1.0. Examining Table 6.3, we find that the size of the interruption is estimated to be over 50 units (downward), and that this estimate is statistically significant. If we make the mistake of expressing the interrupted series as a function of time coded as a before–after dummy variable (Table 6.4), we obtain completely erroneous results. If we use the more conventional procedure, expressing the series as a function of linear time and a before–after dummy for time (Table 6.5), the results still leave much to be desired: The estimated interruption will often be inaccurate under this procedure because the size of the estimate is highly dependent on the nature of any trend that may exist in the series.

Let us return to a consideration of *two* variables interacting and try to imagine what this interaction would involve if the two variables had been *residualized,* that is, cleaned up, through the use of an ARIMA process

```
=================================================================

MTB > ACF 10 C23

   ACF OF C23

            -1.0 -0.8 -0.6 -0.4 -0.2  0.0  0.2  0.4  0.6  0.8  1.0
            +----+----+----+----+----+----+----+----+----+----+
  1  -0.043                          XX
  2  -0.142                        XXXXX
  3  -0.232                      XXXXXXX
  4   0.103                          XXXX
  5   0.137                          XXXX
  6  -0.167                        XXXXX
  7  -0.132                         XXXX
  8   0.162                          XXXXX
  9   0.109                          XXXX
 10  -0.072                         XXX

MTB > PACF 10 C23

   PACF OF C23

            -1.0 -0.8 -0.6 -0.4 -0.2  0.0  0.2  0.4  0.6  0.8  1.0
            +----+----+----+----+----+----+----+----+----+----+
  1  -0.043                          XX
  2  -0.144                        XXXXX
  3  -0.251                      XXXXXXX
  4   0.054                          XX
  5   0.085                          XXX
  6  -0.204                       XXXXXX
  7  -0.102                         XXXX
  8   0.175                          XXXXX
  9   0.002                          X
 10  -0.098                         XXX

=================================================================
```

Figure 6.3. Autocorrelation functions of the residuals of an interrupted time series subjected to an ARIMA process

or some similar process. Because Max Weber had a penchant for introducing elaborate concepts by means of "ideal types," and because he was also a strong advocate of sophisticated statistical tools, he would have no objection to the use of an ideal type to illustrate a statistical method. Sinusoidal functions have proven indispensable in efforts (mainly by econometricians) to estimate patterns and periodicities of time-series data (Chatfield, 1975:110; cf. Gottman, 1981:6–7), and the essential features of a perfect adaptation process – the central concept of this book – are clearly represented by a combination of sine and cosine curves (Figure 6.5). Any theory may be selected from Table 5.1, and if that theory contains a significant time dimension and describes a perfect adaptation process with nearly regular periodicity, then the theory probably has a

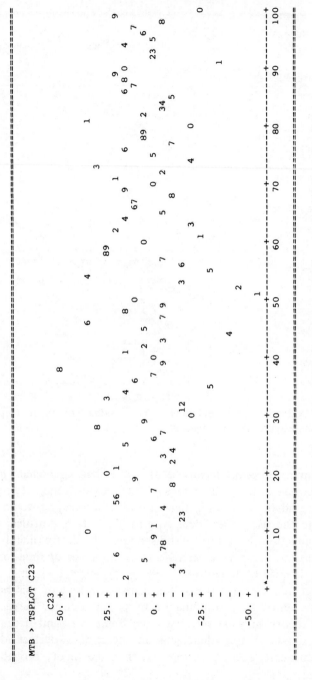

Figure 6.4. Time-series plot of ARIMA residuals with a spike representing an interruption of the series

Table 6.3. *Regression of ARIMA 2,1,0 residuals on a spike variable representing time*

```
=================================================================

MTB > REGR C23 1 'SPIKE'

THE REGRESSION EQUATION IS
C23 = 2.48 - 58.0 SPIKE

    99 CASES USED      1 CASES CONTAIN MISSING VALUES

                              ST. DEV.    T-RATIO =
COLUMN       COEFFICIENT      OF COEF.    COEF/S.D.
                 2.485          1.760        1.41
SPIKE          -57.97          17.51       -3.31

S = 17.42

R-SQUARED = 10.2 PERCENT
R-SQUARED =  9.2 PERCENT, ADJUSTED FOR D.F.

ANALYSIS OF VARIANCE

  DUE TO      DF           SS      MS=SS/DF
REGRESSION    1        3326.5       3326.5
RESIDUAL     97       29435.4        303.5
TOTAL        98       32761.9

=================================================================
```

pattern similar to that of the sinusoidal curves. It is very rarely, however, that real data behave this predictably.

Let the cosine curve represent the problem variable (H), and the sine curve an adaptive mechanism (S). Then, for all pairs of observations in which the lag from H to S involves $\pi/2$ time units (where the X-axis represents time), the correlation of H and S will be 1.00; for all pairs of observations in which lag from S to H involves $\pi/2$ time units, the correlation of S and H will be -1.00. Thus, we appear to have a perfect instance in which a problem *produces* an adaptive effort, whereas the adaptation *diminishes* the initial problem.[1]

The sinusoidal process has additional properties of substantial theoretical and methodological import. First, the autocorrelations for pairs of observations (on a single variable) spanning $\pi/2$ time units are always zero; that as, in a perfect adaptation process the tendency for variables to "cause themselves" over time would be diminished, although, as we shall see, there are highly patterned autocorrelations over lags other than $\pi/2$. Second, the simultaneous or cross-sectional correlation between the sine

Table 6.4. *Regression of interrupted time series on a dummy variable representing time*

```
================================================================

MTB > REGR 'INTTS' 1 'DUMMY'

THE REGRESSION EQUATION IS
INTTS = 52.4 + 28.0 DUMMY

                                ST. DEV.      T-RATIO =
COLUMN        COEFFICIENT       OF COEF.      COEF/S.D.
              52.445            4.613         11.37
DUMMY         27.982            6.523          4.29

S = 32.62

R-SQUARED = 15.8 PERCENT
R-SQUARED = 14.9 PERCENT, ADJUSTED FOR D.F.

ANALYSIS OF VARIANCE

  DUE TO      DF            SS         MS=SS/DF
REGRESSION    1          19575          19575
RESIDUAL     98         104256           1064
TOTAL        99         123830

================================================================
```

Table 6.5. *Regression of interrupted time series on linear time and a dummy variable representing time*

```
================================================================

MTB > REGR 'INTTS' 2 'TIME' 'DUMMY'

THE REGRESSION EQUATION IS
INTTS = 0.74 + 2.03 TIME - 73.4 DUMMY

                                ST. DEV.      T-RATIO =
COLUMN        COEFFICIENT       OF COEF.      COEF/S.D.
              0.736             3.136          0.23
TIME          2.02781           0.09602       21.12
DUMMY        -73.408            5.543        -13.24

S = 13.86

R-SQUARED = 85.0 PERCENT
R-SQUARED = 84.7 PERCENT, ADJUSTED FOR D.F.

ANALYSIS OF VARIANCE

  DUE TO      DF            SS         MS=SS/DF
REGRESSION    2         105207          52604
RESIDUAL     97          18623            192
TOTAL        99         123830

================================================================
```

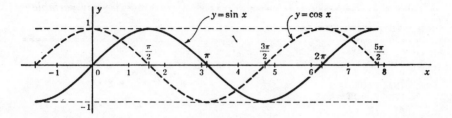

Figure 6.5. Sinusoid illustration of a perfect adaptation process. *Source:* Ralph P. Agnew, *Calculus* (New York: McGraw-Hill, 1962), p. 442.

and cosine values is always zero, suggesting that an erroneous (cross-sectional) test of an adaptation process will tend to generate perfectly disconfirmatory and perfectly incorrect results and suggesting again that functionalist hypotheses can be tested only by dynamic, time-series data. Third, any tendency to "flatten" a perfect adaptation process by averaging one's observations across time periods that exceed the appropriate causal lapse (in this instance) of $\pi/2$ will tend to produce erroneous results. As we shall see, this limitation often accounts for negative conclusions of the sort reported by Szymanski (1973); when, however, this limitation is taken as a caveat, as in a masterful study by Phillips (1979), one often arrives at extraordinary conclusions.

The many fascinating properties of sinusoidal processes can be simulated with standard program packages such as SAS, SPSS, and Minitab. Using the latter, I generated a series of 100 data points, distributed the corresponding sine and cosine values around them, and "shuffled" the data by introducing random disturbances. In effect, I extended Figure 6.5 well beyond the $5\pi/2$ or 7.86 data points where it abjectly disappears and entered the exotic realm (for sociologists) in which we encounter time series that extend across 100 or more points in time. Figure 6.6 is a scattergram showing the relationship between the adaptive variable ('SINE') and the problem variable at the preceding point in time ('COSLAG'). Indeed, the correlation between the two variables is strongly positive, suggesting (but not demonstrating) that high values of the problem variable give rise to increased adaptive efforts. Examining Figure 6.7, in which the problem variable ('COSINE') is expressed as a function of the adaptive variable at the preceding point in time ('SINLAG'), we see a pattern suggesting that the adaptive efforts have an impact: The correlation lagged from adaptation to problem is strongly negative. It is impor-

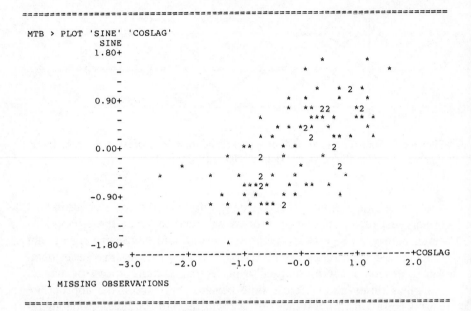

Figure 6.6. Scattergram of the relationship between cosine function and sine function after $\pi/2$ time units

tant to note that the relationships shown in Figures 6.6 and 6.7 could not occur in cross-sectional data. Two variables cannot at once have a positive and negative correlation.

The basic shortcoming of this simulation is that it is too perfect, too mechanical, too unrealistic, although it is incorrect to say, with Irving Zeitlin (1973:14), that ". . . to rely on cycles alone and to ignore history is to deprive oneself of the study of causality." A cycle has a history by definition, and we find the causes of a cycle in roughly the same way that we find causes of other forms of change. In our simulations, however, the data were contrived in a way that creates extremely regular periodicity, highly predictable cycles of a sort that probably do not often occur in real social processes, although sometimes they may. Another problem is that if real time-series data generally behaved this systematically, cyclically, and predictably, it would be possible, and even mandatory if one insists on parsimony, to predict and explain nearly all variations in important social variables with reference to their own past values. Functional interconnectedness would become secondary, if not superfluous. Once again,

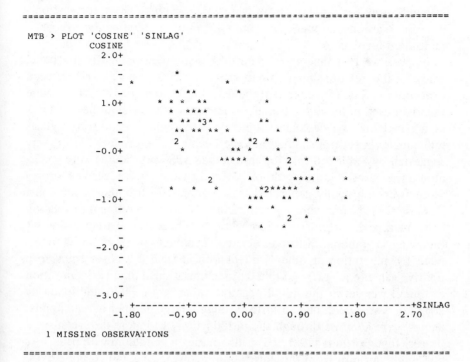

```
MTB  >  PLOT  'COSINE'  'SINLAG'
            COSINE
            2.0+
               -              *
               -  *                    *
               -        * **        *
            1.0+    *  *  *    **          *
               -        *  ****
               -      * **  *3 *        **
               -      ** ** ** *      *
               -    2        *  *2 *    * * *
           -0.0+    *        ** *    *
               -          ***** *   2  *    *
               -                 *  *  *
               -      2      *      ****      *
               -  *   *   *    *2*****   *
            -1.0+          *** **        *
               -          *  *
               -                  2  *
               -              *   *
            -2.0+                  *
               -
               -                        *
               -
            -3.0+
               +---------+---------+---------+---------+---------+SINLAG
              -1.80     -0.90      0.00      0.90      1.80      2.70

         1 MISSING OBSERVATIONS
```

Figure 6.7. Scattergram of the relationship between sine function and cosine function after $\pi/2$ time units

then, we see that it is inherent in the nature of functional analysis not only that it focus on time-series data, but that it focus on messy, irregular, unsystematic, discontinuous, unpredictable, explosive time-series data.

Contrary to Zeitlin's claim (1973:31), perhaps Parsons was right, at least in the limited statistical sense suggested before, when he said (in Zeitlin's paraphrase) that ". . . social equilibrium, the continuity and maintenance of social patterns, is *not* problematic and requires no explanation." Perhaps Parsons said this because he was impressed by the continuity of social forms, because he was not a thoroughgoing Marxian functionalist. For those of us who are, equilibrium becomes a secondary concept, although it retains much of the utility claimed by Parsons. It must be remembered, however, that the alternations of equilibrium and disequilibrium are primarily empirical questions not ideological issues. When we classify a given time series as having a form that is nonstationary, we have demonstrated disequilibrium (or, at least, a "moving equilibrium"). Those social scientists who focus on stationarity may find life a little unexciting, but who is to fault them for that?

Suppose we had time-series data over many data points from a panel study of the relationship between crime victimization (V) and reduced exposure to crime (A); note that the data would be similar in format to the real data used in the divorce analyses presented earlier, and that the units of a panel may be ecological areas or taxonomic categories as well as individuals. In several simulation experiments, data formatted in the way suggested by Table 6.6 (p. 119; based on an SPSS procedure) were generated. First, a set of initial victimization and adaptation (reduced exposure) scores were randomly generated from normally distributed populations. Because these scores were selected randomly, a cross-sectional correlation close to zero is virtually assured. Next, victimization at time 2 was set (allowing for random disturbances) at a negative value (e.g., -0.9) multiplied by adaptation at time 1, adaptation at time 2 was set equal to a positive value (e.g., 1.2) multiplied by victimization at time 1, victimization at time 3 was set at the initial negative value (e.g., -0.9) multiplied by adaptation at time 2, and so forth through a large number of data points. Scores were shuffled through the introduction of random disturbances, a process that Gottman (1981:103) calls "pelting a pendulum with peas." As one might surmise from the illustration involving sine and cosine curves, this simulation produces several notable results:

1. Correlations lagged over one time unit from victimization to adaptation, in conformity with the functionalist hypothesis, are strongly positive. They fall short of unity only to the extent that random error is introduced into the data.

2. Correlations lagged from adaptation to victimization are strongly negative (depending, again, on error terms), conforming to the functionalist hypothesis. Note that each correlation coefficient in either series spans only two points in time. Even if there were strong secular trends in the data, a condition profoundly disturbing to most time-series analyses and requiring some sort of "filtering" (Chatfield, 1975:12), this series of correlation coefficients would remain unchanged. The reason is that at each point in time the secular trend would be represented by a constant, and these constants would grow larger (or smaller) over time; but because the correlations from A to V or from V to A span only a pair of data points and constants do not affect correlations, any secular trend is effectively filtered.

3. All cross-sectional correlations between victimization and adapta-

tion, being essentially linear transformations of the original random series, remain close to zero, thus emphasizing the danger of trying to test dynamic functionalist hypotheses with cross-sectional data.

4. Because victimization and adaptation (it is assumed) are involved in a reciprocal causal process, and because the slope coefficients of these causal relationships may have a product with an absolute value greater than unity (for example, $-0.9 \times 1.2 = |1.08|$), we encounter what Blalock (1969: 82) calls an "unstable negative feedback" process, unstable in the sense that fluctuations of both victimization and adaptation become more violent over time; that is, they have higher amplitudes. This upward spiral continues indefinitely, demonstrating that "the logic of functional explanation" is not incompatible with explosive social change, that a "second-order autoregressive process" (Gottman, 1981:ch.12) can oscillate and expand simultaneously, as a moving equilibrium. On the other hand, increasing amplitude means increasing noise, and noise, as we have suggested, is not usually allowed to grow indefinitely.

5. The rightward margin of our hypothetical table (as in Table 6.6), would contain individual means, over all data points, for victimization and adaptation. It is noteworthy that the correlation between these means will usually be trivially close to zero; in other words, the flattening out of time-series variations, in this instance, would wrongly produce disconfirmatory conclusions. The effect of using averages in one's analysis is to eliminate virtually all the time-series variations. This practice would be tantamount to throwing out one's best data.

6. At the bottom of our hypothetical table for victimization and adaptation (again as in Table 6.6) we would place means and standard deviations for both variables at any given point in time. Correlating these means over the appropriate time lag, as called for by the functionalist hypothesis, is tantamount to obtaining the "ecological" or aggregate relationships between the two variables. In the typical simulation the correlation from victimization lagged to adaptation approaches +1.0; and from adaptation to victimization it approaches -1.0. Again, however, the cross-sectional correlation is trivial. Remembering the "ecological fallacy," we note that it would be easy to write, at the bottom of the table, a series of values for mean victimization and mean adaptation that would *not* be correlated in the way suggested by theory. And yet, since these means would deny us only a single degree of freedom in contriving scores for individual cases, we could find strong corroboration of the theory in the body of the table; in other words, nearly all individual cases could be made to conform to the theory. An additional advantage, then, of "the

logic of functional explanation" is that it forces us to ascertain whether theories operate at the individual, organizational, or systemic levels, or some combination thereof. It is a fine way of reconciling issues of "reductionism." In a moment, for instance, we will see that various Marxian-functionalist hypotheses proposed by Szymanski (1973) may be more applicable at the state or provincial level than at the (aggregate) national level assumed by Szymanski.

7. If there is insufficient temporal variation either in individual scores or in the series of means for each data point, then the analysis cannot proceed. Assessing the size of such variations would probably involve an index such as the ratio of standard deviations to means, known as the "coefficient of variation" (Blalock, 1979:84). When variables are constructed in such a way that their means hover around zero, this is not a meaningful index; the index applies only to ratio variables. In any case, one should always begin a time-series analysis by plotting one's data on a graph as a way of determining whether sufficient variation occurs.

8. When we examine autocorrelations of victimization and adaptation – that is, the correlation of each variable with itself at a later time – we discern a characteristic pattern. The autocorrelations over a single time unit tend to be small. For instance, the correlation of victimization at time t with itself at time $t+1$ tends to be trivial because this correlation is merely the product of two other correlations: that of victimization at time t with adaptation at time t, and that of adaptation at time t with victimization at time $t+1$. Such a pattern is typical of series that have approximately the properties of sinusoidal curves: The latter always have autocorrelations of zero when time lag is held at $\pi/2$.

9. When we examine a complete correlogram (a graph in which autocorrelations are plotted against all possible lags [Chatfield, 1975:25; Cook and Campbell, 1979:235–93]), a more subtle pattern, a recognizable signature, begins to emerge. Over a single time lag, as we have seen, the correlation of victimization with itself is trivial. Over two time lags, it approaches -1.0 (with minimal random disturbance); three time lags, trivial; four time lags, again approaching 1.0; five time lags, again trivial; and so forth. This clear pattern of weak, high, or low correlations, then, starting with the correlation (called "identity") of victimization with itself at time 1 is identity, zero or weak, low (i.e., approaching -1.00), zero or weak, high, zero or weak, low, zero or weak, high, and so forth, ad infinitum. The same pattern holds for adaptation. The appropriate lag time for causal analysis, then, is the length of the "high" to "high" cycle divided by 4. (Note, again, that the correlogram for a perfect sinusoidal

function would be identity, 0.0, −1.0, 0.0, 1.0, 0.0, −1.0, and so on, and the appropriate lag time for causal analysis would be $2\pi/4$ or $\pi/2$.) Most functionalist processes, if they operated as theorists imply, would exemplify such patterns in their correlograms. For any cross-lagged analysis in which autocorrelations are strong, of course, it is necessary to control them (Bohrnstedt, 1969).[2] It is important to remember that if lag times are selected wrongly, it is possible to create a reversal of one's expected findings, an intriguing outcome for which Gottman (1981:16) has provided a delightful analogy: Such a result is comparable to what happens in a motion picture when the lagged relationship between the camera's shutter speed and the rate of rotation of a wagon wheel makes it appear that the wheel is rotating in reverse or is not moving at all. When this happens in sociology, the screeching is rarely heard.

In social research using real data the patterns exemplified by our simulation would be obscured by a wide range of disturbances; again we see the dialectic of stability/instability. Victimization and adaptive behavior are not simple linear functions of one another with a fixed lag time of a single unit and with autocorrelations and cross-sectional correlations close to zero. All sorts of exogenous disturbances exist in the real world, and lag times (e.g., the time required for a person or organization to reduce exposure to crime) may vary substantially around an average value that we would have to discern. Nor is it essential that lag times be held equal from H to S and back to H; allowing "realistic" variations in lag times merely alters correlograms and other indices in patterned, recognizable ways. In one simulation, for instance, it was assumed that two time units would be required for victimization to influence adaptive behavior. Results of this simulation, although generally similar to those preceding, differ in several ways that we would probably discern through examination of autoregression signatures and other forms of evidence. In any case it is important to "play with one's data," and one should never lose sight of the need to control for trend, autocorrelation, extraneous variables, and so forth.

It should be observed, finally, that ascertaining appropriate lag times is not entirely a methodological problem: It is equally a theoretical problem. In recent work by Phillips (1979), for example, it is shown that widely reported suicides by prominent individuals seem to create an increase in traffic deaths, with a lag time of about three days. This research was a test of imitative, or "crowd contagion," theories of Tarde and LeBon, and it is strongly implied by these theories that imitative effects occur rapidly: If Phillips had not had the benefit of daily traffic death rates (available for four states only) his research could not have been properly done, and it is especially noteworthy that when Phillips flattened out his data by calculating weekly traffic death rates (let alone the usual annual rates!) the apparent imitative effects were nearly lost. Bowers and Pierce (1980) show a similar short lag time for effects of capital punishment.

In planning one's data-gathering procedures, then, it is well to take the advice of Markus (1979:54): ". . . the measurement period [should be] less than the time required for a causal effect [sic] to occur . . . ."

2. Malefactions Marxist and otherwise, with hope

Table 6.6 contains data that illustrate the pitfalls of research of the sort undertaken by Szymanski (1973), in which insufficient attention is given to dynamic aspects of functional analysis. The data pertain to economic stagnation (unemployment) and military spending for a number of nations. Because military spending is thought to be an adaptation to economic stagnation (Szymanski, 1973), the data are organized just as they would be in the case of the victimization simulation. The SPSS program called REPORT is recommended as an efficient way of organizing the data. For Table 6.6 REPORT generated a variable called UNST, which identifies and lists those nations for which the standard deviation of unemployment over time (SDU), divided by the mean of unemployment over time (MOU), produces a relatively high variability score (VOU). When the same procedure is followed for military spending, it turns out that only three nations have sufficient variability on both unemployment and defense spending to be of use: Austria, Holland, and West Germany. (Denmark has many missing data.) For each of these nations an upward trend in unemployment seems to be associated with a downward trend in defense expenditures, but the data do not permit much in the way of generalization.

We discover, then, that a meaningful time-series analysis is precluded by the nature of the data. Defense spending as a proportion of total government expenditure cannot be construed as a temporal variable during the period from 1968 to 1976, either for individual nations (with few exceptions) or for the capitalist system as a whole; we simply do not have sufficient variation through time to permit the typical hypotheses of dynamic functionalism, and we therefore know that adaptive adjustments of spending cannot be occurring over time periods as short as a few years. Mean proportions spent by each nation on defense over the nine-year period are vastly larger than the standard deviations for the same vari-

Table 6.6. *Economic stagnation and military spending*

UNST	COUNTRY	U68	U69	U70	U71	U72	U73	U74	U75	U76	MOU	SDU	VOU
1													
	AUST	1.5	1.5	1.4	1.6	2.3	1.9	2.3	4.4	4.4	2.4	1.1	.48
	DENM	999	999	999	999	999	1.1	2.5	6.0	6.1	999	999	999
	HOLL	1.9	1.4	1.1	1.6	2.7	2.7	3.6	5.2	5.5	2.9	1.5	.53
	WGER	1.5	.90	.70	.80	1.1	1.2	2.6	4.7	4.6	2.0	1.5	.75
VALI		3	3	3	3	3	4	4	4	4	3	3	3
MEAN		1.6	1.3	1.1	1.3	2.0	1.7	2.7	5.1	5.1	2.4	1.4	.59
STDE		.23	.32	.35	.46	.83	.74	.58	.70	.79	.42	.22	.14

UNST	COUNTRY	U68	U69	U70	U71	U72	U73	U74	U75	U76	MOU	SDU	VOU
0													
	ASTR	2.9	2.8	2.4	2.1	1.9	1.6	1.5	2.0	2.0	2.1	.46	.21
	BELG	4.5	3.6	2.9	2.9	3.4	3.6	4.0	6.7	8.6	4.5	1.8	.41
	FINL	4.0	2.8	1.9	2.3	2.5	2.3	1.7	2.2	4.0	2.6	.79	.30
	GRBR	2.5	2.4	2.6	3.5	3.8	2.7	2.6	4.1	5.8	3.3	1.1	.32
	ISRA	6.1	4.5	3.8	3.5	2.7	2.6	3.0	3.1	3.6	3.7	1.0	.28
	ITAL	3.5	3.4	3.2	3.2	3.7	3.5	2.9	3.3	3.7	3.4	.24	.07
	JAPA	1.2	1.1	1.2	1.2	1.4	1.3	1.4	1.9	2.0	1.4	.30	.22
	NORW	1.1	1.0	.80	.80	1.0	.80	.70	1.3	1.3	.98	.21	.21
	SWED	2.0	1.7	1.4	2.0	2.0	1.9	1.5	1.4	1.2	1.7	.29	.17
	USA	3.6	3.5	4.9	5.9	5.6	4.9	5.6	8.5	7.7	5.6	1.6	.28
VALI		10	10	10	10	10	10	10	10	10	10	10	10
MEAN		3.1	2.7	2.5	2.7	2.8	2.5	2.5	3.4	4.0	2.9	.78	.25
STDE		1.5	1.1	1.3	1.4	1.4	1.2	1.5	2.4	2.6	1.4	.58	.09

UNST	COUNTRY	D68	D69	D70	D71	D72	D73	D74	D75	D76	MOD	SDD	VOD
1													
	AUST	.30	.27	.25	.23	.21	.20	.16	.14	.14	.21	.05	.26
	DENM	.15	.13	.12	.11	.10	.10	.10	.10	999	999	999	999
	HOLL	.22	.20	.21	.21	.19	.18	.17	.17	.16	.19	.02	.11
	WGER	.20	.20	.18	.18	.17	.16	.15	.15	.15	.17	.02	.11
VALI		4	4	4	4	4	4	4	4	3	3	3	3
MEAN		.22	.20	.19	.18	.17	.16	.14	.14	.15	.19	.03	.16
STDE		.06	.06	.05	.05	.05	.04	.03	.03	.01	.02	.02	.08

UNST	COUNTRY	D68	D69	D70	D71	D72	D73	D74	D75	D76	MOD	SDD	VOD
0													
	ASTR	.09	.08	.07	.07	.07	.06	999	999	999	999	999	999
	BELG	.20	.20	.18	.18	.17	.17	.16	.16	.16	.18	.01	.09
	FINL	.10	.09	.09	.09	.09	.09	.09	.09	.08	.09	.00	.05
	GRBR	.31	.28	.27	.27	.26	.25	.25	.22	.23	.26	.03	.10
	ISRA	999	.68	.72	.70	.68	.79	.74	.77	999	999	999	999
	ITAL	.17	.16	.16	.16	.15	.15	.17	.15	.15	.16	.01	.05
	JAPA	.09	.09	.09	.09	.09	.09	.09	.08	.08	.09	.00	.05
	NORW	.24	.23	.23	.21	.20	.19	.19	.19	.18	.21	.02	.10
	SWED	.19	.18	.16	.16	.15	.15	.14	.14	999	999	999	999
	USA	.46	.44	.40	.36	.34	.33	.32	.31	.30	.36	.05	.15
VALI		9	10	10	10	10	10	9	9	7	7	7	7
MEAN		.21	.24	.24	.23	.22	.23	.24	.23	.17	.19	.02	.08
STDE		.12	.19	.20	.19	.18	.21	.20	.21	.08	.10	.02	.04

Percent unemployed: United Nations <u>Statistical Yearbook</u>, 1977, Table 22. Data are provided either from labor force sample surveys or from employment office statistics. Since both series are available for Norway and Sweden, only employment office data were used. For Belgium, data refer to those "wholly employed."

Defense spending as proportion of total government expenditure: United Nations <u>Yearbook of National Accounts Statistics</u>, 1977, Table 7a.

able, and autocorrelations are close to 1.00. There is, however, substantial variation at any given time in average annual defense expenditure *among* the "wealthiest capitalist countries" (Szymanski, 1973:1) for which data are available: Austria allocates only 7 percent of its governmental expenditure to defense, whereas Israel allocates 73 percent. Because there is also substantial variation in corresponding values for unemployment–from a low of 0.98 percent in Norway to a high of 5.58 percent in the United States–it is tempting merely to correlate these two static measures despite the fact that, as we have seen, the flattened time series found in the right marginal column of the table would tend not to reflect any dynamic processes within the body of the table. And functionalist theory pertains primarily to the latter.

The major "finding" possible with this set of data, then, is the correlation of .39 between a static measure of unemployment and a static measure of defense spending. Although this is precisely the sort of finding cited by Szymanski in testing the Marxian-functionalist hypothesis of a nexus between military spending and economic stagnation, the data are not sufficiently dynamic to permit a test of the hypothesis in functionalistic format; it is as if the data had a certain Sumnerian invariability (cf. M. Zeitlin, 1974:1453). The same result occurs when defense spending is defined as total defense expenditure divided by gross domestic product: The high autocorrelations preclude detailed analysis, but once again a relationship exists between static measures of the two variables (Table 6.7). The finding of a positive relationship between defense spending and unemployment contradicts Szymanski's finding of a negative relationship, and relatively short-term adaptive processes do not seem to occur here either.[3]

One finds many instances in the literature in which autocorrelation (the momentum that characterizes many social variables) is proposed as an adequate explanation. This practice is illegitimate when one is interested in change (i.e., the tendency for variables *not* to be governed by their own momentum, their own past values). Human ecology, says Hawley (1984:912), ". . . posits an external origin of change, for a thing cannot cause itself. Change is induced when an environmental input, that is, new information, impinges on and is synthesized with existing information." In an attempt to apply the "comparative method" to the United States and Canada, Lipset (1970:39) proposes that

Although many factors in the history of these nations have determined the current variations between them, three particular factors may be singled out: the varying origins of their political systems and national identities, varying religious traditions, and different frontier experiences. In general terms, the value orienta-

Table 6.7. *Unemployment and defense spending*

Country	Average Unemployment in Percentages, 1968–76	Average Defense Spending as Proportion of GDP, 1968–75
Australia	2.37	.03
Austria	2.13	NA
Belgium	4.47	.03
Denmark	NA	.02
Finland	2.63	.02
Great Britain	3.33	.05
Israel	3.66	NA
Italy	3.38	.02
Japan	1.41	NA
Netherlands	2.86	.03
Norway	0.98	.03
Sweden	1.68	.04
United States	5.58	.07
West Germany	2.01	.03

r = .55
Source: See Table 13.

tions of English-speaking Canada stem from a counterrevolutionary past, a continuing need to differentiate itself from the United States, the influence of monarchical institutions, a dominant Anglican religious tradition, and a less individualistic and more governmentally controlled frontier expansion than was present on the American frontier.

The basic problem with Lipset's approach is that it tries to explain "current variations" such as the strong conservatism (on selected criteria) of Canadian values by invoking the same variations as they have appeared historically. This explanation is unabashedly tautological; it holds that Canada is conservative for being conservative, and Lipset's method would be far more effective if his excellent descriptive material were supplemented by the variation-and-selective-retention paradigm. When he tells us, for instance, that

the absence of an aristocratic stratum following the Revolution left the United States free to develop a socially as well as economically dominant class of merchants and manufacturers whose desire for wealth was uninhibited by norms denigrating hard work and the accumulation of capital (1970:62)

he affords an opportunity to examine unique organizational forms produced and perpetuated mainly in the United States; but it is an opportunity that Lipset does not pursue.

In brief, self-replication, despite its apparent explanatory power in ge-
netics, explains very little in the social realm. When we hear that "the
cause of war is war itself," or that there is a self-perpetuating "culture of
poverty," we are once again in a tautological situation.

Slightly more convincing illustrations of dynamic functional analysis
may be drawn from research on capital punishment. Over the last decade
or so, a substantial amount of research has addressed the deterrence
doctrine (Gibbs, 1975), that is, the hypothesis that threatened and/or
actual punishments are an effective means of suppressing deviant behavior. The deterrence hypothesis involves an alleged adaptation process;
therefore, one version of the deterrence hypothesis – that which holds that
capital punishment may deter violent crime – has been included in Table
5.1. Research on capital punishment has become highly sophisticated in
that it utilizes elaborate time-series data (Blumstein et al., 1978; Bowers
and Pierce, 1980; Ehrlich, 1975) and uses methods such as two-stage least
squares (Namboodiri et al., 1975:492–532) in which it is clearly recognized (cf. Figure 5.1) that while sanctions may influence deviance, deviance may have a reciprocal impact on sanctions (Kleck, 1979; Passell,
1975). In other words, a handful of deterrence studies reflect Durkheim's
awareness of the inherent interactional and dynamic aspects of functionalist hypotheses; the remaining studies are vitiated by their failure to incorporate these properties into the analysis (cf. Faia, 1982). It is likely that
in the future the most powerful forms of deterrence research will use
time-series data on delict–sanction rates for many jurisdictions at many
ecological levels, and will routinely test for reciprocal interaction; in
short, the data of such studies will be amenable to the format of Table
6.6, with the understanding that a "case" may consist of a nation, state,
city, or other aggregation for which rates are available. The use of rates
forces us to avoid (or move beyond) individuals as the unit of analysis, as
Mayhew (1980) insists we must.

We conclude, then, that the first step in analyzing social change is to
separate change from measurement unreliability and from autocorrelation
and to ascertain the lag times over which real changes tend to occur; we
then try to explain these changes with reference to other variables. And
apropos of organizational survival, it should be noted that whenever survivorship is made an explicit part of adaptation theories, life-table data
can readily be fit into a format such as that of Tables 6.6 and 6.7, and can

then be used to test theories of social survivorship. Suppose, for instance, that instead of a series of cases (e.g., countries) in these tables, we were to list a series of ecological areas (or broad taxonomic categories) each of which contained a large number of organizations of a given type. The homeostatic variable (H) would be any of several measures of survivorship derived through life-table analysis. (Life tables would have to be made cross-sectionally for each of many data points.) The structural or adaptive variable (S) would be an organizational feature thought to have an impact on survivorship. (In this instance the structural variable would be subject to disturbances, as opposed to the usual situation in which the homeostatic variable is subject to disturbances.) If these variables showed sufficient temporal variation to justify application of the variation-and-selective-retention model – if, in other words, the data were sufficiently dynamic – we would again be able to exploit "the logic of functional explanation:" Disturbances of the structural variable would produce *increased* social selectivity (i.e., reduced survivability), and increased social selectivity would tend to *reduce* the initial disturbance by selecting against it in the finest Darwinian manner. Again we would observe, with appropriate lag times, the typical functionalist pattern of positive correlations interwoven with negative correlations; despite Levy and Cancian's claim (1968:37), we would observe "reciprocal" and "self-regulating" relationships. It is important to note, however, that, contrary to Zeitlin (1973: ch. 1), functionalist hypotheses do not always involve social survivorship; many structures serve interests that have no demonstrable bearing on social survivorship, and some structures may survive despite the fact that they serve neither interests nor survivorship.

An Advanced Beginner's Bibliography on Time-Series Analysis

For several works listed, the numbers following authors' names indicate my opinion as to order of difficulty, with the more difficult works having higher numbers.

Atkin, R. et al. 1977. *Child Development* 48:944–52. "Cross-lagged panel analysis of sixteen cognitive measures at four grade levels."

Blalock, Hubert M. (3) 1969. Englewood Cliffs: Prentice-Hall. *Theory Construction.* Chapters 5 and 6.

Chatfield, Christopher (11) 1975. New York: Wiley. *The Analysis of Time-Series: Theory and Practice.*

Coleman, James S. (12) 1968. New York: McGraw-Hill. "The mathematical study of change." pp. 428–78 in Hubert M. and Ann B. Blalock (eds.), *Methodology in Social Research.*

Cook, Thomas D. and Donald T. Campbell (4) 1979. Chicago: Rand McNally. *Quasi-Experimentation: Design & Analysis Issues for Field Settings.* Chapters 5, 6, and 7.

Dhrymes, Phoebus J. (13) 1970. New York: Harper and Row. *Econometrics.* Section 10.4.

Gottman, John M. (6) 1981. New York: Cambridge University Press. *Time-Series Analysis: A Comprehensive Introduction for Social Scientists.*

Hannan, Michael T. and Alice A. Young (8) 1977. San Francisco: Jossey-Bass. "Estimation in panel models: results on pooling cross-sections and time series," pp. 52–83 in David R. Heise (ed.), *Sociological Methodology 1977.*

Hanushek, Eric A. and John E. Jackson. 1977. New York: Academic. *Statistical Methods for Social Scientists.* Chapter 6.

Heise, David R. (6) 1970. San Francisco: Jossey-Bass. "Causal inference from panel data," pp. 3–27 in Edgar F. Borgatta and George W. Bohrnstedt (eds.), *Sociological Methodology.*

Hull, C. Hadlai and Norman H. Nie (eds.) (9) 1981. New York: McGraw-Hill. *SPSS Update 7–9.* Chapter 2

Jessor, R. and S. L. 1977. New York: Academic Press. *Problem Behavior and Psychosocial Development: A Longitudinal Study of Youth.*

Kemeny, John G. et al. (1) 1962. Englewood Cliffs: Prentice-Hall. *Finite Mathematics With Business Applications.* Chapter IV.

Lave, L. B. and E. P. Seskin. 1977. Baltimore: Johns Hopkins University. *Air Pollution and Human Health.*

Markus, Gregory B. (2) 1979. (mimeograph.) University of Michigan. "Models for the analysis of panel data."

Namboodiri, N. Krishnan et al. 1975. New York: McGraw-Hill. *Applied Multivariate Analysis and Experimental Designs.* Chapter 11.

Ostrom, Charles W. Jr. 1978. Beverly Hills: Sage. *Time Series Analysis: Regression Techniques.*

Pelz, Donald C. and Robert A. Lew (7) 1970. San Francisco: Jossey-Bass. "Heise's causal model applied," pp. 28–37 in Edgar F. Borgatta and George W. Bohrnstedt (eds.), *Sociological Methodology 1970.*

Roberts, Harry V. (5) 1981. Chicago: SPSS. "Signs and symptoms of spurious correlation in time-series analysis." *Proceedings of the Fifth Annual SPSS Users and Coordinators Conference.*

SAS Institute. 1979. Raleigh, NC: SAS Institute. *SAS User's Guide, 1979 Edition.* Chapters on AUTOREG, SPECTRA, and SYSREG.

Singer, Burton and Seymour Spilerman. *American Journal of Sociology* 82:1–54. "The representation of social processes by Markov models."

Tuma, Nancy B. and Michael T. Hannan. 1979. *American Journal of Sociology* 84:820–54. "Dynamic analysis of event histories."

Part III. L'envoi

As Karras handed him the stole, the exorcist added, "Is there anything at all you would like to ask now, Demian?"

Karras shook his head. "No. But I think it might be helpful if I gave you some background on the different personalities that Regan has manifested. So far, there seem to be three."

"There is only one," said Merrin softly, slipping the stole around his shoulders.

Wm. P. Blatty, *The Exorcist*

There can be only one social science.

A. R. Radcliffe-Brown, *A Natural Science of Society*

. . . there is no place
that does not see you.
You must change your life.

– Rainer Rilke

7. Toward an integrated social science paradigm

N. J. Demerath III (1967:501–18) has defended functionalism against its detractors by pointing out that the latter have often been guilty of the "synecdochic fallacy"; that is, they have identified specific types of functionalism and treated them as if they represented functionalism in general. They have permitted the part to represent the whole (a synecdoche, by definition), and their strident critiques of functionalism are thus applicable only to specific formulations (or even to tangential issues, as we shall see in the appendix) and not to functionalism in general. In distinguishing among types of functionalism, Demerath identifies relatively simple bivariate theories as "structuralistic" and the more elaborate multivariate theories (e.g., theories of deviance and social control in their usual formulations) as "functionalistic." A similar distinction once was drawn by Gouldner, who "has taken the further step of aligning the two options with particular theorists," Merton and Parsons (Demerath, 1967:504–5):

. . . system concepts play a pivotal role in both their formulations of functional theory. It will be noted, however, that the nature of their commitment to a system model differs, Parsons' being what may be called a total commitment, while Merton's can be regarded as a strategy of minimal commitment . . . . In brief, for Merton functional analysis is focused on some delimited unit of human behavior or belief, with a view to accounting either for its persistence or change by establishing its consequences for environing social or cultural structures . . . .

In contrast to Merton, Parsons does not focus on the explanation of empirically delimited units of social behavior or belief, but instead centers attention directly on analysis of the contextual structure as system . . . . Parsons' assumption is that it is impossible to understand adequately any single pattern except by referring it to some larger systemic whole. He, therefore, assumes that the *whole* system must be conceptually constituted prior to the investigation and analysis of specific patterns. In consequence, Parsons is led forthwith to the analysis of the *total* anatomy of social systems in an effort to identify their constituent elements and relationships.

As Lazarsfeld (1958, 1967) explains, the transformation of bivariate into multivariate causal theories – in this case, the transformation of Mertonian into Parsonian theories – is essentially a matter of adding antecedent and/or intervening variables, and this process, says Lazarsfeld, constitutes "explanation." Clearly, the first question to raise about a Mertonian structuralistic theory is whether it is possible to extend the theory, as Bredemeier (1955) once suggested, by adding antecedent and/or intervening variables. Let us then define a multivariate theory as one involving three or more variables associated with one another in a determinable (or identifiable) causal pattern. If Demerath and Gouldner are correct, it should be possible to classify functional theories, and perhaps other kinds of theories, according to the bivariate–multivariate dimension.

1. Value-added aspects of social science theories

We shall assume that virtually all sociological propositions are classifiable on the bivariate–multivariate dimension. Furthermore, propositions are classifiable as to whether they claim some sort of temporal order, as many "process" theories and many causal theories do, especially those of the path-analytic variety. For any sociological proposition, then, we could ask whether it is (1) causal or noncausal (associational), (2) multivariate or bivariate, (3) time-ordered or cross-sectional, (4) functionalistic or non-functionalistic. These several dimensions, of course, are not entirely independent of one another: For instance, if a functional proposition explains a structure with reference to its consequences while also positing feedback paths from the consequences to the structure, then all functionalist propositions by definition involve causation, and it is contradictory to assert, as does Moran (1982:45), that one can succeed ". . . in demonstrating functional relationships, but not in establishing causality." Essentially the same error is made by Zeitlin (1973:8) when he says that causation ". . . is precisely what traditional functionalism has not concerned itself with" (cf. Garbarino, 1977:60). Similarly, any functionalist proposition, as we have seen, almost necessarily involves time ordering of data, thus nearly precluding a functional (or Mertonian structuralist) proposition that is not time ordered. On the other hand, the presence of time-series data predicts nothing about the multivariate–bivariate distinction or about the causal–noncausal distinction; nor does the presence of a given number of variables enable us to predict whether causal interpretations have been made. If the four dichotomies were entirely independent of one another (as defined), we would have 16 distinctive logical possibilities for classifying any given proposition. However, six of these possibilities are ruled out by definition in that they denote functionalist proposi-

Table 7.1. *A hypothetical Guttman scale of sociological propositions*

ITEM..		FUNCTION		ORDERED		MULTIVAR		CAUSAL		TOTAL
RESP..		0	1	0	1	0	1	0	1	
C		I		I		I		I		
O	4	0	7	0	7	0	7	0	7	7
M		---ERR		I		I		I		
P		I		I		I		I		
L	3	11	1	0	12	1	11	0	12	12
E		---ERR		I		I		I		
X		I		I		I		I		
	2	20	0	15	5	3	17	2	18	20
		I		I		---ERR		I		
		I		I		I		I		
	1	23	0	22	1	22	1	2	21	23
		I		I		I		---ERR		
		I		I		I		I		
	0	38	0	38	0	38	0	38	0	38
SUMS		92	8	75	25	64	36	42	58	100
PCTS		92	8	75	25	64	36	42	58	
ERRORS		0	1	0	6	4	1	4	0	16

```
100 CASES WERE PROCESSED
  0 (OR  0.0 PCT) WERE MISSING


STATISTICS..

COEFFICIENT OF REPRODUCIBILITY = 0.9600
MINIMUM MARGINAL REPRODUCIBILITY = 0.7225
PERCENT IMPROVEMENT = 0.2375
COEFFICIENT OF SCALABILITY = 0.8559
```

tions without time order and/or without causal implications, combinations that are disallowed. On the other hand, functionalist propositions (as noted by Gouldner) may be either bivariate or multivariate.

I would surmise that if we were to examine and classify a large number of sociological propositions drawn randomly from the literature, we would discover that most of them are classifiable according to a Guttman scale (here called COMPLEX) consisting of the five types listed in the leftward margin of Table 7.1, a table containing contrived data for 100 propositions so that many frequencies in the table can be treated as percentages. I propose, further, that sociological propositions tend to develop diachronically according to a "value-added" sequence defined by this scale. In other words, we first undertake exploratory data analysis, perhaps observing concomitant variation between pairs of variables and arriving at a finding that would receive a score of zero on our hypothetical Guttman scale. Next, we apply some variant of Mill's methods in order to infer causation (score = 1). At the next step, we (or our critics) invoke additional variables (antecedent or intervening, according to Lazarsfeld) to test for the possible "spuriousness" of the original relationship, thereby escalating to the multivariate level of analysis (score = 2). Then, having established elaborate multivariate causal theories, usually involving a single dependent variable explained with reference to several independent variables, we are ready to seek out time-ordered causal sequences by means of sophisticated methods such as path analysis (e.g., Jencks, 1972; Sewell et al., 1976), for a scale score of 3. Finally, if we were pursuing functionalist hypotheses we would try to discover additional causal sequences – possible feedback paths – from the dependent variable back to some combination of the independent variables, always bearing in mind the possibility of cybernetic control with its typical pattern of regularly oscillating variables;[1] in this case we have a scale score of 4. The existence of such a Guttman scale, along lines suggested by the hypothetical data of Table 7.1, would strongly imply that functional analysis, subsuming other basic forms of sociological analysis, is the most advanced approach to sociological theorizing and not at all characterized by the methodological and theoretical primitiveness attributed to it by Davis (1959: 762), especially in his references to Parsonian functionalism.

Readers with a talent for keeping counts of things may accuse us of cheating in the preparation of Table 7.1: If there are 16 logically possible scoring patterns for our four dichotomies, if the Guttman scale comprises five of these scoring patterns, and if another six are ruled out by the definitional problems noted above, then all errors occurring in the Guttman scale must arise from five sources, as follows:

1. Functionalist, ordered, causal propositions that never go beyond the bivariate level (score = 3).
2. Ordered, causal propositions that remain nonfunctionalist and bivariate (score = 2).
3. Ordered, multivariate propositions that remain nonfunctionalist and noncausal (score = 2).
4. Multivariate propositions that do not become functionalist, ordered, or causal (score = 1).
5. Ordered propositions that remain nonfunctionalist, bivariate, and noncausal (score = 1).

As it turns out, these five error types seem to have a strong potential for disrupting scalability. There are established research traditions and perhaps even "schools of thought" associated with each of the five error-producing propositional forms. Type 1 corresponds to what Gouldner refers to as the "structuralist" variety of functional analysis. The second scoring pattern illustrates a host of studies in which correlations between two time series are assessed with a view to establishing causation (e.g., Pelz and Andrews, 1964). Type 3 scoring patterns are exemplified by "process theories" in which many variables are observed for their concomitance through time, as in the case of "transition theory" in demography. For type 4 it may be said that the phrase "multivariate propositions that do not become functionalist, ordered, or causal" provides an excellent definition of "axiomatic theory" as developed by Zetterberg (1965) and others. Finally, error type 5 illustrates highly simplistic "theories" in which variables are associated through time, with the implication that temporal concomitance somehow implies causation but with little evidence supporting the implication (cf. Roberts, 1981).

For each of these five error-producing patterns the next logical step would be to move toward the upper scoring levels of our Guttman scale. The absence of such movement makes many of the forms of theory exemplified by the five types appear to be sterile, degenerate forms. Any theory of the axiomatic genre (e.g., Gibbs and Martin, 1962; Hage, 1965; Schwirian and Prehn, 1962), for instance, seems to cry out for some effort toward causal interpretation, toward a time ordering of events, and toward functionalist explanation based on circular causation and cybernetic regulation. Similarly, even though "analytical induction," as developed by Robinson (1951) and others, has the pattern of scale type 1 and would therefore not be a source of error in our hypothetical Guttman scale, theories based on analytical induction usually seem to be strong candidates for extension by means of multivariate formulations, time ordering, and functionalist interpretation. For instance, whereas analytical induction tries to establish X as a necessary condition for Y (Robinson, 1951) and tries to formulate this relationship as an absolute, invariable sociological law, functionalism asks whether Y ever has an impact on X and whether this impact could exemplify an absolute, invariable sociological law involving circular causation and self-regulation.

If a Guttman scale of sociological propositions were shown to exist, and if this scale corresponded to the diachronic, value-added sequence suggested above, it would provide a concise way of defining what to Davis is the "neglected" and "residual" category of "nonfunctional analysis." Any proposition receiving a score other than 4 on our hypothetical Guttman scale is nonfunctionalist. Given, first, the clear possibility of many types of nonfunctionalist propositions; second, the many levels of sociological analysis ranging from individuals to cohorts of organizations; and third, the existence of a number of broad categories from which sociological variables may be drawn (Hauser and Duncan, 1959:ch. 28; Duncan and Schnore, 1959), the possibilities of nonfunctionalist social theory are infinite. And this infinitude provides us with an infinitude of opportunities for moving toward a functionalist culmination.

For us to exploit these opportunities, it is essential that the discipline aid and abet the "social indicators" movement in every way: We must have time-series data on a host of variables, and time intervals must be short. It is essential that we move inexorably from nonfunctionalist levels of analysis toward a functionalist culmination in which change is explained with reference to dynamic, multivariate causal models involving feedback and self-regulation. When we are confronted by an assertion such as that of Theodore Caplow et al. (1982) that Muncie, Indiana has changed very little over the last 50 years, we should know precisely the sorts of data needed to determine whether the variation-and-selective-retention model is applicable to Muncie, whether any significant thrust toward social change (noise) has been selected against by identifiable mechanisms of social control. If we were to find high stability on a variable such as rate of class exogamy, this stability could potentially be explained in either (or both) of two ways: (1) The incidence rate of class exogamy is controlled through the operation of social norms, or (2) the prevalence rate of such marriages is controlled through social selection. The first option corresponds to the biologist's reproductive selection, and the second to lethal selection; these are precisely the meanings given to the two types of rates in Hollingshead and Redlich's famous study of mental illness (1958). In either case we would find discernible noise at some level of analysis. If the Caplow et al. thesis is wrong, we should be able to chart all specific trends constituting social change, and we should be able to identify mechanisms that select, either through incidence or prevalence, in favor of change. Thus we see again that stability and instability may be manifestations of the same social processes, in this case the processes of social selection.

Many years ago Stuart Chase (1931) wrote a fine volume on Mexico in which he compared the Lynds' work on Muncie with Redfield's work on a Mexican village called Tepoztlán. If we were to make a similar comparison today, we would find that while the thesis of Caplow et al. may be valid for Muncie, it appears that fundamental changes have been taking place in Tepoztlán. Again, the task of dynamic functionalism would be to ascertain precisely what is changing and what is remaining constant about the social structure of Tepoztlán, what the factors are that account for these patterns of change and stability, and whether there are emergent social problems or homeostatic variables that give rise to new adaptive practices. When Lewis (1960:94), for instance, speaks of the increasing ". . . use of doctors instead of curanderos . . .," one is tempted to ask whether there remains a modicum of demand for traditional healers, what the factors are that determine the numbers of curanderos available at a given time, and what kinds of circumstances lead to their being called upon by the sick (Trotter and Chavira, 1981). In other words, a new level of curanderismo may be emerging just as, in an earlier example, a new sex ratio at birth may emerge eventually as a result of sex preselection of children. These same types of questions could be asked about Lewis's claim (1960:94) that recent changes in Tepoztlán have made ". . . the disparity between the incomes of the rich and poor more striking than ever before." In each instance we would benefit from an analysis similar to that of Tuma and Hannan (1979), in which the long-term effects of income-maintenance experiments on marital status were assessed by means of Markov processes with their "steady-state" implications (cf. Lieberson and Fuguitt, 1967).

Finally, if sociological propositions do indeed tend to evolve from relatively low to relatively high scores on our hypothetical Guttman scale, we are forced to conclude that all sociological propositions classified on the four dichotomies of Table 7.1 are either functionalistic or protofunctionalistic. Ironically, this is the tiny grain of truth in Kingsley Davis's assertion that virtually all social scientists are functionalists – the tiny grain from which a thousand flowers yet may bloom.

2. Theory, methods, and the single paradigm

There is nothing either good or bad,
but thinking makes it so.

  – Hamlet, Act ii, sc. 2

There is nothing either important or unimportant,
but beta weights tell us so.

  – Anonymous

Although there are probably as many definitions of social science theory as there are social scientists, one hopes that eventually we will move toward the long-awaited consensus, the "theoretical integration" (Martindale, 1960:ch. 20), that seems to have so much appeal to those who believe, with Ritzer (1980:201–8), that the costs of paradigm differences probably outweigh the benefits. Although my own definition of social science theory has no special magic, it does contain many clues as to how we might achieve integration of the several competing paradigms. My definition, although it tends to evolve, is for the moment as follows:

Social science theory consists of a large set of interrelated propositions, empiri-cally substantiated, and stated at many different levels of abstraction. The func-tions of theory are (1) the systematization of knowledge, (2) prediction, explana-tion, and (perhaps) social control, and (3) the generation of new research hypo-theses.

This definition appeals to me largely because it says nothing about para-digms and does not commit me to any special focus on "social facts" or "social definitions" or "social behavior." This entire volume, in fact, says virtually nothing about paradigms, and yet it clearly implies a range of strategies and tactics that implement each component of this definition. Propositions are interrelated primarily through the application of mathe-matical logic and syllogistic reasoning. Empirical substantiation is essen-tial for any social science that purports to be positivistic and to have verifiable ties to social reality. Elaborate taxonomies that evolve accord-ing to empirical findings are essential to any highly developed science, and nothing kills a science more quickly than the "dead-level abstraction" lamented by great semanticists like Alfred Korzybski (Johnson, 1946) and great sociologists like C. Wright Mills (1959). Prediction, explanation, and social control require procedures that become more or less obvious once one has become committed to a multiple-causation strategy, as most of us have. Finally, we all seek a good source of new hypotheses, and these arise through the inductive and deductive processes involved in making abstract generalizations and deriving concrete applications from them.

Again, I believe that I have been discussing theory throughout this volume and defending what appears to be a theoretical position; yet I have not found it necessary to say anything pejorative about social fact-ists, social definitionists, or social behaviorists. To my mind, the differ-ences among these paradigms were spelled out clearly many years ago by Robert Merton (1957: 87–88):

Much of what is described in textbooks [or theory books] as sociological theory consists of general orientations toward substantive materials. Such orientations involve broad postulates which indicate *types* of variables which are somehow to be taken into account rather than specifying determinate relationships between particular variables. Indispensable though these orientations are, they provide only the broadest framework for empirical inquiry. . . . Such general orientations may be paraphrased as saying in effect that the investigator ignores this *order of fact* at his peril. They do not set forth specific hypotheses.

The chief function of these orientations is to provide a general context for inquiry . . . . They constitute only the point of departure for the theorist. It is his task to develop specific, interrelated hypotheses by reformulating empirical generalizations in the light of these generic orientations.

Once we have decided what must "be taken into account" – a relatively minor decision when we realize that eventually *everything* must be taken into account – we discover that the tasks of "reformulating empirical generalizations" and developing "specific, interrelated hypotheses" become the central challenge. In other words, we first make a relatively unimportant paradigm decision in which we delude ourselves into believing that some particular orientation is more fundamental than the rest, and then we encounter the real problem of trying to make theories that more or less live up to the demanding definition of theory just given.

I believe that the current corps of theory writers (Ritzer is a fine example) provide an important service when they tell us of the many orientations found within the discipline and then begin seeking ways of integrating paradigms, as do several of these writers. Ritzer himself (1980: 212–29) argues that the greatest social scientists of past and present have been "paradigm bridgers," although from time to time, as in the case of Parsons, they may have burned a few bridges. In any case I have become convinced that if the theory writers wish to clarify further the ways in which paradigms may be converging, they would be well advised to put aside, if only for the moment, their volumes of Marx, Durkheim, Weber, and Parsons, and to make a careful, detailed study of, say, the latest SPSS manual (SPSS, Inc., 1983). In reading this manual we discover that, despite a lack of paradigm integration as understood by the likes of Martindale, Ritzer, Irving Zeitlin, or Talcott Parsons, there has been a substantial amount of convergence toward *methods* appropriate for the creation of theories that are not mere defenses of orientations (Wells and Picou, 1981:153–174). The SPSS manual explains clearly how to implement nearly all aspects of our preferred definition of social science theory. It tells us, among many other things, how to conceptualize by means of scale analysis or factor analysis, how to use various kinds of samples in order to obtain results isomorphic with social reality, how to make causal inferences at a multivariate level under a variety of circumstances, how to sort out the structure of a time series, how to make predictions and explanations. It tells us that the infamous paradigm dispute between quantitative and qualitative social science may be swept into the dustbin of history once we understand log-linear methods, another way of handling multiple causation and holistic properties. It tells us how to make appropriately specified causal hypotheses, how to test for interaction among causes, and how to search for nested effects, that is, conditional causes. It tells us how to use analysis of covariance in order to explain *patterns* rather than *variables* (or perhaps to explain pattern variables). It tells us how to escape the conceptual muddiness of assuming that social mobility or status discrepancy have a social significance that is not captured by the variables used to measure them, such as (in the case of mobility) son's SES and father's SES. The SPSS manual, clearly the best theory book I know, is silent only in the realm of taxonomy, although it does provide useful aids to constructing taxonomies, such as factor analysis and Guttman scaling. And therefore I reiterate my earlier suggestion that the American Sociological Association establish a continuing committee on taxonomy.

It is both revealing and inspiring that Ritzer (1980:223), in a discussion of various ways of achieving paradigm integration, makes reference to "triangulation" as one approach, for he understands perfectly well that triangulation has been proposed primarily as a methodological strategy (Webb et al., 1966; Babbie, 1983:97), and only indirectly as a theoretical strategy. I am almost prepared to argue that the whole array of multivariate methods *are* theory (cf. Collins, 1984:344); however, I will merely say that multivariate methods, the integrated methodological paradigm, are such an indispensable (requisite?) part of theory that nobody, whether a factist, a definitionist, or a behaviorist, can make a good theory without them.

Take, for instance, the matter of sex discrimination. I believe that nobody ever fully understood sex discrimination (or any other form of discrimination) without first understanding the logic (if not the practical details) of multivariate statistical modeling. Consider, for instance, how we might undertake a multiple regression analysis of sex discrimination in the salaries of American professors, as surveyed in 1975 by the Carnegie Council on Higher Education. As we prepare SPSS command files, it becomes clear that important conceptual, theoretical, and methodological aspects of discrimination must be stipulated by the commands, and that these problems must be addressed in ways that are clear, specific, and parsimonious.

As a first step, suppose that we wish to examine the salary determination equation for males alone, using as predictors (hereafter called qualifications) the following: having full-time status (FULLTM), having an annual as opposed to a nine-month salary base (ANNUAL), being in the natural sciences (NATSCI) or humanities/social sciences (HUMSS) as opposed to other fields, having a given professorial rank from instructor to professor (RANK), one's recent scholarly publications (LATEPUBL), being affiliated with a relatively poor quality institution (POORQUAL), and seniority (DEGREEYR), defined as the year of one's highest degree. If these determinants do not seem appropriate, then we have a specification problem that we can address unambiguously: Either some of the determinants are conceptually inappropriate, or they do not have anything of importance to do with salaries, or the list is too short. The latter seems to be a particularly strong possiblity. Furthermore, all the continuous variables, such as seniority, are being assessed as to their *linear* impact on salaries, with early career salary gains from seniority (for instance) forced to be the same as later salary gains from the same source. Given the fact that salary increases are often assigned on a percentage basis, this assumption violates reality. If we were to decide how the relationship could be assessed more realistically, the multiple regression model would force us to get very specific about the meaning of "realistic."

Suppose we ascertain that for male professors the mean salary is 6.135. If one checks the codebook for the Carnegie survey one sees that salaries had a range from less than $8,000 to more than $25,000 (for 1974–5), and were coded on a scale from 1 to 10. A mean of 6.135 means that, for men, the average salary (as coded) was just over $16,000. This imprecision involves classic measurement problems: It is hard to get people to state their current salaries with accuracy, and it is nearly impossible to obtain their past salaries with accuracy. The remaining means tell us fascinating things, such as (1) 94 percent of the males are full-time, (2) 31 percent of the males receive salaries on an annual basis, (3) 23 percent are natural scientists, (4) 35 percent are humanities or social science professors, (5) the average rank is 2.8 on a scale where 1 = instructor and 4 = full professor, (6) the average publication rate for recent years is 2.0 on a scale that is coded from 1 to 5, (7) the average score for a poor quality institution is 4.2 on a scale from 1 to 7, and (8) the year of one's highest degree is 7.59, which means about 1961. When we compare these averages against the corresponding averages for women, we see some interesting differences of the sort that we should be able to anticipate on the basis of past research and theory.

Let us examine the nonstandardized salary equation for males:

Variable	Weight
DEGREEYR	−0.20
FULLTM	+1.11
NATSCI	−0.38
ANNUAL	+1.07
LATEPUBL	+0.24
HUMSS	−0.63
POORQUAL	−0.15
RANK	+1.21
(CONSTANT)	+3.32

We observe (in another part of the output) that our several determinants explain about 59 percent of the statistical variation (variance) in salaries, suggesting that our specification may not be complete or that we may be in the presence of luck or whim or free will. Examining another part of the output (not shown), we see that all eight determinants have a significant impact on salaries, although for some determinants (e.g., RANK) the beta weight (a measure of the relative impact of each of the determinants) is large in absolute value. The signs indicate the direction of relationships: for example, a more recent year of receipt of one's highest degree tends to suppress one's salary. The regression constant, 3.32, represents the hypothetical salary received by a male whose qualifications did not lead to any upward or downward adjustment; the corresponding value for women is 2.22, and this difference may be a direct result of sex discrimination. If we wished, we could ascertain the size of this difference of constants for those men and women whose qualifications are precisely at the average; this gap, also, would tell us something about the direct effects of sex discrimination. (To obtain this result, we subtract mean qualification scores from the scores of each individual and do the analysis over again.)

If male salaries were set entirely by the above equation, males would have an average of 6.19 on our salary scale. This finding may not seem exciting, but imagine how interesting it would be to have *female* salaries as predicted by the *male* equation, so that we could compare these predicted salaries against the actual salaries of females. Such a manipulation gets to the heart of sex discrimination by applying a relatively universalistic standard to a group that may have been subjected to a particularistic standard. We would discover that for female professors, the average salary as predicted by the male equation would be 5.15. This is less than the corresponding male value, 6.19, because on our many salary determinants female scores are generally lower than male scores. If the scores on determinants such as professorial rank or field are themselves influenced by discrimination, this is a form of discrimination that we have not yet captured; it requires a reconceptualization of the process and a new specification. However, if we compare the actual female salaries against the female salaries as determined by the male equation, 4.53 versus 5.15, we have isolated a possible locus of sex discrimination in the weights associated with qualifications, although we cannot be dogmatic on this matter until we decide whether the overall equation is an adequate specification.

Summing up, we can say that the differences between the male and female equations tell the story of possible sex discrimination in three ways. First, the difference between the constant terms, 3.32 versus 2.22, tells us where the relative starting points are for male and female salaries, with the understanding that these starting points are adjusted upward or downward on the basis of qualifications and the weights attached to them. Second, we see that the weights also vary in ways that generally favor males: For instance, males get a better payoff for seniority, for having annual contracts, and for having high rank; several smaller differences exist, one or two of which favor females. Third, once we have isolated that part of salary differences due to differences in qualifications such as rank, the next logical step is to ascertain whether acquisition of these qualifications is itself influenced by sex discrimination. If we compare male and female means on all the qualifications, for instance, we note that whereas the average rank for males is 2.82, it is 2.27 for females; whereas 23 percent of the males are natural scientists, only 11 percent of the females are natural scientists; and so forth. It should be possible to write equations for these qualifications that would be properly specified and to use these specifications as a way of assessing whatever discrimination may exist, just as we did in the case of salaries. Notice, however, that it would probably be much easier to write equations for professorial rank than, say, for field, because the former is determined largely within higher education bureaucracies, whereas the latter may go back to childhood.

Once we have estimated the various regression coefficients that represent discrimination, we are in the presence of social facts, of structural conditions and social processes that presumably serve various interests and may, in many instances, have an impact on the survival of organizations. At this point a social definitionist might well be inspired to try to identify the interests served, the intentions fulfilled, and the victims enlightened (or flamboozled) by the social facts of sex discrimination; an attempt is made, in other words, to distinguish between manifest and latent functions. A range of intentions and interests probably has an impact, through feedback, on the social facts of discrimination, maintaining them at a certain level. My own research, for instance, suggests that the traditional 12–15 percent salary discrimination gap for academic women in the United States dropped to about 4–5 per cent over the several years preceding 1973 (Fields, 1974), and I suspect that this gap has more or less stabilized at that new level, much in the manner of curanderismo.

We try, then, to discover ways in which the left side of our regression equation for salaries may influence the several salary-determining factors on the right side. Thus, the regression equation provides us with an operational definition of feedback. After these feedback processes have been modeled, a social definitionist might well inquire as to the relationship between the degree of discrimination and the perception of discrimination. Nowadays a gap as large as 4 or 5 percent probably leads to a discernible level of protest and to demands for change, and a gap approaching zero will probably not long survive either; in other words, we may be dealing with a cybernetically regulated series. A social behaviorist, observing the deliberations, negotiations, and decision-making processes that produce an academic salary schedule, would provide immeasurable aid to the social factists seeking improved specifications, and vice versa. Multivariate methods would help these theorists communicate. Ultimately, the factists, definitionists, and behaviorists would provide vast amounts of positive feedback for one another; in the words of Marvin Harris (1968:561), we would form "one big happy Kula ring."

In a sense I agree with Coser (1975) when he says that modern multivariate methods fall short on the criterion of "substance"; that is, they do not presuppose any particular orientation or specific content, so that if stratification specialists wish to focus on "distributive" rather than "relational" aspects of social class (1975:694), they are free to do so. Contrary to Coser's implication, however, there is nothing about multivariate methods that precludes a focus on relational aspects of class, although his use of this term is a little obscure. If Coser were to carry out the specification process outlined earlier, he would begin to communicate more clearly, he would no doubt produce a series of testable hypotheses, and he would have a potential contribution to stratification theory. He would also realize that, contrary to his initial opinion (1975:692), it is both possible and desirable to ". . . compensate for [or reduce] theoretical weakness by methodological strength," and vice versa. When Coser resorts to the usual platitude about the methodological tail wagging the theoretical dog, he misleads us. Methods are not an appendage of theory, nor is theory an appendage of methods. The relationship between theory and methods is symmetrical.

Briefly, then, a good theoretical model (with its methodological components) creates its own substance, and substance (i.e., the way the empirical world behaves) tells us which models are appropriate. Any creative process, I believe, requires methods that produce substance and allow substance to select and/or modify methods, through feedback. Alexander (1983: xvii–xxv, 8–11) may be correct in pointing to the occasional decoupling of theory and method, but we do not always work this way, and we probably should never work this way. Consider, for instance, the following methodological paradigm, one that also lacks substance:

1. Write a series of eight lines in iambic pentameter; that is, each line must have five feet, with each foot consisting (preferably) of two syllables, the latter stressed. The eight lines should express a basic idea or theme.
2. Let the last syllable of these lines follow the rhyme pattern 1–2–2–1, 1–2–2–1.
3. After the eighth line write six more lines, also in iambic pentameter and with a rhyme pattern 3–4, 3–4, 3–4.
4. The last six lines should express a significant change in the basic idea or theme established by the first eight lines.
5. To get started, select any attractive line in iambic pentameter appearing, say, in a book of poetry.
6. Use imagination and perhaps a rhyming dictionary.

Let us hope that the integrated methodological paradigm encourages graduate students to do social theory as well as the preceding recipe encourages undergraduates to write Petrarchian sonnets.

Appendix. Snafu and synecdoche: historical continuities in functional analysis

This appendix, essentially an elaboration of Chapter 1, is designed to defend the null hypothesis as it is applied, or should be applied, to the relationship between functionalism and the assorted mistakes, misjudgments, prejudices, distortions, and ideologies of its practitioners. In recent years it has been taken as axiomatic that, as one of our current graduate students affirms on his office door, "social science is inevitably moral science." Claims of this kind may turn out to be true, but the problem is that when we treat them as axiomatic we are not strongly inclined to test them. And in the case of functionalism there is usually the additional implication that not only do our biases enter into the theory, but it is the theory itself that creates the biases. The null hypothesis, as usual, states that there is no relationship between functional analysis (or any other form of theory) and the various errors committed by its practitioners. As good scientists, we must adhere to the null hypothesis until we are compelled by strong evidence to abandon it. In my opinion, such evidence does not exist in the history of functional theory.

Although most authors who make reference to Davis's presidential speech emphasize his claim that functional analysis is just another name for general sociology, we saw in Chapter 1 that his argument was more elaborate and far-reaching than the usual summaries imply. What Davis clearly intended was a powerful *indictment* against general sociology, one that has a straightforward, albeit appalling, syllogistic form:

(1) We are all functionalists;

(2) Functionalism is a faulty paradigm;

We all do faulty work.

This book argues vehemently that it is not now true, nor has it ever been true, that all social scientists are functionalists under any detailed conventional definition. Yet, I do agree that many social scientists have attached the label of functionalism, sometimes arbitrarily, to their own unique

142

brand of social inquiry, and that most critics of these various theory groups have committed what Demerath (1967) calls the "synecdochic fallacy": They attack the part as if it were the whole. This book also argues that there are no special methodological weaknesses that distinguish functional analysis from other forms of analysis. If we finally reject the alleged universality of the functionalist paradigm, along with the notion that those who favor this paradigm somehow hobble themselves ideologically or methodologically, we will have rejected both premises of Davis's argument. It is worth remembering, however, that a valid syllogism may have two false premises and still contain a true conclusion.

As we read the not inglorious history of functional analysis, we soon discover that we have entered a Hegelian dream world filled with theses, antitheses, attempted syntheses, and new departures, and that at any given historical moment functionalists of a given variety are struggling vigorously against those of a slightly different variety, or perhaps against a vociferous school of nonfunctionalists or even antifunctionalists. As we listen further to the many strident voices that make up this history, we see the wisdom of Ritzer's claim (1980:201–8) that paradigm disputes probably do more harm than good. To paraphrase two eminent early functionalists, we can say that the history of all hitherto existing functional analysis is the history of paradigm struggles carried on in an uninterrupted, now hidden, now open fight, a fight that each time ended either in a revolutionary reconstitution of the several paradigms or in the common ruin of the contending parties.

Fortunately, ruin has occurred only on a limited scale, although we have witnessed any number of reconstitutions. Most of these seem to have weakened the functionalist paradigm at least as much as they strengthened it. In Harris's excellent chapters on the subject (1968) it becomes clear that historical functionalism has damaged itself in several ways: First, its early overindulgence in organicism, social Darwinism, racism, sexism, and unilinear evolutionary theory (parallelism); second, its subsequent over-reliance on synchronic (cross-sectional) analysis, its occasional repudiation of structural "survivals," its occasional indulgence in hopelessly abstract Hegelian idealism, its apparent conservatism, and its alleged willingness to tolerate questionable research practices. Although I consider most functionalists to be guilty on at least one of these counts, I believe that extenuating circumstances require clemency and perhaps even amnesty. In any case, regardless of how severely we casti-

gate functionalists, we must recognize that the lengthy list of charges
against them does not necessarily tell us anything about the strengths and
weaknesses of functional analysis. The occurrence of an occasional illness
reveals little about the general condition of the organism.

One who wishes to comprehend the wonderful and dreadful panoply of
nineteenth-century functionalism cannot do better than to examine the
thought of a man whose works are said to encompass all the major
intellectual trends of the century, Herbert Spencer. Martindale (1960:65)
gives Spencer credit for having provided the philosophical basis for "positivistic organicism," and a detailed examination of Spencer's organicism
makes it clear that, once we have stripped away a few quaint and perhaps
outrageous notions no longer taken seriously, it subsumes or surpasses all
the essential premises of modern functionalism, including neofunctional-
ism with its revival of social evolutionism. Martindale (1960:67) summarizes Spencer's organic analogy as follows:

(1) society undergoes growth; (2) in the course of its growth, its parts become
unlike (that is, there is a structural differentiation); (3) the functions of society are
reciprocal, mutually independent, and interrelated; (4) like an ordinary organism,
the society may be viewed as a nation of units; and (5) the whole may be destroyed without at once destroying the life of the parts.

I embrace these premises so strongly that I think it fair to say that this
entire volume is merely an elaboration of a few of them. If the sociology
of the twentieth century had been content to pursue the Spencerian premises to their logical conclusions as a way of understanding social dynamics, rather than pointing to the inevitable limitations of the organic analogy and to the many faults, foibles, and egregious claims of Spencer and
his followers, contemporary sociology probably would be in a stronger
position than it is. A perusal of Spencer's sociology – never mind his many
contributions to philosophy, biology, and psychology – shows that it is, as
Lenin once said of Clausewitz's writings on war, a splendid collection of
fine points.

Consider a small sample:

Each advance in [the] nervous system which, using the information coming
through the senses, excites and guides . . . external organs, becomes established
by giving an advantage to its possessor in presence of prey, enemies, and competi-
tors. On glancing up from low types of animals having but rudimentary eyes and
small powers of motion, to high types of animals having wide vision, considerable
intelligence, and great activity, it becomes undeniable that where loss of life is
entailed on the first by these defects, life is preserved in the last by these superi-
orities. The implication, then, is that successive improvements of the organs of

sense and motion, and of the internal co-ordinating apparatus which uses them, have indirectly resulted from the antagonisms and competitions of organisms with one another (Spencer, 1969:80).

Next, he draws the analogy to social systems:

A parallel truth is disclosed on watching how there evolves the regulating system of a political aggregate, and how there are developed those appliances for offence and defence put in action by it. Everywhere the wars between societies originate governmental structures . . . . Observe, first, the conditions under which there is an absence of this agency furthering combination; and then observe the conditions under which this agency begins to show itself (Spencer, 1969:80–81, 269).

Spencer provides a series of such observations. Immediately, then, we find ourselves in the presence of a sophisticated functionalist theory about the growth of state power, and we also note that a large burden of proof falls upon those who insist that functionalism does not come to grips with conflict: One cannot simultaneously criticize Spencer for an overindulgence in social Darwinism and functionalism for a reluctance to address social conflict. In elaborating his theory, Spencer appends some thoughts about political leadership:

As this differentiation by which there arises first a temporary and then a permanent military head, who passes insensibly into a political head, is initiated by conflict with adjacent societies, it naturally happens that his political power increases as military activity continues. Everywhere . . . we find this connexion between predatory activity and submission to despotic rule (Spencer, 1969:84).

In his treatment of social differentiation and "the regulating system," Spencer alludes to one of the major megatrends of contemporary advanced societies:

If, with those early stages in which the rudimentary industrial organization is ruled by the chief, and with those intermediate stages in which, as it develops, it gets a partially-separate political control, we contrast a late stage like our own, characterized by an industrial organization which has become predominant, we find that this has evolved for itself a substantially-independent control (Spencer, 1969:104).

The secular trend, in other words, is toward differentiation of political and economic institutions. To Spencer this differentiation may have seemed fitting and proper, but to the modern Marxian functionalist the issue is fundamental: Do modern multinational corporations possess "global reach," and how does this structural condition serve various interests and fail to serve others? With all his prescience, Spencer anticipates the increasing differentiation and autonomy of large industrial, commercial, and service organizations, and it would be fascinating to know what he would make of the refusal of a major American corporation to sell oil to the United States Navy during the 1973 Arab oil embargo (Barnet and Muller, 1974:77–8).

In his discussion of "social metamorphoses," it becomes clear that Spencer has a strong sense of the sometimes discontinuous character of social evolution:

Verification of the general view . . . is gained by observing the alterations of social structures which follow alterations of social activities; and here again we find analogies between social organisms and individual organisms. In both there is metamorphosis consequent on change from a wandering life to a settled life; in both there is metamorphosis consequent on change from a life exercising mainly the inner or sustaining system, to a life exercising the outer or expanding system; and in both there is a reverse metamorphosis (Spencer, 1969:136).

Warfare remains the engine of social evolution, but with a surprising twist:

The struggle for existence has been an indispensable means to evolution. Not simply do we see that in the competition among individuals of the same kind, survival of the fittest has from the beginning furthered production of a higher type; but we see that to the unceasing warfare between species is mainly due both growth and organization. . . . Mark now, however, that while this merciless discipline of Nature . . . has been essential to the progress of sentient life, its persistence through all time with all creatures must not be inferred. . . . The myriads of years of warfare which have developed the powers of all lower types of creatures, have bequeathed to the highest type of creature the powers now used by him for countless objects besides those of killing and avoiding being killed. His limbs, teeth, and nails are but little employed in fight; and his mind is not ordinarily occupied in devising ways of destroying other creatures, or guarding himself from injury by them. . . . Observe that the inter-social struggle for existence which has been indispensable in evolving societies, will not necessarily play in the future a part like that which it has played in the past (Spencer, 1969:176–7,178).

Notice the irony: The man who coined the phrase "survival of the fittest" (Harris, 1968:128) brings forth a theory that implies a social metamorphosis in which past warmaking adaptations either lose their functionality or evolve in such a way as to take on new nonwarmaking functions. Spencer, then, clearly envisions the occasional disassociation of structure and function (do we then find "survivals?") and makes imaginative use of that disassociation as a mechanism of social transformation. And if Spencer's functionalism does not have any ultimate commitment to social conflict, perhaps more recent versions of functionalism do not, or need not, have any ultimate commitment to social integration, cooperation, and consensus. Similarly, the presumed association of functional analysis with a particular brand of politics may also turn out to be untenable, as Merton (1957: 37–46) once argued. Our politics may be largely a matter of personal predilection, not theoretical necessity.

Although the organic analogy flourished in the latter part of the nineteenth century largely because of the immense successes of Darwinian biology, we should not lose sight of the fact that evolutionary theory in biology owes more to sociology than sociology owes to biology. Harris (1968:114) reminds us that Darwin, Wallace, and Lyell were all avid readers of Malthus and received valuable insights from that imposing, profoundly sociological mind. And instead of calling Spencer a social Darwinist, it would make far more sense to call Darwinism a form of "biological Spencerism" (Harris, 1968:129). *Social* evolutionary theories were widely accepted both by scholars and by large segments of public opinion long before Darwin and Wallace's biological breakthrough, and Darwin and Wallace had deep credibility problems with academicians and public opinion alike that continue to the present day. In any case biology and sociology by the latter half of the nineteenth century had become closely enlaced, and it also had become clear, as it has again in recent years, that sociology gets into trouble when it begins relying too heavily on biology or gives up too much ground to biology.

Take a case in point: In Harris's (1968:129) words,

from the point of view of the history of theories of culture, it is Spencer and not Darwin who bears the greatest share of the onus of having crippled the explanatory power of cultural evolutionary theory by merging and mixing it with racial determinism.

Harris (1968:137) devotes a few excoriating paragraphs to "Lewis Henry Morgan, Racist" and to "Edward Burnett Tylor, Racist," two famous scholars noted primarily for their fine contributions to evolutionary functional analysis. In Spencer's case we should note that his sexism was hardly less appalling than his racism:

That absolute or relative infertility is generally produced in women by mental labour carried to excess, is . . . clearly shown. Though the regimen of upper-class girls is not what it should be, yet, considering that their feeding is better than that of girls belonging to the poorer classes, while in most other respects, their physical treatment is not worse, the deficiency of reproductive power among them may be reasonably attributed to the overtaxing of their brains – an overtaxing which produces a serious reaction on the physique. This diminution of reproductive power is not shown only by the greater frequency of absolute sterility; nor is it shown only in the earlier cessation of child bearing; but it is also shown in the very frequent inability of such women to suckle their infants. In its full sense, the reproductive power means the power to bear a well-developed infant, and to supply that infant with the natural food for the natural period. Most of the flat-chested girls who survive their high-pressure education are incompetent to do this (Spencer, 1867–8:485–6).

These ridiculous claims, of course, are highly distasteful to all contemporary scholars except those who run about obtaining correlations of IQ and breast size. One might point out in Spencer's favor, however, that he intended his thoughts on fecundity (and its reduction) to be an answer to the "dismal" views of Malthus (Harris, 1968:127). It is most comforting to discover that neither Spencer nor Morgan nor Tylor was ever able to demonstrate how racism or sexism were inevitable deductions from the postulates of evolutionary functionalism. The truth is, they are not. In Harris's view (1968:140), all these aberrations arise mainly out of confusion:

In his *Anthropology* (1899), the first textbook in the field, Tylor displays little understanding of the difference between racial and cultural capacities. . . . In this fashion, the greatest figures of late-nineteenth-century anthropology fell under the spell of racial determinism. Even when the racial factor simply hovered over a discussion without actually coming to roost, it crippled the attempt to apply scientific methods to sociocultural phenomena.

It is arguable, then, that the worst nineteenth-century snafus of the second wave of functionalists (following the likes of Locke, Smith, and Malthus) resulted from the fact that biology was very much in the air. Similarly, the stigmata that have affixed themselves to contemporary North American versions of functional analysis may have arisen out of the prevailing *political* climate of recent decades:

The very dates of the steep rise of interest in functionalism among [recent] sociological theorists also suggest that it may have some ideological import. It arose after 1940 and with particular speed after World War II. Moreover, its ranks have been increasingly swelled by deserters from social behaviorism – an evidently liberal position. The rise of sociological functionalism thus coincides with the return of the Republican Party to power, the return to religion, the rise of McCarthyism, and other typical manifestations of a postwar conservative reaction. Whether these are just accidental correlations or not, it is certainly true that ideological factors are now far less important for the structure of sociological theory than was once the case (Martindale, 1960:520).

I doubt that ideology is now *less* important than heretofore, primarily because I see so little evidence of its past significance as an inescapable determinant or consequence of one's theoretical strategies. I have yet to discover evidence that the conservatism of a scholar such as Spencer was a necessary consequence of his positivistic organicism, I do not see how the "integrative" functionalism (and its associated politics) of recent years is compatible with the conflict functionalism (and its associated politics) of the Spencerians, I have grave doubts that the arrival into the functionalist camp of liberal social behaviorists had a large political impact on either field (cf. Faia, 1974), and I do not see any reason to believe that Martindale is calling our attention to anything except "accidental correlations," as he himself surmises. An accidental correlation, of course, does not lead us to reject the null hypothesis.

On the matter of Spencer's distrust of government, his consequent laissez-faire predilections, and the relationship of these to his sociological theories, Barnes (1948:129) has provided the definitive alternative hypothesis. Spencer, he says, had an "anti-authority complex" exacerbated by experiences of childhood, especially his "domination by male relatives, and his confirmed neurotic tendencies." We must also remember, says Barnes, that Spencer came from a ". . . dissenting family and was reared in that atmosphere." It seems, says Barnes, "that his attitude toward government must have had a deep-rooted emotional foundation, since it diverged materially from some of the vital premises of his general philosophy." I realize that this sort of psychohistory may have fallen out of fashion lately, but it explains Spencer's politics far more plausibly than does his advocacy of evolutionary positivistic organicism. If anybody ever returns a diagnosis of neuroticism in the case of Talcott Parsons, the thesis that politics are sharply constrained by theories, or vice versa, will receive yet another deserved and devastating setback.

The Spencerian system dominated functionalist sociology during the first several decades of the present century, and this fact is clearly evidenced in the works of Durkheim and Vilfredo Pareto. Most contemporary social scientists have a deep and detailed appreciation of Durkheim's functionalism (it is cited throughout this volume), but Pareto has fallen into an oblivion as total, and as inexplicable, as that of Spencer. For a time in the United States Pareto received a careful reading and had a profound impact (Lazarsfeld, 1970:104):

The entry [of functionalism] into sociology came about through a collaboration of Talcott Parsons, then a young teacher at Harvard, with his senior colleague, L. J. Henderson, a biologist, who jointly studied and admired the books of Wilfredo Pareto. From the Harvard group a galaxy of sociologists emerged, mainly Americans . . . . The 'official' publication for this period is Parsons' *The Social System* . . . Robert Merton's 'Manifest and Latent Functions' . . . represents an historical turning point inasmuch as it takes a functional position but at the same time tries to carve out yet unsolved problems. Practically every subsequent publication quotes Merton's paper. It consists of two main parts. The first summarizes and criticizes what one might call early radical functionalism. It may be reduced to three prevailing postulates:

a. Specific social items are functional for the entire social system;
b. All social items fulfill sociological functions;
c. The items are consequently indispensable.

A careful reading of Merton's text shows that he does not at all claim that such radical functionalism ever existed.

Although an examination of Merton's work is inappropriate at this point, it is appropriate to examine Pareto's functionalism with a view toward seeing whether he was a major source of "early radical functionalism," a question which, despite the terminology, is tantamount to asking whether Pareto – as tradition would have it – was the "Marx of the bourgeoisie." If I were a member of the bourgeoisie, I would be mildly discomfited by Pareto's famous remark that "history is a cemetery of the aristocracies," by his "law" about emerging economic conditions that reduce income inequality (Lopreato, 1980:xvii), and by his claim that in the United States ". . . the chief actual instrument of governing . . . is the political 'machine' " and that "the administration in power 'looks after' the interests of the speculators and often without any explicit understanding with them" (1980:336).

Let us begin by clarifying the central issue: Anybody who accepts the postulate of universal functionality tends to see any given social structure as having strong persistence, a persistence that surely goes beyond the inertia characterizing a structural "survival." As we have implied in an earlier discussion, structures have functionality either because they serve interests or because they contribute to survivorship or both. If universal functionality prevails, it prevails because whenever we try to eliminate even those structures that appear to be "survivals" – say, the Electoral College in the United States – we typically encounter strong resistance from assorted interest groups. The postulate of universal functionality does not necessarily commit its adherents to some sort of antichange orientation or to laissez-faire politics. The postulate has the virtue that once we understand what it means, we realize that it is subject to empirical test: We merely try to eliminate a structure and observe what happens (Stinchcombe, 1968: passim). And even when change is resisted, it clearly is not ruled out: An efficient internal-combustion engine has universal functionality in that each part plays a crucial role and has persistence due to the causal impacts of many other parts, but we can readily improve the behavior of an engine by adding a turbocharger, or we can stop an engine the easy way by cutting the ignition or the hard way by taking hold of the flywheel.

I have always believed that many of the laissez-faire philosophers were merely warning us against grabbing flywheels, and I therefore believe that Harris (1968:534–5) goes too far when he says that

[there is] an analogy between the entire synchronic functionalist movement and the classical laissez-faire doctrines of economics. . . . This analogy . . . is an undeniable consequence of both the Malinowskian and Radcliffe-Brownian versions of [radical] functionalism that every sort of institution, from witchcraft to war, receives its due as a functional contribution to the welfare and maintenance of the social system. . . .

I believe that an objective appraisal of the contribution of the structural-functionalists requires one to acknowledge the streak of intellectual know-nothingism which flourished in their work despite the ostensible emphasis upon scientism and orderliness. . . .

The point . . . is not to criticize the functionalists for their political and ethical beliefs, about which we are at any rate very badly informed. The know-nothingism to which I refer is a scientific rather than an ethical problem. It is an affliction which leads the functionalists to ignore . . . the amount of order that human history exhibits. . . . It fails to come to grips with the fact that the evolutionary careers of . . . sociocultural systems consist of an array of eminently functional structures, all doomed to extinction.

Perhaps these charges can be made against Malinowski and (more debatably) against Radcliffe-Brown, but they can hardly be sustained against Spencer, who never insisted upon universal functionality and whose laissez-faire proclivities cannot possibly have been derived from the antievolutionism of later British social anthropologists; Spencer obviously did not subscribe to it. Nor can the charges be sustained against Pareto. Even Malinowski and Radcliffe-Brown did not play down the evolutionary themes because of some latent commitment to know-nothingism or to laissez-faire politics, but rather because they wished to disassociate themselves from the ethnocentric evolutionary theories of some of their predecessors and to escape the recrudescence of social Darwinism, racism, and sexism that had stained the escutcheons of Spencerian theory. Harris himself (1968:54) points to one of the positive consequences of the self-regulating laissez-faire model when he says that, as exemplified in the works of Jeremy Bentham, James Mill, David Ricardo, and John McCulloch, it contributed to ". . . the perpetuation of the scientific ap-

proach." And returning to the image of an internal-combustion engine –
the "GM analogy" (Parsons, 1937:31,230; cf. Parsons, 1954:238) in contrast to the organic analogy – we realize that the properties of self-
regulation do not preclude an occasional overhaul.

As for Pareto, perhaps we should begin by questioning the ugliest of
the political accusations against him, that he somehow aided and abetted
the Italian fascist movement. In Lopreato's assessment (1980:xix–xx),
Pareto realized by 1922

that fascism was a fleeting phenomenon, greatly inferior to the socialist faith, and
defined fascism as a complex of factors destined to "remain secondary and subor-
dinate to the great factors of social evolution". . . .
However, his political theory speaks the loudest. Pareto was a political skeptic.
His theory of revolution conveys a powerful message: all regimes become deca-
dent and nasty as they mature. He was also a humanist who fought ceaselessly for
democracy of the Swiss variety, for freedom of religion and the press, against
racism and anti-semitism, for freedom of any sort of organization. If that is the
stuff that fascists are made of, then Pareto was indeed one of them.

As we explore his theoretical writings, we discover that Pareto developed a system of social thought that was soon to be recognized by
another famous Harvard professor, Sorokin (1928:37–62), as a brilliant
"quantitative description of the functional interdependence of social
phenomena" that eschewed "one-sided causation" and insisted upon a
dynamic analysis of phenomena called "residues" and "derivations,"
which Pareto (1980:164) defines as follows:

The residues are manifestations of sentiments. The derivations comprise logical
reasonings, unsound reasonings, and manifestations of sentiments used for purposes of derivation: they are manifestations of the human being's hunger for
thinking. If that hunger were satisfied by logico-experimental reasonings only,
there would be no derivations; instead of them we should get logico-experimental
theories. But the human hunger for thinking is satisfied in any number of
ways. . . .

Although I agree with Sorokin (1928:61) when he says that Pareto's
residues are not clearly defined, I am willing to accept his suggestion
that we consider the residues to be more or less synonymous with "economic interests;" actually, I would be happy to equate the residues with
the "basic needs" of Malinowski or perhaps with a host of needs,
wishes, sentiments, and drives that I vaguely remember memorizing as a
graduate student, including security, new experience, recognition, response, hunger, vanity, sex, fear, health, wealth, sociability, knowledge,
beauty, righteousness; the list goes on forever, or at least it did at one

time. In short, to understand Pareto we must be attuned to the possibility that social structures – and even Pareto's derivations, which are primarily mental phenomena – serve an assortment of interests, be they biological or derived.

In an early discussion of Pareto, Sorokin invites us to undertake the appropriate time-series analyses of the residues and derivations when he points out (1928:53) that the residues have a lower "tempo" and "amplitude" of change than do the derivations, a topic discussed in Chapter 4. He also believes that given the instability of the derivations there must be a substantial amount of functional equivalence among them (1928:54), thereby calling our attention to an idea that has become a central aspect of modern functional analysis:

> In the past the residue of obedience was manifested principally in a subordination to the kings, priests, and nobility. Now these are slandered, but the residue remains and manifests itself in an obedience to the demagogues, leaders of labor unions, captains of industry, and so forth. The "dresses" are different, but the residue is the same. The residue for imposing uniformity on the members of society has been manifested in the past in religious intolerance, in . . . attacks on private property, divorces, short skirts, and so on. Now we are tolerant in this respect, but instead we have an intolerance toward drinking (prohibition), and toward any criticism of the actions of reformers . . . and so on. Derivations have changed, but the residues remain.

The importance of these insights is not vitiated by the fact that each of them may be wrong. They are important because they exemplify the principles of functional equivalence, possible substitutability, and the occasional disassociation of structure and function that may produce structural survivals.

To me, the strength of Pareto's (1980) form of functionalism derives from features that are merely elaborated upon in the present volume: the sharp distinction between objective and subjective aspects of social behavior (5–6,19); the strong emphasis on "rationalization and non-logical conduct" (ch. III), a thesis that is the harbinger of the later concept of "latent functions;" the serious questioning of social darwinism as an exclusionary sociological orientation (109–10); the incisive analysis of what appears to be a "strain toward consistency" among the mental processes that make up the derivations (168); the awareness of reciprocal causation among the residues and among the derivations and between these two categories (215); the recognition of afunctionality, that is, the possibility of survivals with the many insights they provide into social change (221) and the opportunities they provide for introducing social change; the anticipation of Chambliss's (1966) distinction between "instrumental" and "expressive" forms of deviance, and an appreciation of the special difficulties encountered in trying to suppress the latter (229); the theory of revolution, based on the "circulation of elites" and the confrontation of competing elites (272–9); the clear comprehension of the human ecological perspective as set forth much later in the POET paradigm (280); a clear understanding of the place of "oscillations" in history (357–64).

Again, I must provide a sample of the many functionalist hypotheses found in Pareto's work. Consider, first, the functions of baptism and the derivations surrounding them:

> Christians have the custom of baptism. If one knew the Christian procedure only one would not know whether and how it could be analyzed. Moreover, we have an explanation of it: we are told that the rite of baptism is celebrated in order to remove original sin. . . . If we had no other facts of the same class to go by, we should find it difficult to isolate the elements in the complex phenomenon of baptism. But we do have other facts . . . The pagans too had lustral water, and they used it for purposes of purification. If we stopped at that, we might associate the use of water with the fact of purification. But other cases of baptism show that the use of water is not a constant element. Blood may be used for purification, and other substances as well. . . . So the circle of similar facts widens, and in the great variety of devices and in the many explanations that are given for their use the thing which remains constant is the feeling, the sentiment, that the integrity of an individual which has been altered by certain causes, real or imaginary, can be restored by certain rites (p.116).

This analysis makes a sharp distinction between what later came to be known as manifest and latent functions. It also demonstrates the utility of taxonomies that recognize the common elements among apparently disparate phenomena.

On the functions of the death penalty, he writes:

> Erroneous, therefore, are all those reasonings which, from the fact that a penalty is ineffective from the standpoint of logical conduct, conclude that it is ineffective in general. It is erroneous . . . to argue that the death-penalty is ineffective because logically, directly, it does not restrain a man from committing murder. The penalty works in a different way. In the first place . . . it does away with the murderer. . . . Then again it serves indirectly to invigorate sentiments of horror for crime (Pareto, 1980:230).

Again, we encounter a potential multiplicity of functions. If "horror for crime" has anything to do with deterrence, I have doubts about this particular hypothesis (Faia, 1982); it does, nevertheless, anticipate modern work on the effects of capital punishment. It is too bad that Pareto never conducted evaluation research on the effects of capital punishment, for then he would have been forced to say much more about the meaning and measurement of "horror for crime." Pareto's nonempirical predilections, unfortunately, carried over into the Parsonian traditions of functional analysis in the United States.

On the functions of protectionism, in cost–benefit format, he says:

Mathematical economics . . . supplied proof that, in general, the direct effect of protection is a destruction of wealth. For many economists the destruction of wealth is an "evil". . . . But before such a proposition can be granted the indirect economic effects and the social effects of protection have to be known. Keeping to the former, we find that protection, by transferring a certain amount of wealth from a part, *A* of the population to part *B,* through the destruction of a certain amount of wealth, *q,* is economically detrimental to a population as a whole; if it increases by a quantity greater than *q,* the operation is economically beneficial. But one has to distinguish between dynamic effects, which ensue for a brief period of time after protection has been established for a certain length of time. A distinction must further be drawn between the effects on productions that are really susceptible of increase, such as manufactures in general, and the effects on productions not so susceptible of increase, such as the agricultural (p.320).

In reading this argument, one is reminded of Merton's distinction between eufunctions and dysfunctions, and the net balance between them.

As suggested earlier, there has been for many years a sort of Hegelian dialectic among functionalists and between functionalists and their many detractors. In the early decades of this century, when the positivistic organicism of Comte, Spencer, Morgan, Tylor, Durkheim, Pareto and others began to disintegrate, the breach was filled quickly by a host of "trait diffusionists," mainly in Europe, and by the Boasian movement in the United States with its strong emphasis on idiographic interpretations of particular cultures, its strong distrust of nomothetic evolutionary theories with their typical unilinear postulates, and its understandable distaste for the racism and sexism of the organicists (Martindale, 1960:456; Harris, 1968:267). It is arguable, however, that the diffusionists, Boasians, and antievolutionists overreacted, and it was left for Bronislaw Malinowski and A. R. Radcliffe-Brown to attempt a reasonable, balanced synthesis, prior to the point, of course, where they begin fighting each other.

Martindale (1960:459) summarizes Malinowski's brand of functionalism as follows:

(1) it is accepted . . . as an axiom that human beings have needs for food, reproduction, shelter, etc.; (2) it is assumed that human drives are physiological but

restructured by acquired habit; (3) culture is conceived as a conditioning apparatus which through training in skills and norms amalgamates nature with nurture; (4) it is taken as fundamental that man never deals with his difficulties alone; he organizes . . . ; (5) the symbolism of language is a component in all technology and social organization; (6) cultural satisfaction of primary biological needs imposes secondary imperatives on man; (7) the functional theory postulates that the system of production, distribution, and consumption must be carried on even in the most primitive of communities.

This orientation seems to place an unduly strong emphasis on biology, and I therefore agree with Harris's (1968:531,561) point that Malinowski's scheme falters on the fact that we cannot adequately explain cultural variations with biological constants. Radcliffe-Brown expressed the same misgivings (Harris, 1968:515), thereby generating a lively series of altercations with Malinowski.

As he develops his theory further, Malinowski raises compelling questions about the unilinear predilections of earlier functionalists, about their use of the comparative method as a way of comprehending the distant history of human societies, and about the use of survivals as keys to the past. Malinowski's critics have accused him of adopting a horribly constraining synchronic approach to cultural anthropology – remember Harris's reference to the know-nothingism of the Malinowskians – but Malinowski himself (1944:16,175–6; 1982:60) makes it clear that his position is far from simplistic:

Modern anthropology started with the evolutionary point of view. In this it was largely inspired by the great successes of the Darwinian interpretations of biological development, and by the desire of cross-fertilizing prehistoric findings and ethnographic data. Evolutionism is at present rather unfashionable. Nevertheless, its main assumptions are not only valid, but also they are indispensable to the field-worker as well as to the student of theory. The concept of origins may have to be interpreted in a more prosaic and scientific manner, but our interest in tracing back any and every manifestation of human life . . . remains . . . legitimate. . . . I believe that ultimately we will accept the view that "origins" is nothing else but the essential nature of an institution like marriage or the nation, the family or the state, the religious congregation or the organization of witchcraft . . . .

Functionalism, I would like to state emphatically, is neither hostile to the study of distribution, nor to the reconstruction of the past in terms of evolution, history or diffusion.

Although I have trouble with Malinowski's equivocation over the meaning of "origins," I do not discern here an attitude of total hostility toward history; perhaps Malinowski was guilty only of taking seriously Pareto's contention (1980:77) that "in general the unknown has to be explained by the known, and the past is therefore better explained by the present than the present is by the past . . ." Nevertheless, Malinowski's outright rejection of the idea of survivals (1944:27–28, 142), with its consequent deemphasis on social evolution, seems to leave him wide open to the charge of pernicious know-nothingism and perhaps even to the charge of "conservative" bias in the form of a closed-minded insistence on the universal functionality of social structures:

There is . . . one point on which the various older schools have committed a sin of commission . . . . This is the uncritical and, at times, even anti-scientific concept of "dead-weights" or cultural fossils in human culture. . . . In evolutionary theories, such dead-weights appear under the guise of "survivals." . . . . When a habit ceases to be rewarded, reinforced, that is, vitally useful, it simply drops out. This is . . . our criticism of "survival," meaningless traits, irrelevant form, and similar concepts used as illegitimate devices of argument in the reconstructive work of certain evolutionary or diffusionist theories.

I suspect that the electoral college, among many other structures I could mention, is no longer "vitally useful," and I wish Malinowski were here to explain why it has not yet "dropped out." When he presents his famous allegory of the fork (1944:118), which to Harris (1968: 553) has the delightful implication that we understand a fork by paying heed ". . . to the service it renders in conveying food to the mouth," I wish that Malinowski were able to join me at my favorite Hollywood bar, order a bottle of retsina and a small dish of feta cheese, and then ask for a knife, or even a fork or a spoon, to slice the cheese. He would be told that, under a California law regarding the placing of eating utensils on bars, he must use his fingers. Between the retsina and the cheese, I would insist in a hostile way that he reformulate his allegory of the fork.

In a book unfriendly toward Malinowski, Jarvie (1967:187) explains Malinowski's rejection of survivals as having been essential to his continued warm relations with the Trobrianders, among whom he could hardly commit the indiscretion of suggesting that elements of the culture were superfluous. My initial reaction to Jarvie was one of incredulous outrage combined with the conviction that I would be willing to accompany Malinowski on our hypothetical Hollywood pub crawl no matter what he might say about the electoral college. But I soon realized that Jarvie's hypothesis is at least as plausible as Barnes's hypothesis, cited earlier, regarding Spencer's alleged neuroticism, and that both these hypotheses are more plausible than the usual contention that a theoretician's eccentricities must result from his theories.

The apparent problem, however, is that Malinowski correctly discerns the abuses of the earlier evolutionists, not to mention the diffusionists and the Boasians, and then proceeds, in the manner of so many of his predecessors, to overreact. I do not insist that the electoral college is a survival, but I maintain that we cannot tell whether it is or is not unless we have several "natural experiments" in which a serious attempt is made to eliminate it. If the resistance turns out to be nonexistent or weak or readily overcome, then the electoral college is shown to have been a survival, provided one can discern its historical functions. When Harris argues (1968:171,232) that the nineteenth-century evolutionary theories, for all their faults, were not nearly so unilinear and ethnocentric as we often imagine, that on the other hand the inherent linearity of technological development imposes a degree of linearity on social evolution, and that brilliant, neglected minds of the last century (for instance, Adam Ferguson [Harris, 1968:30]) did excellent work involving evolutionary stages, we are tempted to ignore Malinowski's warnings altogether and to begin anew to examine history in the Spencerian manner. In writing history we surely must avoid the worst of Malinowski's failings, especially his insistence on universal functionality and his application of an equilibrium model so misleading that, prior to World War II, he made the prediction (in Harris's view, an absurd prediction [1968:557,561]) that Europeans and their African colonial subjects "were about to become part of one big happy Kula ring." Perhaps Harris is not altogether fair when he says that "it is in large measure because Malinowski could not shake loose from the functionalist emphasis upon equilibrium that his theory never gets off the ground" (1968:559), but it does seem clear that Malinowski had a deplorable tendency to hobble himself in ways that were totally unnecessary. His presupposition against survivals is perhaps the best example.

Radcliffe-Brown's many warnings against "conjectural" history seem far better balanced than those of Malinowski. Radcliffe-Brown recognizes (1952:50), with Pareto, that the trouble with conjectural history

is not that it is historical, but that it is conjectural. History shows us how certain events or changes in the past have led to certain other events or conditions, and thus reveals human life in a particular region of the world as a chain of connected happenings. But it can do this only when there is direct evidence for both the preceding and succeeding events or conditions and also some actual evidence of their interconnection. In conjectural history we have direct knowledge about a state of affairs existing at a certain time and place, without any adequate knowledge of the preceding conditions or events . . . .

Radcliffe-Brown simply backs away from an attempt to explain the origins of the "Omaha" system of kinship (1952:85), arguing that "the only possible way of answering the question why a particular society has the social system that it does have is by a detailed study of its history over a sufficient period, generally several centuries. For the tribes with which we are here concerned the materials for such a history are entirely lacking" (1952:85). I find this attitude appropriate and, indeed, inescapable whenever we raise questions that we cannot answer: It is adopted throughout this book in connection with the question of survivorship of social systems and, specifically, in Chapter 2, where Tylor's thought experiments on the origins of the incest taboo are discussed. In the latter case, I try to make it clear that the Tylor theory is merely an exercise in conjectural history, albeit a most enlightening one.

As for equilibrium, there is for Radcliffe-Brown (1952:43) nothing magical about it:

One . . . necessary condition of continued existence [of social systems] is that of a certain degree of functional consistency amongst the constituent parts of the social system. Functional consistency is not the same thing as logical consistency; the latter is one special form of the former. Functional inconsistency exists whenever two aspects of the social system produce a conflict which can only be resolved by some change in the system itself. . . . No social system ever attains to a perfect consistency, and it is for this reason that every system is constantly undergoing change.

Perhaps Gregg and Williams (1948) have a point in accusing Malinowski of being charmed and seduced by the notion of "functioning harmonious wholes," but they cannot make a similar charge against Radcliffe-Brown.

Radcliffe-Brown (1952) produced a series of excellent papers about the functions of such phenomena as classificatory kinship systems (66–67), informal "joking" relationships between persons of different generations (96), totemism (132), and magic (ch. VII). The flavor of this work is captured nicely by the following remarks about joking relationships of individuals with their parents and grandparents:

The social tradition is handed down from one generation to the next. For the tradition to be maintained it must have authority behind it. The authority is therefore normally recognized [sic] as possessed by members of the preceding generation and it is they who exercise discipline. As a result of this the relation between persons of the two generations usually contains an element of inequality . . . . The unequal relation between a father and his son is maintained by requiring the latter to show respect to the former. . . .

When we turn to the relation of an individual to his grandparents and their brothers and sisters we find that in the majority of human societies relatives of the second ascending generation are treated with very much less respect than those of the first ascending generation . . . .

Authority, then, is respected over age, knowledge, and experience – perhaps another instance in which the famous Davis–Moore theory (1945) falters. As we assess Radcliffe-Brown's many similar insights, our only disappointment is his insistence that because "societies do not die in the same way that animals die . . ." (1935:398), it follows that ". . . the function of a social activity is to be found by examining its effects upon individuals" (1935: 400). Radcliffe-Brown, in other words, substitutes crania for Malinowski's broader range of biological factors. He should have dealt much more with the survival of social organizations.

Incidentally, the moment we begin to examine survivorship, entertaining hypotheses about structural features that may enhance or impede the viability of organizations, or may have no impact at all, we have resolved the issue of universal functionality in a way that would surely please Radcliffe-Brown, whose approach did not ". . . require the dogmatic assertion that everything in the life of every community has a function" (1935:399). And once functionalists recognize the existence of dysfunctions, any bias toward stability is effectively removed.

All these preliminaries bring us to Talcott Parsons. Various secondary sources provide excellent summaries of Parsons's copious writings at various stages of his career (Abrahamson, 1981: ch. 3; Martindale, 1960: 484–90; Ritzer, 1983: ch. 7; Toby, 1977; Turner, 1974: ch. 3; Zeitlin, 1973: chs. 2, 3). My own summary incorporates these and adds several points that appear to have been neglected:

1. Action – "the structures and processes by which human beings form meaningful intentions and implement them in concrete situations" (Parsons, 1977:249) – involves a goal, a motivation, a situation, and normative regulation (Abrahamson, 1981:47). These four characteristics may be illustrated by describing a man driving to a lake to go fishing: "fishing is the goal; driving there takes effort requiring motivation; the car, the road, and so on, describe the situation; and the way the man drives down the road reflects normative regulation" (Abrahamson, 1981:47). Actions combine to form subsystems: personality, the social system, culture, and the "organism" (Turner, 1974:40). A social system, or society, is a large-scale, persistent, independent system of action consisting of status roles and meeting various prerequisites; institutions consist of integrated and standardized status roles (Martindale, 1960:488).

2. Role expectations can be analyzed by means of the "pattern variables:" affectivity versus affective neutrality, self-orientation versus collectivity-orientation, universalism versus particularism, achievement versus ascription, and specificity versus diffuseness (Martindale, 1960:489). The polarities of social action to which these variables call our attention may be defined, respectively, as follows: "to seek immediate gratification or exert restraint . . . ; to pursue private goals or collective interests . . . ; to treat people (or objects) as elements of a class, or according to their unique qualities . . . ; to emphasize given attributes of people (or objects), or their performance . . . ; to respond to restricted situational qualities, or to general features" (Abrahamson, 1981:49; cf. Turner, 1974:36).

3. During a period when Parsons emphasized requisite analysis (Turner, 1974:39), action systems were deemed to present four "survival problems" involving the four functions known by the acronym AGIL: *Adaptation* "involves the problem of securing from the environment sufficient facilities and then distributing these facilities throughout the system." *Goal attainment* is ". . . the problem of establishing priorities among system goals and mobilizing system resources for their attainment." *Integration* is ". . . the problem of coordinating and maintaining viable interrelationships among system units." *Latency* refers to ". . . two related problems: pattern maintenance and tension management," with the first pertaining to the operation of sanction systems, the second to ways of dealing with "internal tensions and strains of actors in the social system" (Turner, 1974:39).

4. Among the four action subsystems (culture, social structure, personality, and organism) there is a cybernetic hierarchy of control, with ". . . culture informationally circumscribing the social system, social structure informationally regulating the personality system, and personality informationally regulating the organismic system" (Turner, 1974:41). Interrelationships among the four action systems generally involve "exchange media" such as money, power, and influence.

5. Although *The Structure of Social Action*, Parsons's first major work, opens with the question, "Who now reads Spencer?" and continues with a critique of Spencerian evolutionary theory, more recent work by Parsons (1977) revives and reexamines the issue of social evolution.

For something like 30 years, starting around 1940, Parsons's work was a dominant paradigm in American and perhaps European sociology. In Alexander's view (1983:7) the strength of Parsonian thought derives mainly from its multidimensionality, that is, from its tendency to focus on the interactions of biology, personality, society, and culture. The cybernetic continuum, operating through various exchange media, makes possible a degree of integration of highly disparate social phenomena, so that society is seen as constituting the ultimate form of Spencer's "coherent heterogeneity." Parsons's predilection for multidimensionality made him a strong believer in the benefits of paradigm integration in the social sciences (Alexander, 1983: 45, 152; Parsons, 1937: x; Parsons, 1954:223), although his efforts, ironically, have probably caused more contention than consensus. Nevertheless, Parsons's early claim (1937) that a synthesis of Marshall, Pareto, Durkheim, and Weber would be the best strategy for the modern social sciences remains essentially correct, especially if the synthesis contains an appropriate element of Marxism. In Toby's estimation (1977:2) *The Structure of Social Action* has served to correct the tendency of positivism to neglect values and the tendency of idealism to neglect environmental conditions.

Although Parsons never attempted a systematic formulation of functional analysis in the style of Merton (1957: ch. 1), the functionalist premises are adumbrated throughout his works, primarily in the form of abstract hypotheses and generalizations that, given Parsons's limited interest in empirical verification, were rarely tested at the level of concrete phenomena. The cybernetic continuum (Alexander, 1983:29) places us squarely in the functionalist realm of discourse. Parsons's numerous discussions of the socialization of sex roles in schools (Alexander, 1983:141; Parsons, 1951:240–3) and in the nuclear family (Alexander, 1983:57), although they bear the taint of sexism, involve the central functionalist imagery of structural conditions having an impact on social integration. Parsons's requisite analysis, with all its assorted untenabilities, appears early in his writings not merely in connection with the four-functions thesis (AGIL) but in the clever and unique argument that various combinations of the pattern variables may be functionally improbable if not impossible (Parsons, 1951: 152,160; cf. Heise, 1967). Parsons has a clear imagery of "structured strain" and its ability to produce adaptive efforts or to disrupt stability. He occasionally interprets social systems from the standpoint of what I call the GM analogy (Parsons, 1937:31, 230), and he never seems to regard reciprocating engines, at least, as being inherently smooth running. His insistence that utilitarian theory is built upon the mistaken notion of "randomness of ends," and that this venerable theory therefore fails to explain ends adequately (1937:59–60, 231), forces us to examine reciprocal interaction between ends and other aspects of the social system, and this is clearly a functionalist endeavor. When

Parsons (1937:346) points to Durkheim's thesis on the "anteriority" of social facts, implying that many social facts therefore do not have utilitarian value for given actors, he inadvertently introduces the important concept of structural survivals and the possibility of a disassociation of structure and function. Despite his commitment to requisite analysis, Parsons (1951:167–77) has a clear recognition of the possibility of functional alternatives. His understanding of net balance is reflected in an analysis of the cybernetic regulation of gambling (1951:307). Finally, Parsons has a surprising comprehension of the interaction of theory and research and of the ways in which this interaction may arrive at functionalist culminations (1954:219), and his discussion of accountability (1977:212) shows a strong appreciation of evaluative research – functional analysis par excellence.

In his history of anthropological thought, Harris (1968:99) says of the field of phrenology that its ". . . measurements were notoriously imprecise, and the entire system functioned as a kind of projective test in which the observer could match his prejudices to arbitrary eminences and ridges on his subject's head." Those who have examined the eminences and ridges of Parsonian thought often have brought with them similar sets of prejudices and presuppositions, and if we rely too heavily on these secondary sources in evaluating Parsons's work we risk being badly misled. My own exercises in Parsonian phrenology have led to the following catalog of anti-Parsonian allegations:

1. A large part of Kingsley Davis's presidential address (1959), although inapplicable to functional analysis generally, may have been applicable to Parsons. For instance, Parsons has little to say about ways in which proof by covariation could be used in testing hypotheses drawn from requisite analysis.

2. At least in the early stages of his career, it was Parsons's intention to provide a powerful critique of positivism and its excessive emphasis on environmental determinism (Alexander, 1983:xx). Parsons argues (1937:111–21) that the central weakness of the Malthusian theory (as reflected, also, in Darwinism) is its "anti-intellectual" presumption that human volition does not count for much, that human will can hardly overcome the dismal laws of the Malthusian population dynamic. Parsons believed that behaviorist psychology suffered from a similar affliction. When Parsons joins forces with Alfred Marshall to revive a strongly voluntaristic theory of human action, he throws the pendulum far too strongly in the direction of idealism. The carefully measured voluntarism of Malthus's second edition, with its recognition that human volition may

be able to substitute preventive checks for positive checks (death), would have been a far better model for Parsons to incorporate. The persistent directionality, the asymmetry, of Parsons's cybernetic hierarchy – with power, information, and other media flowing predominantly ". . . down from the cultural system . . ." into the "societal community," into the polity and the economy, into personality systems, and finally into the "behavioral organism" (Toby, 1977:8,9; cf. Parsons, 1977:234–5) – places before our eyes, again, the baleful image of Kant's deluded dove. Parsons cannot justify this image any more than Harris (1968: 4) can justify his own antithesis of the fundamental, dominant role of technoenvironmental and technoeconomic factors. It is likely that Parsons's nonempirical orientation derives from his belief in the preeminence of subcranial phenomena, and the same may be said of his insistence that social norms be defined in terms of ideals and values (1951:56) rather than on the basis of observations of behavior. Alexander (1983:85) may be correct in commending Parsons's "interchange" model for having avoided the Marxian asymmetry of base and superstructure, but it cannot be gainsaid that Parsons introduces some powerful asymmetries of his own. Alexander (1983:439) mentions Jan Loubser's concerns about Parsons's inability to assign "weights" to social phenomena, but throughout the Parsonian system one encounters implicit, a priori, and nonempirical weights.

3. The modal accusation against Parsons is that he had "political" predilections. Many readers who have made a careful analysis of *The Social System*, while remaining a little cavalier in their treatment of other Parsonian works, have had understandable problems with the statement that

it is essential to the conception of the interaction process . . . and of the theorem of the institutional integration of motivation . . . that the stabilization of the processes of mutual orientation within complementary roles is a fundamental 'tendency' of interaction (1951:481).

Parsons does not help the situation – in fact, he aggravates it further – when he tells us that the stability postulate is a theoretical assumption and not an empirical generalization (1951:481), as if there were some inescapable discontinuity between the theoretical and empirical realms of analysis. Parsons further argues that social systems, having properties of equifinality, are often able to tolerate ". . . fluctuations in the factors of the environment" while maintaining "certain constancies of pattern, whether this constancy be static or moving" (1951:482). (Ignore the fact that a "moving constancy" is not precisely an instance of stability, or that for every instance of equifinality one can easily identify a departure from equifinality.) One soon begins to wonder how Parsons reconciled his "law of inertia" (1951: 482) with the voluntaristic notion of human action. Perhaps the best instance of an unreasonable adherence to stability and inertia in Parsons's work is his theory of sex roles and their allocation within nuclear families. These writings do indeed exemplify what feminists have called a "functional freeze" (Friedan, 1963). I do not see any reason to summarize this untenable theory in these pages; it is set forth and elaborated upon in several places (Parsons, 1951:193, 241, 503–5; 1954:96–98; Parsons et al., 1955: ch. II).

In Parsons's defense it should be pointed out that his analyses of specific instances or mechanisms of social change do not insist on a tendency toward stability. *The Social System* presents an array of conditions and processes capable of producing change from *within* a society, including selection against untenable combinations of the pattern variables (1951: 152), several forms of structural strain (1951: 179–200), deviant behavior (1951:206), the extreme malleability of the human infant (1951:336, 508), a general strain toward consistency in values (1951:383), new religious ideas, genetic change (1951:493), and the changeability of functions performed by given structures (again, a prospect of survivals), as in the example of horses (1951: 511). And perhaps Parsons's best statements about *external* sources of change are found in the extraordinary series of essays on the historical evolution of Germany and Japan and on the prospects of social engineering in these societies after 1945 (Parsons, 1954). Parsons echoes Spencer in recognizing warfare as a powerful mechanism of change, he sees very few limits on the ability of the victors to impose change on the vanquished, and he rarely seems to worry about unanticipated consequences of fundamental though carefully designed change. The Morgenthau plan, calling for the dismantling of German industry, apparently did not strike Parsons as being carefully designed (1954:264).

Perhaps the clearest instance of Parsons's "political" bias occurs in his handling of the question of "separation of ownership and control" in advanced capitalist societies. Eventually it becomes starkly obvious that Parsons's basic strategy in addressing this issue is to *deduce*, from his general principle of increasing social differentiation, that a separation of property and power must be proceeding apace. If the basic AGIL functions are carried out by complex social structures that become sharply distinct from one another, if educational institutions over time become more and more sharply separated from kinship, if the separation of religion and politics is an inexorable trend in the more advanced societies (Parsons, 1977: 52–65, 102–8, 145–6, 194), then surely there must be an emergent bifurcation of ownership and control. The thesis is reiterated in several places (Parsons, 1951:509,514; 1977: 198; cf. Alexander, 1983: 136). A large empirical literature, of course, has challenged this thesis (Useem, 1984:26–58).

4. It is perhaps critical of Parsons, though I have doubts, to mention Irving Zeitlin's claim (1973: ch. 3) that it was the better of the "two Parsons" who had written the profound analysis of Nazi Germany and its historical antecedents; that the turgid, theoretical Parsons of *The Social System* is mercifully held in abeyance when specific social processes or problems are under investigation. Alexander (1983:415) points out that ". . . after 1960 Parsons never referred to the [pattern] variables in his systemic writings," and yet these variables had apparently been a fundamental part of Parsons' conceptual apparatus in earlier years. As developed by Zeitlin, the two-Parsons thesis is designed to cast aspersions on the abstractly conceptual and theoretical Parsons, as compared to the Parsons of the *Essays*. I must confess that I too enjoy the *Essays* far more than *The Social System*, but that is just my own bias. In any case if there are two Parsons, let us make the most of them. As I consider the issue of Parsons's alleged plurality – what Alexander (1983:318) calls the "standard argument that Parsons's interesting empirical essays have little connection to his 'grand theory' " – I am reminded of a delightful graffito that I encountered not long ago:

> Roses are red,
> Violets are blue,
> I'm schizophrenic,
> And so am I.

In summary, I find once more that there is no necessary nexus between a general commitment to the functionalist paradigm and the assorted warts and moles of a given functionalist. Regarding Parsons, Alexander inadvertently states the same thesis when he tells us (1983:44) that it is possible to discuss Parsons's "most basic orientations . . . without reference to functionalism . . . ." In a later, more explicit, passage (1983:103), Alexander tells us that while the functionalist paradigm is sometimes thought to " . . . overemphasize the role of values," it is his intention "to show that Parsons's value analysis is neither so reductionist nor so conflationary" – at least, any tendency to overemphasize values did not derive from Parsonian functionalism. On the matter of Parsons's political values,

Alexander not only denies that they derive from the functionalist paradigm, he also argues (1983:133) that Parsons's critics

> have, for the most part, distorted these values themselves. Parsons is not an "organicist," and neither is he an "individualist." He can be labelled a "conservative" only if we adopt the most present-minded, antihistorical framework. Parsons' life-long polemic against the nominalism and utilitarianism of the Anglo-Saxon democratic tradition resembles Durkheim's, and his synthetic counterproposal . . . has proved almost as difficult for critics to understand.

Although Alexander (1983:186) does recognize in Parsons's work an "a priori acceptance of stability," he believes that this postulate is ". . . not necessarily connected to Parsons's presuppositions, his functional model, his ideological commitments, or his empirical understanding of the process of social change." In short, it is another part of Parsons's conceptual apparatus that must eventually have been abandoned.

Notes

Chapter 1

1. In a discussion of "negative feedback and functional analysis," Coleman (1968:440) defines an "equilibrium value" for a variable called x_1 and explains negative feedback as follows:

   > . . . when x_1 is below its equilibrium value, it will increase to the equilibrium. . . . When such negative feedback exists, then there is a chain of effects, somewhat as follows:

   $$x_1 \rightarrow x_2 \rightarrow x_3 \rightarrow x_1$$

   > where there is an odd number of negative effects. That is, x_1 may affect x_2 positively, which affects x_3 positively, which affects x_1 negatively. This would produce a system that would come to stable equilibrium.

   In later chapters, we shall encounter many theories involving negative feedback.

2. See Faia (1967, 1968) for a concept of social norms that tries to avoid the reliance on public opinion found in the typical social problems textbook. Also compare Moran's claim (1982:60) that ". . . an ethnoecological approach fails to consider 'latent functions'," despite the fact that such functions ". . . might be precisely the ones that are crucial to a population's survival . . . ."

Chapter 2

1. Some support has been found in recent years for the "biological degeneration" theory of the incest taboo (Dobzhanski, 1970:156–7; Wilson, 1975:78–79). Dobzhanski, however, claims that "the increase of the incidence of hereditary diseases in the offspring of marriages between relatives . . . over that in persons not known to be related is slight – so slight that geneticists hesitate to declare such marriages disgenic." In any case White's objection to the biological degeneration theory, largely based on the fact that certain tribes are "unaware of the relationship between sexual intercourse and pregnancy" (1948:417), is irrelevant: The biological degeneration theory may well describe a *latent* function, and, as we saw in Chapter 1, people do not always know what they are doing even (or especially) when they are making babies.

   A sociological alternative to Tylor, of course, is that violations of the incest taboo would disrupt *internal* family relationships (Davis, 1949:401–4; cf. Bredemeier, 1955).

   Tylor's theory regards exogamy as a variable, not a universal. Similarly, Collins (1975:236) points out that incest may be treated as a variable in studies of contemporary societies:

The problem becomes more tractable by treating it as a matter of variations. . . . incest taboos are only one form of a larger class of controls over sexuality, along with rules on adultery and exogamy more generally. The strength and extensiveness of these controls depends on the form of social organization. The more wide-reaching taboos are found where extensive kinship organizations are the basis for strong economic and political ties . . . . Incest, adultery, and exogamy rules all reflect particular kinds of sexual property, and the power relations within which they are embedded.

While providing no data, Collins raises interesting questions. For instance, among fathers and brothers whose assertion of sexual property rights is so strong that they have a "dispensation" to "kill rapists of their daughters and sisters" (1975:236), is incest more likely? If so, then we are forced to the paradoxical conclusion, implicit in Collins's treatment, that incest has the function of reaffirming sexual property rights.

2. The requirement that a woman marry a brother of her deceased husband.
3. The requirement that a man marry a sister of his deceased wife.
4. I have always found it most unrewarding to encounter theorists who say, for instance, that a necessary condition for the existence of any society is an economic system. Such a statement merely defines an abstract universal, and this is not an exciting accomplishment. When Goldschmidt (1966:87) tells us that "sharing" is a requisite and then gives us the unenlightening news that ". . . it is precisely my point that the institutions for goals-sharing vary from one culture to another, but that some means of doing so is to be found in all," we wish that the variations could be more strongly emphasized than the abstract universality. The same deficiency characterizes the work of Levy (1952: e.g., 191): It is not terribly exciting to be told that "effective control of disruptive forms of behavior" is found everywhere; what we need to know is why it is that a given type of society has a given type of social control system, and not another. Neither Malinowski nor Parsons, I assume, could conceive of a human society without an economic system. Yet, this empty search for universals is attributed to Malinowski, Parsons, and others by Sztompka (1974), for example, who discusses these scholars in the context of requisite analysis. Thus, in Table 2.1, I speak of the absence or deficiency of alleged prerequisites.

If the social sciences were to develop a plausible list of prerequisites sufficiently concrete to avoid being obvious universals, it would then be possible to use our understanding of prerequisites as a heuristic tool, much in the manner of biologists. For instance, although it was once thought that the nasal glands of various marine birds had the function of producing a secretion that would wash irritating salt water away from the nasal area, it now appears that this gland functions to reduce the salinity of internal bodily fluids, thereby enabling these birds to ingest large amounts of sea water (Schmidt-Nielsen 1979:328–331). Having an awareness of the prerequisite of salinity regulation, Schmidt-Nielsen and his collaborators were able to search for any structure with an output highly correlated with the saline content of bodily fluids. Eventually, the investigators hit upon the nasal gland. A similar strategy is used by Goldschmidt (1966:87–117), who considers it the most distinctive aspect of his brand of functionalism.

In any case I hope that other eastern European functionalists do not give requisite analysis the deference found in Sztompka's work. It may tend to make them unduly conservative.

5. In an insightful passage, Campbell (1969:78) argues that the principle of "simultaneity of invention" – the notion that material and nonmaterial inventions (variations) tend to occur in several places at once – suggests underlying social mechanisms behaving in predictable ways and perhaps constituting an important mechanism of social variation.

Note that such processes would be quite different from those of genetic mutation, because the latter apparently occur randomly.

6. "Darwinian," in this case, is defined in terms of lethal selection.
7. For a discussion of boundaries as an essential aspect of the concept of social norms, see Faia (1967:392–3). Stinchcombe (1968:223) discusses borders from the standpoint of territoriality, but throughout his discussion it is clear that interaction patterns are much more important than maps in ascertaining the location of borders.

Indeed, if space is man's new frontier, it will raise fascinating questions about borders. If Gerard O'Neill is correct in arguing that future excess human population will be relocated in space colonies constructed primarily of lunar material, such colonies will raise a host of questions regarding social control. Would the nation-state system survive such a development, or would individual space colonies be entirely self-sufficient (i.e., characterized by extremely sharp boundaries) so that earth-bound political systems would not wish to challenge their sovereignty? Would some sort of dependency be maintained as a means of preserving dominance of terrestrial political systems? See Gerard K. O'Neill (1974; 1975). I believe it was Lawrence of Arabia who once warned that a ruler shou.d never allow artillery troops to have more than a few hours' ammunition, if he wishes to preserve his sovereignty. On the other hand, it could have been Machiavelli.

8. From an interactionist standpoint, separation of husband and wife may be much more significant than divorce. Although separation data are available in the 1887–1906 survey, they are not as complete as the divorce data. Unfortunately, legal facts are probably more likely to be recorded than social facts.

Chapter 3

1. All data for Table 3.2 are from the United States Government Printing Office (1961).
2. Such life-table values have an interesting property known as *bonus effect*. If 10-year-old marriages, on the average, arrive at divorce at an age of 15.98 years, then their duration is $15.98 - 8.74 = 7.24$ years greater than that of the average newly established marriage. Thus, a marriage lasting 10 years has demonstrated a certain vigor merely by surviving for so long a time. Vigor, in fact, can be measured by taking the ratio of bonus effect to current age,

$$V_x = \frac{x + e_x - e_0}{x}$$

In the above instance,

$$V_{10} = \frac{7.24}{10} = 0.724$$

For marriages at age 15,

$$V_{15} = \frac{15 + 4.02 - 8.74}{15} = 0.69$$

and so forth. In the case of congressional tenure, the vigor of congressmen entering their fifth term of office is

$$V_5 = \frac{5 + 4.43 - 3.82}{5} = 1.12$$

and for those entering the tenth term,

$$V_{10} = \frac{10 + 3.22 - 3.82}{10} = 0.940$$

and so forth. In functional analysis generally, it is appropriate to relate vigor to the age of social organizations (cf. Stinchcombe, 1965). Although the correlation of vigor and life expectancy may be high, approaching 1.0, there are many instances in which the pattern of termination rates is such that high vigor may be associated with low life expectancy. In third-world life tables, for instance, young adults have high vigor with relatively low life expectancies. Data involving vigor could be organized by the method presented in Table 6.6 and associated text. Finally, it is important to note that the vigor of social entities of a given age could be taken as an index of the success of their various adaptive strategies (cf. Hannan and Freeman, 1977:937), a concept to be discussed later in some detail.

Chapter 4

1. Examples of curvilinear theories (or hypotheses) not involving time are (1) the rank-size rule, relating the size of a given city to its rank among all cities of a nation (Petersen, 1975:489); (2) the cube-root law of assembly sizes, relating the size of national legislatures to the size of the "active population" for a number of contemporary nations (Taagepera, n.d., Figure 1); (3) the cube law relating the proportion of votes cast for a given party to the proportion of seats won by the same party (Benson, 1963:36–37); (4) Durkheim's theory relating social integration to the suicide rate (Pierce, 1967); (5) a theory relating "cross-pressures" to rates of political participation (Faia, 1967:407–12); (6) the Nimkoff–Middleton theory relating family type (independent vs. extended) to degree of spatial mobility (Marsh, 1967:73–74); finally, several additional examples are found in Hage (1972:92,102–6).
2. The SAS User's Guide (1979) contains a discussion of SPECTRA, a subroutine that performs time-series analyses designed to discover periodicities and other temporal patterns.
3. A comparison of Malthus (first edition) and the Club of Rome world model illustrates all the important points made in Chapter 1.

Chapter 5

1. Hagstrom (1965) uses Durkheim's theory of the division of labor to explain the formation of new academic departments in highly competitive situations.
2. This estimate may turn out to be low in the case of mainland China, which is implementing a one-child family ideal.
3. See Henry and Short (1954) for an exploration of the possibility that suicide and homicide may act as functional alternatives.

Chapter 6

1. For an illustration of a nearly perfect adaptation process modeled on the famous Lotka–Volterra predator-prey interaction equations, see McNaughton and Wolf (1973, ch. 10) and Solbrig (1979:382–397). An example of supply-demand interaction is discussed in Cook and Campbell (1979:313). Intentions to purchase "no doubt 'caused'

purchases a year later." For television sets the correlation from intentions to purchases a year later was .75, and from purchases to intentions a year later, −.57. Purchases, in other words, reduce subsequent intentions. In the language of functionalism, demand stimulates supply and supply diminishes demand (cf. Blalock, 1969:50–59).

2. Bohrnstedt (1969) argues against use of difference scores as a way of controlling auto-correlation, and in favor of residualizing all relevant variables. Difference scores often reflect regression effects: A high value for a variable at time 1 will tend to be followed by a negative difference score for $t_2 − t_1$, and a low value at time 1 will tend to be followed by a positive difference score. On the other hand, if variance holds up over time, there must be sources of variation that create counterregression effects. It helps to visualize these matters: If, for instance, one were repeatedly to drop to the floor a very large number of coins, the resulting spread of the coins would be more or less constant, assuming no variation in one's dropping technique. Those coins near the outer edge of the distribution on a given throw would tend to be closer to the middle of the distribu-tion on the next throw; however, coins near the middle of the distribution on a given throw would tend to spread further on a subsequent throw.

   Bohrnstedt argues that a simple autoregressive equation could potentially explain all the difference scores, and an explanation based on autoregressive equations would arguably be more parsimonious than one invoking another independent variable. In this type of situation, if regression over time tended to outweigh counterregression the time series would move toward zero variance. Thus, in any instance where variance holds up over time (as in the stationarity condition), we have ipso facto evidence that extraneous variables (and/or measurement unreliability) are creating new variations.

3. Several research projects currently underway at William and Mary are designed to test specific adaptation hypotheses. The first involves an effort to test the Szymanski eco-nomic stagnation–military spending hypothesis at the state level (see Mintz and Hicks, 1984). (If Congress does indeed "throw money" at areas of economic stagnation, and given the fact that Congress, as a "designed system" [Henshel, 1976], meets annually, there should be discernible lead and lag times of about one year [cf. Griffin et al., 1985].) The second involves a life-table analysis of tenure (or survivorship) of members of the House of Representatives and asks, among other things, how the homeostatic constant (H) of 435 members is maintained by adaptations either in the size of freshman cohorts, by adjustments of survival rates, or both. The third assesses the interaction between the sex discrimination gap in salaries of college faculty members and periodic adjustments intended to reduce the discrimination gap; it also asks whether contextual factors, such as the presence of a merit system with close ties between merit and reward, have an impact on salary dissatisfaction among those for whom there are merit–reward disparities. The fourth project has to do with attendance patterns. It asks whether declining attendance at NFL football games increases the likelihood of local TV blackouts, with the latter then tending to increase attendance at future games. (For the years 1973–75, NFL broadcast decisions were regulated by federal law, and that law can be looked upon as expressing an adaptation theory of sorts.) The final project assesses the relationship between violent crimes such as homicide and the rate at which convicted criminals receive death sentences.

Chapter 7

1. Kelley et al. (1967) have suggested that variations in voter turnout reflect primarily local differences in the ease of voter registration, a proposition classifiable as multivari-

ate and causal, but neither ordered nor functionalist. The next logical step would be to determine whether increasing voter turnout (a variation) over an appropriate lag would have any impact through the political process on voter registration. In this instance one would not be surprised to find positive feedback illustrating Skinner's (1981) formulation of the social selection process.

References

Aberle, D. F., A. K. Cohen, A. K. Davis, M. J. Levy, Jr., and F. X. Sutton. 1950. "The functional prerequisites of a society." *Ethics* 60:100–11.

Abrahamson, Mark. 1981. Englewood Cliffs: Prentice-Hall. *Sociological Theory: An Introduction to Concepts, Issues, and Research.*

Alexander, Jeffrey C. 1982. Berkeley: University of California. *Theoretical Logic in Sociology, Volume I: Positivism, Presuppositions, and Current Controversies.*

Alexander, Jeffrey C. 1983. Berkeley: University of California. *Theoretical Logic in Sociology, Volume IV: The Modern Reconstruction of Classical Thought: Talcott Parsons.*

Alexander, Jeffrey C. 1984. "Social-structural analysis: some notes on its history and prospects." *Sociological Quarterly* 25: 5–26.

Allison, Paul D., J. Scott Long, and Tad K. Krauze. 1982. "Cumulative advantage and inequality in science." *American Sociological Review* 47:615–25.

Ashby, W. Ross. 1968. Chicago: Aldine. "Regulation and control," pp. 296–303 in Walter Buckley (ed.), *Modern Systems Research for the Behavioral Scientist.*

Atkin, R., R. Bray, M. Davison, S. Herzberger, L. G. Humphreys, and U. Selzer. 1977. "Cross-lagged panel analysis of sixteen cognitive measures at four grade levels." *Child Development* 48: 944–52.

Babbie, Earl. 1983. Belmont, CA: Wadsworth. *The Practice of Social Research.*

Balkin, Steven. 1979. "Victimization rates, safety and fear of crime." *Social Problems* 26: 343–58.

Banks, J. A. 1954. London: Routledge and Kegan Paul. *Prosperity and Parenthood: A Study of Family Planning Among The Victorian Middle Classes.*

Baran, Paul A. and Paul M. Sweezy. 1966. New York: Monthly Review Press. *Monopoly Capital.*

Barnes, Harry Elmer. 1948. Chicago: University of Chicago Press. *An Introduction to the History of Sociology.*

Barnet, Richard J. and Ronald E. Muller. 1974. New York: Simon and Schuster. *Global Reach.*

Bartky, Ian R. 1984. "A comment on 'the standardization of time' by Zerubavel." *American Journal of Sociology* 89:1420–25.

Benson, Oliver. 1963. "The use of mathematics in the study of political science," pp. 30–57 in James C. Charlesworth (ed.), *Mathematics and the Social Sciences.* American Academy of Political and Social Sciences.

Berelson, Bernard and Gary A. Steiner. 1964. New York: Harcourt, Brace. *Human Behavior.*

Berry, Wendell. 1981. San Francisco: North Point Press. *The Gift of Good Land.*

Bierstedt, Robert. 1960. "Sociology and humane learning." *American Sociological Review* 25: 3–9.

Black, Theodore and Thomas Orsagh. 1978. "New evidence on the efficacy of sanctions as a deterrent to homicide." *Social Science Quarterly* 58: 616–31.

Blalock, Hubert M. 1969. Englewood Cliffs: Prentice-Hall. *Theory Construction.*

Blalock, Hubert M. 1979. New York: McGraw-Hill. *Social Statistics.*

Blau, Peter M. 1977. "A macrosociological theory of social structure." *American Journal of Sociology* 83: 26–54.

Blau, Peter M. 1980. New York: Free Press. "Contexts, units, and properties in sociological analysis," pp. 31–66 in Hubert M. Blalock Jr. (ed.), *Sociological Theory and Research.*

Blumstein, Alfred, Jacqueline Cohen, and Daniel Nagin, eds. 1978. Washington, D.C.: National Academy of Sciences. *Deterrence and Incapacitation: Estimating the Effects of Criminal Sanctions on Crime Rates.*

Bohrnstedt, George W. 1969. San Francisco: Jossey-Bass. "Observations on the measurement of change," pp. 113–33 in Edgar F. Borgatta and George W. Bohrnstedt (eds.), *Sociological Methodology.*

Bowers, William J. and Glenn L. Pierce. 1980. "Deterrence or brutalization: what is the effect of executions?" *Crime and Delinquency* 26: 453–484.

Boyd, Lawrence H. and Gudmind R. Iversen. 1979. Belmont, CA: Wadsworth. *Contextual Analysis.*

Braithwaite, Richard B. 1955. New York: Cambridge University Press. *Scientific Explanation.*

Bredemeier, Harry C. 1955. "The methodology of functionalism." *American Sociological Review* 20: 173–80.

Brinton, Crane. 1965. New York: Random House. *The Anatomy of Revolution.*

Bureau of the Census. 1908. *Marriage and Divorce, 1887–1906* (Part II, General Tables). Washington, D. C.

Cahen, Alfred. 1968. New York: AMS. *Statistical Analysis of American Divorce.*

Campbell, Colin. 1982. "A dubious distinction? An inquiry into the value and use of Merton's concepts of manifest and latent function." *American Sociological Review* 47: 29–44.

Campbell, Donald T. 1969. "Variation and selective retention in socio-cultural revolution." *General Systems* XIV: 69–85.

Caplow, Theodore, Howard M. Bahr, Bruce A. Chadwick, Reuben Hill, and Margaret Holmes Williamson. 1982. Minneapolis: University of Minnesota. *Middletown Families.*

Carroll, Glenn R. 1984. "Organizational ecology." *Annual Review of Sociology* 10:71–93.

Chambliss, William J. 1966. "The deterrent influence of punishment." *Crime and Delinquency* 12: 70–75.

Chase, Stuart. 1931. New York: Literary Guild. *Mexico: A Study of Two Americas.*

Chatfield, Christopher. 1975. New York: Wiley. *The Analysis of Time Series: Theory and Practice.*

Cherlin, Andrew. 1978. "Remarriage as an incomplete institution." *American Journal of Sociology* 84: 634–50.

Cherlin, Andrew. 1981. Cambridge: Harvard University Press. *Marriage, Divorce, Remarriage.*

Chronicle of Higher Education. 1982. XXIV:10. "Dying institutions: researchers have ignored an unpleasant topic."

Church, T. 1976. "Plea bargaining, concessions and the courts: analysis of a quasi-experiment." *Law and Society Review* 10: 377–410.

Churchill, Betty C. 1955. "Age and life expectancy of business firms." *Survey of Current Business* 35:15–19.

Cohen, Albert K. 1955. Glencoe: Free Press. *Delinquent Boys.*

Cohen, Morris R. 1959. New York: Free Press. *Reason and Nature.*

Cohen, Yehudi A. 1964. Chicago: Aldine. *The Transition from Childhood to Adolescence.*

Coleman, James S. 1968. New York: McGraw-Hill. "The mathematical study of change," pp. 428–78 in Hubert M. Blalock and Ann B. Blalock (eds.), *Methodology in Social Research.*

Coleman, James S., Elihu Katz, and Herbert Menzel. 1966. Indianapolis: Bobbs-Merrill. *Medical Innovation: A Diffusion Study.*

Collins, Randall. 1975. New York: Academic Press. *Conflict Sociology.*

Collins, Randall. 1984. San Francisco: Jossey-Bass. "Statistics versus words," pp. 329–62 in Randall Collins (ed.), *Sociological Theory.*

Collins, Randall. 1985. New York: Oxford University Press. *Three Sociological Traditions.*

Cook, Thomas D. and Donald T. Campbell. 1979. Chicago: Rand McNally. *Quasi-Experimentation: Design and Analysis Issues for Field Settings.*

Coser, Lewis A. 1956. Glencoe: The Free Press. *The Functions of Social Conflict.*

Coser, Lewis A. 1975. "Presidential address: two methods in search of a substance." *American Sociological Review* 40:691–700.

Croxton, Frederick E., Dudley J. Cowden, and Sidney Klein. 1967. New York: Prentice-Hall. *Applied General Statistics.*

Davis, James A. 1957. Chicago: National Opinion Research Center. *A Study of Participants in the Great Books Program.*

Davis, James A. 1980. "Conservative weather in a liberalizing climate: change in selected NORC general social survey items." *Social Forces* 58: 1129–56.

Davis, Kingsley. 1949. New York: Macmillan. *Human Society.*

Davis, Kingsley. 1959. "The myth of functional analysis as a special method in sociology and anthropology." *American Sociological Review* 24: 757–72.

Davis, Kingsley and Wilbert E. Moore. 1945. "Some principles of stratification." *American Sociological Review* 10: 242–49.

Demerath, Nicholas J. 1976. New York: Harper and Row. *Birth Control and Foreign Policy.*

Demerath, Nicholas J., III. 1967. New York: Free Press. "Synecdoche and structural-functionalism," pp. 501–18 in N. J. Demerath III and Richard A. Peterson (eds.), *System, Change, and Conflict.*

Dentler, Robert A. and Kai T. Erickson. 1959. "The functions of deviance in groups." *Social Problems* VII: 98–107.

Dhrymes, Phoebus J. 1970. New York: Harper and Row. *Econometrics.*

DiTomaso, Nancy. 1982. " 'Sociological reductionism' from Parsons to Althusser: linking action and structure in social theory." *American Sociological Review* 47:14–28.

Dobzhansky, Theodosius. 1970. New York: Bantam Books. *Mankind Evolving.*

Dollard, John, Neal E. Miller, Leonard W. Doob, O. H. Mowrer, and Robert R. Sears. 1939. New Haven: Yale University Press. *Frustration and Aggression.*

Dougherty, James E. and Robert L. Pfaltzgraff, Jr. 1971. New York: Lippincott. *Contending Theories of International Relations.*

Dumont, Arsène. 1890. Paris: Lecrosnier et Babé. *Dépopulation et Civilisation: Etudes Démographiques.*

Duncan, Otis Dudley. 1961. "From social system to ecosystem." *Sociological Inquiry* 31:140–9.

Duncan, Otis Dudley. 1963. "Axioms or correlations?" *American Sociological Review* 28:452.

Duncan, Otis Dudley and Leo F. Schnore. 1959. "Cultural, behavioral, and ecological perspectives in the study of social organization." *American Journal of Sociology* LXV: 132–46.

Durkheim, Emile. 1938. Glencoe: The Free Press. *The Rules of Sociological Method.*

Durkheim, Emile. 1951. New York: Macmillan-Free Press. *Suicide.*

Easterlin, Richard A. 1980. New York: Basic. *Birth and Fortune: The Impact of Numbers on Personal Welfare.*

Ehrlich, Isaac. 1975. "The deterrent effect of capital punishment: a question of life and death." *American Economic Review* 65: 397–417.

Faia, Michael A. 1967. "Alienation, structural strain, and political deviancy: a test of Merton's hypothesis." *Social Problems* 14: 389–412.

Faia, Michael A. 1968. "On alienation, structural strain, and deviancy: a reply." *Social Problems* 16: 117–20.

Faia, Michael A. 1974. "The myth of the liberal professor." *Sociology of Education* 47:171–202.

Faia, Michael A. 1982. "Willful, deliberate, premeditated, and irrational: reflections on the futility of executions." *State Government* 55: 14–21.

Fararo, Thomas J. 1973. New York: John Wiley and Sons. *Mathematical Sociology.*

Fields, Cheryl M. 1974. "Women struggle to catch up." *Chronicle of Higher Education* VIII (August): 9.

Ford, Daniel. 1985a. "U.S. command and control–part I." *New Yorker* LXI: (April 1): 43–91.

Ford, Daniel. 1985b. "U.S. command and control–part II." *New Yorker* LXI: (April 8): 49–92.

Forrester, Jay W. 1971. Cambridge, MA: Wright-Allen. *World Dynamics.*

Freeman, John and Michael T. Hannan. 1983. "Niche width and the dynamics of organizational populations." *American Journal of Sociology* 88:1116–45.

Frejka, Tomas. 1973. New York: Wiley. *The Future of Population Growth: Alternative Paths to Equilibrium.*

Freund, Julien. 1968. New York: Pantheon. *The Sociology of Max Weber.*

Friedan, Betty. 1963. New York: Norton. *The Feminine Mystique.*

Friedrichs, Robert W. 1970. New York: Free Press. *A Sociology of Sociology.*

Furstenburg, Frank. 1976. New York: Macmillan. *Unplanned Parenthood: The Social Consequences of Teen-age Childbearing.*

Galbraith, John K. 1971. New York: American Library. *The New Industrial State.*

Gans, Herbert. 1972. "The positive functions of poverty." *American Journal of Sociology* 78:275–89.

Garbarino, Merwyn S. 1977. Prospect Heights, IL: Waveland Press. *Sociocultural Theory in Anthropology.*

Garofalo, James. 1977. Washington, D.C.: Superintendent of Documents. *Public Opinion About Crime.*

Gibbs, Jack P. 1972. Hinsdale, IL: Dryden. *Sociological Theory Construction.*

Gibbs, Jack P. 1975. New York: Elsevier. *Crime, Punishment, and Deterrence.*

Gibbs, Jack P. and Walter T. Martin. 1962. "Urbanization, technology, and the division of labor: international patterns." *American Sociological Review* 27:667–77.

Goldschmidt, Walter. 1966. Berkeley: University of California Press. *Comparative Functionalism.*

Goode, William J. and Paul K. Hatt. 1952. New York: McGraw-Hill. *Methods in Social Research.*

Gottman, John M. 1981. New York: Cambridge University Press. *Time-Series Analysis: A Comprehensive Introduction for Social Scientists.*

Gould, Stephen J. 1982. "Darwinism and the expansion of evolutionary theory." *Science* 216: 380–7.

Gouldner, Alvin W. 1970. New York: Basic Books. *The Coming Crisis of Western Sociology.*

Gove, Walter R. 1975. New York: Wiley. *The Labelling of Deviance.*

Granovetter, Mark. 1984. "Small is bountiful: labor markets and establishment size." *American Sociological Review* 49:323–34.

Gregg, Dorothy and Elgin Williams. 1948. "The dismal science of functionalism." *American Anthropologist* 50:594-611.

Griffin, Larry J., Joel Devine, and Michael Wallace. 1985. "One more time: militarizing the U.S. budget: reply to Jencks." *American Journal of Sociology* 91: 384–391.

Hage, Jerald. 1965. "An axiomatic theory of organizations." *Administrative Science Quarterly* 19: 289–320.

Hage, Jerald. 1972. New York: Wiley. *Techniques and Problems of Theory Construction in Sociology.*

Hagstrom, Warren O. 1965. New York: Basic. *The Scientific Community.*

Haldane, J.B.S. 1969. Freeport, New York: Books for Libraries Press. *The Marxist Philosophy and the Sciences.*

Hammond, Phillip E. 1981. "Reply to Anderson." *Contemporary Sociology* 10: 350.

Hammond, Phillip E. and Kirk R. Williams. 1976. "The protestant ethic thesis: a socio-psychological assessment." *Social Forces* 54: 579–89.

Hannan, Michael T. and John Freeman. 1977. "The population ecology of organizations." *American Journal of Sociology* 82: 929–64.

Hannan, Michael T. and John Freeman. 1984. "Structural inertia and organizational change." *American Sociological Review* 49: 149–64.

Hannan, Michael T. and Alice A. Young. 1977. San Francisco: Jossey-Bass. "Estimation in panel models: results on pooling cross-sections and time series," pp. 52–83 in David R. Heise (ed.), *Sociological Methodology 1977.*

Hanushek, Eric A. and John E. Jackson. 1977. New York: Academic. *Statistical Methods for Social Scientists.*

Hardin, Garrett. 1959. New York: Rinehart. *Nature and Man's Fate.*

Harris, Marvin. 1968. New York: Crowell. *The Rise of Anthropological Theory.*

Harris, Marvin. 1979. New York: Random House. *Cultural Materialism.*

Hauser, Philip M. and Otis Dudley Duncan. 1959. Chicago: University of Chicago. *The Study of Population.*

Hawley, Amos H. 1950. New York: The Ronald Press. *Human Ecology.*

Hawley, Amos H. 1984. "Human ecological and Marxian theories." *American Journal of Sociology* 89:904–17.

Heise, David. 1967. "Cultural patterning of sexual socialization." *American Sociological Review* 32:726–39.

Heise, David. 1969. "Separating reliability and stability in test-retest correlations." *American Sociological Review* 34: 93–101.

Heise, David. 1970. San Francisco: Jossey-Bass. "Causal inference from panel data," pp. 3-27 in Edgar F. Borgatta and George W. Bohrnstedt (eds.), *Sociological Methodology 1970.*

Hempel, Carl G. 1959. Evanston: Row, Peterson. "The logic of functional analysis," pp. 271-307 in Llewellyn Gross (ed.), *Symposium on Sociological Theory.*

Henry, Andrew F. and James F. Short, Jr. 1954. Glencoe: The Free Press. *Suicide and Homicide.*

Henshel, Richard L. 1976. Indianapolis: Bobbs-Merrill. *On the Future of Social Prediction.*

Himmelfarb, Gertrude. 1960. New York: Modern Library. "Introduction," pp. xiii–xxxvi in Thomas Robert Malthus, *On Population.*

Hoff, C. J. and A. E. Abelson. 1976. Stroudsburg, PA: Dowden. "Fertility," pp. 128–46 in Paul T. Baker and M. A. Little (eds.), *Man in the Andes.*

Hollingshead, August B. and Fredrick C. Redlich. 1958. New York: Wiley. *Social Class and Mental Illness.*

Homans, George C. 1941. "Anxiety and ritual: the theories of Malinowski and Radcliffe-Brown." *American Anthropologist* 43: 164–72.

Homans, George C. 1962. New York: The Free Press. *Sentiments and Activities: Essays in Social Science.*

Jarvie, I. C. 1967. Chicago: Regnery. *The Revolution in Social Anthropology.*

Jencks, Christopher et al. 1972. New York: Basic Books. *Inequality.*

Jessor, R. and S. L. 1977. New York: Academic. *Problem Behavior and Psychosocial Development: A Longitudinal Study of Youth.*

Johnson, Wendell. 1946. New York: Harper. *People in Quandaries.*

Kamens, David H. 1977. "Legitimating myths and educational organization: the relationship between organizational ideology and formal structure." *American Sociological Review* 42: 208–19.

Kasarda, John D. 1974. "The structural implications of social system size." *American Sociological Review* 39:19–28.

Kasarda, John D. and Patrick D. Nolan. 1979. "Ratio measurement and theoretical inference in social research." *Social Forces* 58: 212–27.

Kelly, K. Dennis and William J. Chambliss. 1966. "Status consistency and political attitudes." *American Sociological Review* 31:375–82.

Kelly, Stanley Jr., Richard E. Ayres, and William G. Bowen. 1967. "Registration and voting: putting first things first." *American Political Science Review* 61: 359–79.

Kemeny, John G., Arthur Schleifer, Jr., J. Laurie Snell, and Gerald L. Thompson. 1962. Englewood Cliffs: Prentice-Hall. *Finite Mathematics With Business Applications.*

Klapp, Orrin E. 1978. New York: Cambridge University Press. *Opening and Closing: Strategies of Information Adaptation in Society.*

Kleck, Gary. 1979. "Capital punishment, gun ownership, and homicide." *American Journal of Sociology* 84: 882–910.

Koestler, Arthur. 1964. New York: Macmillan. *The Act of Creation.*

Kramnick, Isaac. 1972. "Reflections on revolution: definition and explanation in recent scholarship." *History and Theory* XI: 26–63.

Kreps, Gary A. 1984. "Sociological inquiry and disaster research." *Annual Review of Sociology* 10:309–30.

Kreps, Gary A. 1986. Gorizia, Italy: Franco Angeli. "Classical themes, structural sociology, and disaster research." In Russell R. Dynes and Carlo Pelanda (eds.), *Sociology of Disasters: Contribution of Sociology to Disaster Research.*

Kuhn, Alfred. 1974. San Francisco: Jossey-Bass. *The Logic of Social Systems.*

Langton, John. 1979. "Darwinism and the behavioral theory of sociocultural evolution: an analysis." *American Journal of Sociology* 85:288–309.

Lave, L. B. and E. P. Seskin. 1977. Baltimore: Hopkins. *Air Pollution and Human Health.*

Lazarsfeld, Paul F. 1958. "Evidence and inference in social research." *Daedalus* 87: 99–130.

Lazarsfeld, Paul F. 1967. New York: Random House. "Concept formation and measurement," pp. 144–202 in Gordon J. DiRenzo (ed.), *Concepts, Theory and Explanation in the Behavioral Sciences.*

Lazarsfeld, Paul F. 1970. Paris: Mouton/Unesco. "Sociology," pp. 61–165 in *Main Trends of Research in the Social and Human Sciences.*

Lazarsfeld, Paul F. and Wagner Thielens. 1958. Glencoe: The Free Press. *The Academic Mind.*

Leach, E. R. 1951. Cambridge: Harvard University Press. *Political Systems of Highland Burma.*

Lenski, Gerhard. 1966. New York: McGraw-Hill. *Power and Privilege.*

Lernoux, Penny. 1977. "Paraguay: aborigines face destruction." *Washington Post* (June 14): A13.

Levy, Marion J. 1952. Princeton, NJ: Princeton University Press. *The Structure of Society.*

Levy, Marion J., Jr. and Francesca M. Cancian. 1968. New York: Macmillan. "Functional analysis," pp. 21–43 in David L. Sills (ed.), *International Encyclopedia of the Social Sciences.*

Lewis, Oscar. 1960. New York: Holt, Rinehart, and Winston. *Tepoztlán: Village in Mexico.*

Lieberson, Stanley and Glenn V. Fuguitt. 1967. "Negro-white occupational differences in the absence of discrimination." *American Journal of Sociology* 73: 188–200.

Lippitt, Ronald and Ralph K. White. 1958. New York: Holt. "An experimental study of leadership and group life," pp. 496–511 in E. E. Maccoby et al. (eds.), *Readings in Social Psychology.*

Lipset, Seymour M. 1970. New York: Doubleday Anchor. *Revolution and Counterrevolution: Change and Persistence in Social Structures.*

Locke, Harvey J. 1951. New York: Holt. *Predicting Adjustment in Marriage: A Comparison of a Divorced and Happily Married Group.*

Lofland, John and Lyn H. 1984. Belmont, CA: Wadsworth. *Analyzing Social Settings: A Guide to Qualitative Observation and Analysis.*

Lopreato, Joseph. 1980. Minneapolis: University of Minnesota. "Introduction," pp. xiii–xliv in Vilfredo Pareto, *Compendium of General Sociology.*

Loubser, Jan J., R. C. Baum, A. Effrat, and V. M. Lidz, editors. 1976. New York: The Free Press. *Explorations in General Theory in Social Science.* Two volumes.

Lundberg, Ferdinand. 1969. New York: Bantam. *The Rich and the Super-Rich.*

Malinowski, Bronislaw. 1944. Chapel Hill: University of North Carolina. *A Scientific Theory of Culture.*

Malinowski, Bronislaw. 1948. New York: Doubleday Anchor. *Magic, Science, and Religion.*

Markus, Gregory B. 1979. Ann Arbor: University of Michigan (mimeo.). "Models for the analysis of panel data."

Marschak, Jacob. 1959. "Efficient and viable organizational forms." *General Systems* IV: 137–43.

Marsh, Robert M. 1967. New York: Harcourt, Brace. *Comparative Sociology.*

Martindale, Don. 1960. Boston: Houghton Mifflin. *The Nature and Types of Sociological Theory.*

Matras, Judah. 1973. New York: Prentice-Hall. *Populations and Societies.*

Mauss, Armand L. 1975. New York: Lippincott. *Social Problems as Social Movements.*

Mayer, Thomas F. and William R. Arney. 1974. San Francisco: Jossey-Bass. "Spectral analysis and the study of social change," pp. 309–55 in Herbert L. Costner (ed.), *Sociological Methodology 1973–74.*

Mayhew, Bruce H. 1980. "Structuralism vs. individualism: part 1, shadowboxing in the dark." *Social Forces* 59: 335–75.

Mayhew, Bruce H. 1983. "Hierarchical differentiation in imperatively coordinated associations." *Research in the Sociology of Organizations* 2: 153–229.

McCarthy, John D. and Dean R. Hoge. 1984. "The dynamics of self-esteem and delinquency." *American Journal of Sociology* 90:396–410.

McKelvey, Bill. 1982. Berkeley: University of California. *Organizational Systematics: Taxonomy, Evolution, Classification*.

McNaughton, Samuel J. and Larry L. Wolf. 1973. New York: Holt. *General Ecology*.

Meadows, Dennis L. et al. 1974. Cambridge: Wright-Allen. *Dynamics of Growth in a Finite World*.

Merton, Robert K. 1957. New York: The Free Press. *Social Theory and Social Structure*.

Merton, Robert K. and Robert A. Nisbet. 1961. New York: Harcourt, Brace. *Contemporary Social Problems*.

Mills, C. Wright. 1959. New York: Oxford University Press. *The Sociological Imagination*.

Mintz, Alex and Alexander Hicks. 1984. "Military Keynesianism in the United States, 1949–1976: disaggregating military expenditures and their determination." *American Journal of Sociology* 90:411-17.

Moran, Emilio F. 1982. Boulder, CO: Westview. *Human Adaptability*.

Namboodiri, N. Krishnan, Lewis F. Carter, and Hubert M. Blalock, Jr. 1975. New York: McGraw-Hill. *Applied Multivariate Analysis and Experimental Designs*.

National Center for Health Statistics. 1973. Washington, D.C.: Superintendent of Documents. *100 Years of Marriage and Divorce Statistics: United States, 1867–1967*.

National Center for Health Statistics. 1979. Washington, D.C.: Superintendent of Documents. *Divorces by Marriage Cohort*.

Nisbet, Robert A. 1966. New York: Basic. *The Sociological Tradition*.

O'Neill, Gerard K. 1974. "Colonization of space." *Physics Today* 27: 32–40.

O'Neill, Gerard K. 1975. "Space colonies and energy supply to the earth." *Science* 190: 943–7.

Pareto, Vilfredo. 1980. Minneapolis: University of Minnesota Press. *Compendium of General Sociology*. (Abridged by Giulio Farina.)

Parsons, Talcott. 1933. New York: Macmillan. "Malthus, Thomas Robert," pp. 68–69 in *Encyclopedia of the Social Sciences*, Vol. 10.

Parsons, Talcott. 1937. New York: Free Press. *The Structure of Social Action*.

Parsons, Talcott. 1951. Glencoe: The Free Press. *The Social System*.

Parsons, Talcott. 1954. New York: Free Press. *Essays in Sociological Theory*.

Parsons, Talcott et al. 1955. Glencoe: The Free Press. *Family, Socialization, and Interaction Process*.

Parsons, Talcott. 1977. Englewood Cliffs: Prentice-Hall. *The Evolution of Societies*.

Passell, Peter. 1975. "The deterrent effect of the death penalty: a statistical test." *Stanford Law Review* 28: 61–80.

Pelz, Donald C. and Frank M. Andrews. 1964. "Detecting causal priorities in panel study data." *American Sociological Review* 29: 836–48.

Pelz, Donald C. and Robert A. Lew. 1970. San Francisco: Jossey-Bass. "Heise's causal model applied," pp. 28–37 in Edgar F. Borgatta and George W. Bohrnstedt (eds.), *Sociological Methodology 1970*.

Petersen, William. 1975. New York: Macmillan. *Population*.

Petersen, William. 1979. Cambridge: Harvard University Press. *Malthus*.

Phillips, David P. 1979. "Suicide, motor vehicle fatalities, and the mass media: evidence toward a theory of suggestion." *American Journal of Sociology* 84: 1150–74.

Piddocke, Stuart. 1969. Garden City, New York: Natural History Press. "The potlatch system of the Southern Kwakiutl," pp. 130–56 in A. P. Vayda (ed.), *Environment and Cultural Behavior.*

Pierce, Albert. 1967. "The economic cycle and the social suicide rate." *American Sociological Review* 32: 457–62.

Radcliffe-Brown, Alfred R. 1935. "On the concept of function in social science." *American Anthropologist* 37:394–402.

Radcliffe-Brown, Alfred R. 1952. Glencoe: Free Press. *Structure and Function in Primitive Society.*

Ritzer, George. 1980. Boston: Allyn and Bacon. *Sociology: A Multiple Paradigm Science.*

Ritzer, George. 1983. New York: Knopf. *Sociological Theory.*

Roberts, Harry V. 1981. Chicago: SPSS. "Signs and symptoms of spurious correlation in time-series analysis." Proceedings of the Fifth Annual SPSS Users and Coordinators Conference.

Robinson, W. S. 1951. "The logical structure of analytical induction." *American Sociological Review* 16: 812–18.

Rossi, Peter H., Howard E. Freeman, and Sonia R. Wright. 1979. Beverly Hills: Sage. *Evaluation: A Systematic Approach.*

Ruibal, Rodolfo. 1967. Belmont, Calif.: Dickinson. *The Adaptations of Organisms.*

Ryder, Norman B. 1964. "Notes on the concept of a population." *American Journal of Sociology* 69: 447–63.

Sanders, Donald H. 1981. New York: McGraw-Hill. *Computers in Society.*

SAS Institute. 1979. Raleigh, NC: SAS Institute. *SAS User's Guide.*

Schlesinger, Arthur M. 1949. New York: Macmillan. *Paths to the Present.*

Schmidt-Nielsen, Knut. 1979. Cambridge: Cambridge University Press. *Animal Physiology: Adaptation and Environment.*

Schober, Charles P. 1984. *Accumulative Advantage among American Academicians.* Unpublished M.A. thesis, College of William and Mary.

Schram, Sanford F. and J. Patrick Turbett. 1983. "Civil disorder and the welfare explosion: a two-step process." *American Sociological Review* 48:408–14.

Schwirian, Kent P. and John W. Prehn. 1962. "An axiomatic theory of urbanization." *American Sociological Review* 27: 812–25.

Serrón, Luis A. 1980. Norman, Oklahoma: University of Oklahoma. *Scarcity, Exploitation, and Poverty: Malthus and Marx in Mexico.*

Service, Elman R. 1962. New York: Random House. *Primitive Social Organization: An Evolutionary Perspective.*

Sewell, William H., Robert M. Hauser, and David L. Featherman. 1976. New York: Academic Press. *Schooling and Achievement in American Society.*

Shils, Edward A. and Morris Janowitz. 1970. Glenview, IL: Scott Foresman. "Cohesion and disintegration in the Wehrmacht," pp. 183–94 in Thomas E. Lasswell et al. (eds.), *Life in Society.*

Sigelman, Lee and Samuel Bookheimer. 1983. "Is it whether you win or lose? Monetary contributions to big-time college athletic programs." *Social Science Quarterly* 64:347–59.

Skinner, B. F. 1981. "Selection by consequences." *Science* 213: 501–04.

Skocpol, Theda. 1979. New York: Cambridge University Press. *States and Social Revolutions.*

Smelser, Neil J. 1962. New York: The Free Press. *A Theory of Collective Behavior.*

Smith, Tom W. 1982. University of Chicago: National Opinion Research Center. *Annotated Bibliography of Papers Using the General Social Surveys* (4th edition).

Solbrig, Otto T. and Dorothy L. 1979. Reading, MA: Addison-Wesley. *Introduction to Population Biology and Evolution.*

Sorokin, Pitirim. 1928. New York: Harper and Row. *Contemporary Sociological Theories.*

Sorokin, Pitirim A. and Robert K. Merton. 1937. "Social time: a methodological and functional analysis." *American Journal of Sociology* XLII: 615–29.

Spencer, Herbert. 1867. New York: Appleton. *The Principles of Biology,* Volume 2.

Spencer, Herbert. 1969. Hamden, CT: Archon Books. In Stanislav Andreski (ed.), *Principles of Sociology.*

SPSS, Inc. 1983. New York: McGraw-Hill. *User's Guide: SPSSX.*

Stapleton, Vaughan, David P. Aday, Jr., and Jeanne A. Ito. 1982. "An empirical typology of American metropolitan juvenile courts." *American Journal of Sociology* 88:549–64.

Stinchcombe, Arthur L. 1965. New York: Rand McNally. "Social structure and organizations," pp. 142–93 in James G. March (ed.), *Handbook of Organizations.*

Stinchcombe, Arthur L. 1968. New York: Harcourt Brace. *Constructing Social Theories.*

Stinchcombe, Arthur L. 1983. New York: Academic. *Economic Sociology.*

Stockwell, Edward G. and Charles B. Nam. 1963. "Illustrative tables of school life." *Journal of the American Statistical Association* 58: 1113–24.

Stouffer, Samuel. 1940. "Intervening opportunities: a theory relating mobility and distance." *American Sociological Review* 5: 845–68.

Stycos, J. Mayone. 1974. New York: Grossman. *Margin of Life: Population and Poverty in the Americas.*

Sztompka, Piotr. 1974. New York: Academic Press. *System and Function.*

Szymanski, Albert. 1972. "Malinowski, Marx, and functionalism." *Insurgent Sociologist* 2:35–43.

Szymanski, Albert. 1973. "Military spending and economic stagnation." *American Journal of Sociology* 79: 1–14.

Szymanski, Albert. 1976. "Racism and sexism as functional substitutes in the labor market." *Sociological Quarterly* 17: 65–73.

Taagepera, Rein. (unpublished) Irvine, CA: University of California. "Is it time for a 600 member House?"

Takahashi, Joseph S. and Martin Zatz. 1982. "Regulation of circadian rhythmicity." *Science* 217: 1104–11.

Taller de sociología urbana. 1982. Xalapa, Veracruz: Universidad veracruzana. "Wayne Cornelius, un yanqui en las cortes de la revolución urbana mexicana." *Márgenes 3–4: revista de la facultad de sociología:* 190–215.

Thornberry, Terence P. and R. L. Christenson. 1984. "Unemployment and criminal involvement: an investigation of reciprocal causal structures." *American Sociological Review* 49:398–411.

Toby, Jackson. 1977. Englewood Cliffs: Prentice-Hall. "Parsons' theory of social evolution," pp. 1–23 in Talcott Parsons, *The Evolution of Societies.*

Toffler, Alvin. 1980. New York: Morrow. *The Third Wave.*

Trotter, Robert T. and Juan A. Chavira. 1981. Athens, Georgia: University of Georgia Press. *Curanderismo: Mexican American Folk Healing.*

Tufte, Edward R. 1974. Englewood Cliffs: Prentice-Hall. *Data Analysis for Politics and Policy.*

Tuma, Nancy B. and Michael T. Hannan. 1979. "Dynamic analysis of event histories." *American Journal of Sociology* 84:820–54.

Turnbull, Colin M. 1972. New York: Simon and Schuster. *The Mountain People.*

Turner, Jonathan H. 1974. Homewood, IL: Dorsey. *The Structure of Sociological Theory.*

184   *References*

Turner, Jonathan H. and Alexandra Maryanski. 1979. Homewood, IL: Dorsey. *Functionalism.*

United States Government Printing Office. 1961. Washington, D.C. *Biographical Directory of the American Congress.*

Useem, Michael. 1984. New York: Oxford University Press. *The Inner Circle.*

Wallace, Walter L. 1969. Chicago: Aldine. *Sociological Theory.*

Walster, Elaine, G. Wm. Walster, and Ellen Berscheid. 1978. Boston: Allyn and Bacon. *Equity: Theory and Research.*

Webb, Eugene J., Donald T. Campbell, Richard D. Schwartz, and Lee Sechrest. 1966. Chicago: Rand McNally. *Unobtrusive Measures.*

Weick, Karl E. 1981. Temple University. "Evolutionary theory as a backdrop for administrative practice," pp. 106–41 in Herman D. Stein (ed.), *Organization and the Human Services.*

Weller, Robert H. and Leon F. Bouvier. 1981. New York: St. Martin's. *Population: Demography and Policy.*

Wells, Richard H., and J. Stephen Picou. 1981. Washington, D.C.: University Press of America. *American Sociology: Theoretical and Methodological Structure.*

Westoff, Charles F. and Ronald R. Rindfuss. 1974. "Sex preselection in the United States: some implications." *Science* 184: 633–36.

White, Leslie A. 1948. "The definition and prohibition of incest." *American Anthropologist* 50: 416–34.

Wiley, David E. and James A. 1970. "The estimation of measurement error in panel data." *American Sociological Review* 35: 112–17.

Wilson, Edward O. 1975. Cambridge: Harvard University Press. *Sociobiology: A New Synthesis.*

Wright, James D., Peter H. Rossi, and Kathleen Daly. 1983. New York: Aldine. *Under the Gun: Weapons, Crime, and Violence in America.*

Wyer, Jean C. and Clifton F. Conrad. 1984. "Institutional inbreeding reexamined." *American Educational Resources Journal* 21:213–25.

Young, Frank. 1965. New York: Bobbs-Merrill. *Initiation Ceremonies.*

Zeitlin, Irving M. 1973. Englewood Cliffs: Prentice-Hall. *Rethinking Sociology: A Critique of Contemporary Theory.*

Zeitlin, Maurice. 1974. "On 'military spending and economic stagnation.' " *American Journal of Sociology* 79:1452–56.

Zelnik, Melvin, Young J. Kim, and John F. Kantner. 1979. "Probabilities of intercourse and conception . . ." *Family Planning Perspectives* 11:177–83.

Zerubavel, Eviatar. 1982. "The standardization of time: a sociohistorical perspective." *American Journal of Sociology* 88: 1–23.

Zetterberg, Hans L. 1965. New York: Bedminster. *On Theory and Verification in Sociology.*

INDEX

**The Arnold and Caroline Rose Monograph Series
of the American Sociological Association**

J. Milton Yinger, Kiyoshi Ikeda, Frank Laycock, and Stephen J. Cutler: *Middle Start: An Experiment in the Educational Enrichment of Young Adolescents*
James A. Geschwender: *Class, Race, and Worker Insurgency: The League of Revolutionary Black Workers*
Paul Ritterband: *Education, Employment, and Migration: Israel in Comparative Perspective*
John Low-Beer: *Protest and Participation: The New Working Class in Italy*
Orrin E. Klapp: *Opening and Closing: Strategies of Information Adaptation in Society*
Rita James Simon: *Continuity and Change: A Study of Two Ethnic Communities in Israel*
Marshall B. Clinard: *Cities with Little Crime: The Case of Switzerland*
Steven T. Bossert: *Tasks and Social Relationships in Classrooms: A Study of Instructional Organization and Its Consequences*
Richard E. Johnson: *Juvenile Delinquency and Its Origins: An Integrated Theoretical Approach*
David R. Heise: *Understanding Events: Affect and the Construction of Social Action*
Ida Harper Simpson: *From Student to Nurse: A Longitudinal Study of Socialization*
Stephen P. Turner: *Sociological Explanation as Translation*
Janet W. Salaff: *Working Daughters of Hong Kong: Filial Piety or Power in the Family?*
Joseph Chamie: *Religion and Fertility: Arab Christian–Muslim Differentials*
William Friedland, Amy Barton, and Robert Thomas: *Manufacturing Green Gold: Capital, Labor, and Technology in the Lettuce Industry*
Richard N. Adams: *Paradoxical Harvest: Energy and Explanation in British History, 1870–1914*
Mary F. Rogers: *Sociology, Ethnomethodology, and Experience: A Phenomenological Critique*
James R. Beniger: *Trafficking in Drug Users: Professional Exchange Networks in the Control of Deviance*
Jon Miller: *Pathways in the Workplace: The Effects of Race and Gender on Access to Organizational Resources*
Andrew J. Weigert, J. Smith Teitge, and Dennis W. Teitge: *Society and Identity: Toward a Sociological Psychology*
Russell Thornton: *We Shall Live Again: The 1870 and 1890 Ghost Dance Movements as Demographic Revitalization*